THE PICKTON FILE

ALSO BY STEVIE CAMERON

Ottawa Inside Out (1989)
On The Take (1994)
Blue Trust (1998)
The Last Amigo (2001)

Stevie Cameron

THE PICKTON FILE

ALFRED A. KNOPF CANADA

PUBLISHED BY ALFRED A. KNOPF CANADA

Copyright © 2007 Stevie Cameron

Knopf Canada and colophon are trademarks.

www.randomhouse.ca

All photographs in this book are copyright Stevie Cameron
unless otherwise indicated.

Library and Archives Canada Cataloguing in Publication

Cameron, Stevie
The Pickton file / Stevie Cameron.

Includes index.
ISBN 978–0-676–97953–4

1. Pickton, Robert William. 2. Serial murders—British Columbia.
3. Serial murder investigation—British Columbia. 4. Serial
murderers—British Columbia. 5. Murder victims—British Columbia—
Vancouver. I. Title.

HV6535.C33P64 2007   364.152'30971133   C2007–902423–8

Text design: CS Richardson

First Edition

Printed and bound in the United States of America

10 9 8 7 6 5 4 3 2 1

FOR DAVID

CONTENTS

DOWNTOWN EASTSIDE COMMUNITIES

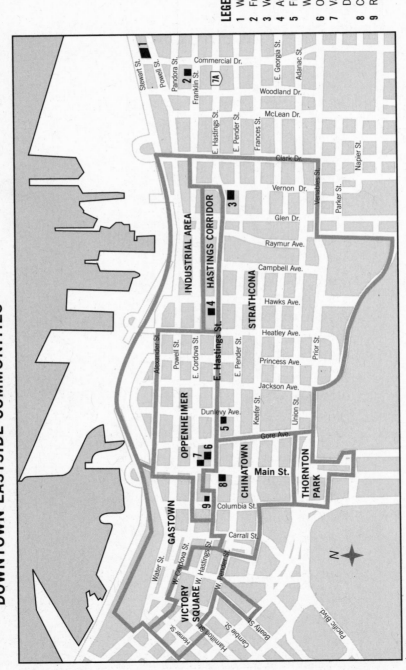

LEGEND
1 West Coast Reduction
2 Franklin Stroll
3 Vernon Rooms
4 Astoria Hotel
5 First United Church / WISH
6 Ovaltine Café
7 Vancouver Police Department
8 Carnegie Centre
9 Radio Café

Stewart St.
Powell St.
Pandora St.
Franklin St.
Commercial Dr.
7A
E. Georgia St.
Adanac St.
Woodland Dr.
McLean Dr.
E. Hastings St.
E. Pender St.
Frances St.
Clark Dr.
Vernon Dr.
Venables St.
Parker St.
Napier St.
Glen Dr.
Raymur Ave.
Campbell Ave.
Hawks Ave.
Heatley Ave.
Prior St.
Princess Ave.
Jackson Ave.
Keefer St.
Union St.
Dunlevy Ave.
Gore Ave.
INDUSTRIAL AREA
HASTINGS CORRIDOR
STRATHCONA
Alexander St.
Powell St.
E. Cordova St.
E. Hastings St.
E. Pender St.
OPPENHEIMER
CHINATOWN
Main St.
THORNTON PARK
Columbia St.
Carrall St.
GASTOWN
Water St.
W. Cordova St.
W. Hastings St.
W. Pender St.
VICTORY SQUARE
Homer St.
Hamilton St.
Cambie St.
Beatty St.
Pacific Blvd.
N

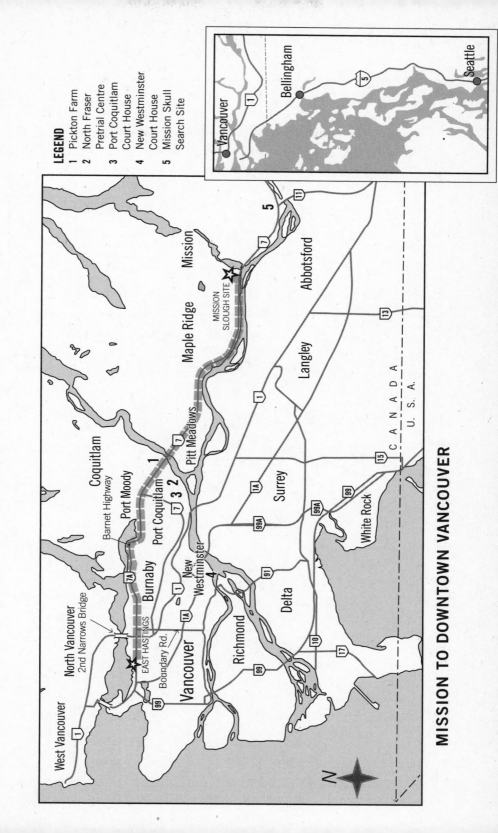

MISSION TO DOWNTOWN VANCOUVER

LEGEND
1 Pickton Farm
2 North Fraser
  Pretrial Centre
3 Port Coquitlam
  Court House
4 New Westminster
  Court House
5 Mission Skull
  Search Site

Seattle

Bellingham

Vancouver

5

1

West Vancouver

North Vancouver
2nd Narrows Bridge

EAST HASTINGS

Boundary Rd.

99

1A

1

1A

91

Richmond

99

Delta

10

17

99

White Rock

99A

99A

15

Surrey

1A

1

Langley

13

Abbotsford

CANADA

U. S. A.

7A

Barnet Highway

Coquitlam

Port Moody

Burnaby

New
Westminster

4

Port Coquitlam

7

3 2

1

7

Pitt Meadows

Maple Ridge

Mission

MISSION
SLOUGH SITE

5

11

7

N

THE PIG FARM AND PORT COQUITLAM

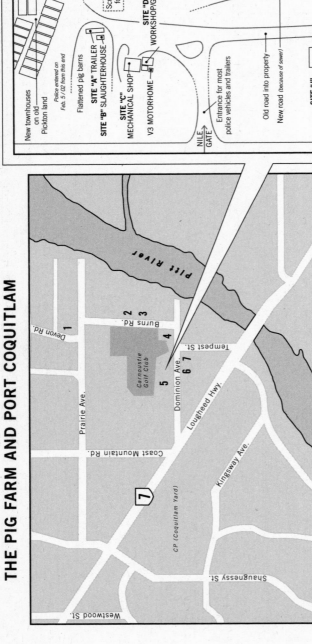

Devon Rd.

Prairie Ave.

Coast Mountain Rd.

Burns Rd.

Tempest St.

Dominion Ave.

Lougheed Hwy.

Kingsway Ave.

Shaughnessy St.

Westwood St.

PITT RIVER

Carnoustie Golf Club

CP (Coquitlam Yard)

1 2 3 4 5 6 7

Inset map

New townhouses on old Pickton land

Police entered on Feb. 5/02 from this end

Flattened pig barns

Sewage lagoons *(drained)*

Screeners for soil

SITE "A" TRAILER
SITE "B" SLAUGHTERHOUSE

SITE "C" MECHANICAL SHOP

V3 MOTORHOME

SITE "D" WORKSHOP/GARAGE

CARNOUSTIE GOLF CLUB

NILE GATE

Entrance for most police vehicles and trailers

Old road into property

New road *(because of sewer)*

PRIVATE HOMES

SITE "I" BARN

SITE "H" LONG STORAGE SHED

SITE "F" DAVE PICKTON'S FARMHOUSE

WEST ◄──── DOMINION AVENUE ────► EAST

HOME DEPOT

HOME DEPOT PARKING LOT

HEALING TENT

HELLS ANGELS CLUBHOUSE

LEGEND
1 Albert and Vera Harvey's blueberry farm, 3640 Devon Rd.
2 Dave Pickton's rancher house, 2600 Burns Rd.
3 Piggy's Palace, 2522 Burns Rd.
4 Bill Malone's house (former Barrett house)
5 Pig Farm, 963 Dominion Ave.
6 Healing Tent
7 Hells Angels Clubhouse

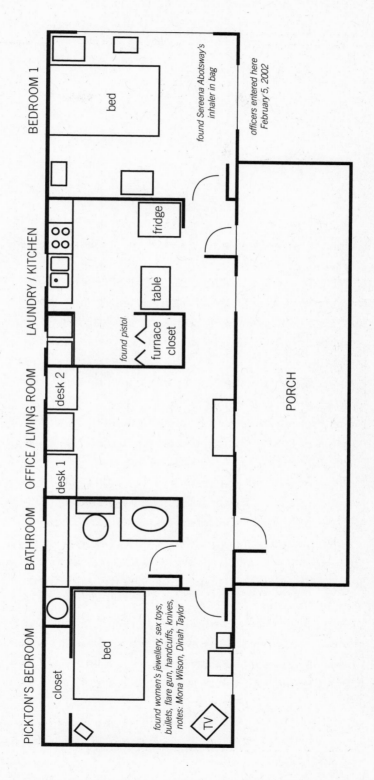

PICKTON'S BEDROOM   BATHROOM   OFFICE / LIVING ROOM   LAUNDRY / KITCHEN   BEDROOM 1

closet

bed

TV

found women's jewellery, sex toys, bullets, flare gun, handcuffs, knives, notes: Mona Wilson, Dinah Taylor

desk 1

desk 2

furnace closet

table

found pistol

fridge

bed

found Sereena Abotsway's inhaler in bag

officers entered here February 5, 2002

PORCH

ROBERT PICKTON MOBILE HOME INTERIOR *(Based on a drawing by Jane Wolsak.)*

PICKTON INDEX

Number of women on official police list of missing women
  since 1978: 65

Number of women who have turned up alive: 4

Number of women Pickton is charged with killing: 26

Age range of the women Pickton is charged with killing: 20 to 46

Number of tips received by the Missing Women Task Force:
  12,700

Number of pages that would be in the investigation's database
  if they printed it out: 2 million

Number of exhibits seized by police: 600,000

Number of DNA samples processed by the RCMP crime labs:
  200,000

Number of swabs used to capture DNA: 400,000

Number of cubic yards of soil sifted by investigators: 383,000

Number of RCMP crime labs used: 6—in Vancouver,
  Edmonton, Regina, Winnipeg, Ottawa and Halifax

Number of media involved: about 378 accredited for trial

Number of journalists showing up every day of the trial:
  between 2 and 6

Number of prosecutors working for the Crown in court: 7

Number of defence lawyers working for Pickton in court: 11

Cost of investigation to date: about $100 million

Number of judges involved in the case so far: 4

Number of Crown witnesses: about 240

Number of vehicles to bring Pickton to court: 3

Population of the Downtown Eastside: about 17,000

Number of single-room occupancy rooms in the Downtown
Eastside: about 5,000

Monthly shelter allowance for people on welfare: $375

Monthly rent for SRO room in the Downtown Eastside: $375

Monthly living allowance for people on welfare: $185

Number of addicts in the Downtown Eastside: between 4,000
and 5,000

Rate of injection drug-users in the Downtown Eastside with
hepatitis C: 9 out of 10

Rate of injection drug-users in the Downtown Eastside who are
HIV positive: 3 out of 10

Average amount spent per day on drugs (mostly cocaine, crack
cocaine, heroin and crystal meth): $200–$400

Number of detox beds for men in the Downtown Eastside: 23

Number of detox beds for women in the Downtown Eastside: 6

FOREWORD

I remember the sense of relief I felt when I learned in the late spring of 2002 that Stevie Cameron was starting research for a book about the case of Vancouver's missing women. I was in the middle of a move—washing floors, packing boxes and listening to CBC Radio—and heard Stevie being interviewed. I'd read two of her books, *Ottawa Inside Out* and her mammoth bestseller *On the Take,* and knew her to be a tenacious reporter with impressive investigative skills. It would take someone with her ability to do justice to the story, which will ultimately conclude, we all hope, with justice for the missing women and justice—in the sense of action—for women who, as a result of their addictions and other problems, remain vulnerable to twisted men.

The story of Vancouver's missing women is a big one. It spans several decades and multiple police jurisdictions and involves over sixty women. I knew twenty of the women who went missing from the streets of the Downtown Eastside. I met them while I worked at WISH, a drop-in centre for sex trade workers, housed in the back of the First United Church on East Hastings Street. WISH is an acronym for Women's Information Safe House. Ina Roelants named the centre when she helped start it up in 1982. She encouraged women to phone their families on a regular basis and thought some might hesitate to call home if the place they were calling from could be identified as a drop-in centre for sex trade workers. A true champion of marginalized women, Ina operated WISH from five p.m. to twelve a.m., five nights a week, for five years, taking home only $100 a month for her efforts. Ina died from bone cancer in March 2005, leaving behind a legacy of support for street-entrenched women that remains unparalleled on the Downtown Eastside.

I've listened to many stories about the women who have gone missing. My earliest recollection dates back to 1998, when Sereena Abotsway told me the police had mistaken her for Angela Jardine. Angela Jardine and Sereena Abotsway were regulars at WISH. According to Sereena, Angela's parents had been trying to report her missing for months, only to be told their daughter was alive and well and working as a prostitute in the Downtown Eastside. Eventually, it was established that the Angela spottings were a case of mistaken identity. Both Angela and Sereena were white women who could have passed for Native; both had brown hair, were in their twenties and were of similar height and weight. Sereena wasn't fazed. She knew many of the women who went missing from this neighbourhood. In 2001, Sereena Abotsway herself was reported missing; in 2002, both Angela's and Sereena's DNA was found on the Pickton farm. Robert Pickton was later charged with their murders.

The women at WISH talked about the events that led them onto the streets of Vancouver's drug ghetto. Many told horrifying tales of child abuse—parents or caregivers who exploited them sexually, physically and emotionally when they were young. Some battled with mental health issues that entrenched them in a downward spiral of addiction and poverty. Others were lured into addiction and the sex trade by boyfriends who introduced them to drugs.

When I began working at the drop-in centre, I knew little about addiction, street life or the sex trade. My previous job had been in the communications field, where I spent a great deal of time office-bound, sitting in front of a computer. At WISH, I worked with a group of women in continual flux. Some women were regulars and came to the centre every night; some would come only once or twice a week. Others were more irregular in their attendance and would come a few days in a row, then skip a week or two. I approached all the new women who came into the centre to welcome them and give them a quick rundown on dinner hours and accessing the showers in the women's bathroom.

Some nights were quiet, others were more animated. Women would sometimes charge through the doors, fleeing from men who were chasing them: drug dealers they owed money to, or violent men who prey upon sex trade workers. Surprisingly, the men pursuing them would stop when they reached the doors of First United. I worked without security, and there wasn't much in place to protect myself or the clients, so we were fortunate that there was respect at street level for the institution that housed the drop-in centre.

Clients sometimes asked me to help them report women who had gone missing. In most cases, the clients had previously approached the police but were upset because there had been no follow-up. One afternoon, early in 2000, I was alone in the church foyer, preparing for the usual six o'clock dinner rush. A client named Ashwan banged on the locked church doors. I let her in. She was crying and out of breath. "Tiffany didn't come home last night. Something's wrong." Ashwan and Tiffany Drew were best friends and shared a room at the

Hazelton Hotel, less than a block from the centre. When they came into WISH, the friends would eat dinner, experiment with makeup and do their hair. I asked Ashwan if it was possible that Tiffany had spent the night at someone's house. Perhaps she hadn't made it home yet. No, Ashwan explained. Ashwan and Tiffany knew that women were going missing from the Downtown Eastside, and they had agreed to check in regularly and let each other know they were safe. Many women at WISH were using the buddy system for the same reason: women were going missing from the neighbourhood at an alarming rate.

I paged a local police officer who visited the centre on a weekly basis. He came by later that night and talked with Ashwan and me. As Ashwan told the officer about Tiffany's disappearance, he didn't take notes or seem concerned. The best he could do, he said, was check with the welfare office in a couple of weeks to see if Tiffany picked up her cheque. Ashwan remained steadfast. "Something has happened to Tiffany. I know it has."

Weeks turned into months, and still there was no sign of Tiffany Drew. Each night, Ashwan returned to the centre worried about her friend. "Tiffany's still missing. She's still missing."

The police officer continued to make regular weekly visits to the drop-in centre. Every time Ashwan saw him, she'd ask him about Tiffany Drew. Had he found out whether Tiffany was collecting her cheques? No, he hadn't gotten around to checking. Ashwan would cry after these conversations. "Why won't he go looking for her?"

Months later, Ashwan and I were told by the same police officer that Tiffany was in a recovery facility and didn't want us to bother her—that if Tiffany were to speak to me or

Ashwan it could trigger a relapse. Tiffany might start using drugs again and jeopardize her recovery. Ashwan shook her head. "Tiffany would never say something like that."

In 2002, Tiffany Drew's DNA was discovered on the Pickton farm and Robert Pickton was charged with her murder. Ashwan maintains, "Tiffany was my best friend. She wouldn't have gone away without telling me."

Why the cop told Ashwan and me that Tiffany Drew was in a recovery facility, when in fact she was not, will always be a mystery to me. But when I look back now, I can see that his actions, or lack thereof, were a manifestation of the attitudes held by police, politicians and the civic leaders ruling Vancouver at the time. To them, women on the Downtown Eastside were unimportant and did not demand a search effort when they went missing.

Not all the police officers I knew were indifferent to the women I worked with. Al Arsenault and Toby Hinton functioned more like advocates for marginalized women than beat cops. In 1998, Al and Toby, with five other Vancouver police officers, formed the Odd Squad, a non-profit organization whose main mandate is drug use prevention through awareness and education. A year after they got started, the Odd Squad, in conjunction with the National Film Board of Canada, produced *Through a Blue Lens,* a gritty documentary chronicling the lives of addicted men and women living on the Downtown Eastside. *Through a Blue Lens* was shown to audiences around the world and became the National Film Board of Canada's all-time most successful documentary.

April Reoch was a participant in the documentary. A pretty, petite, fair-skinned Native woman then in her mid-twenties, April had come from the Squamish Reserve, about 160 kilometres north of Vancouver. She hoped that, by telling her story in the Odd Squad documentary, she could prevent others from making the same mistakes she had. April's life as an addicted woman had been hell—it had robbed her of the ability to raise her son and had exposed her to profound levels of violence.

On December 25, 2000, April Reoch's friend Danny Dee phoned Al and Toby to tell them that April had been expected home on the reserve to celebrate Christmas with her son but hadn't arrived. Danny was upset, as he'd heard a radio newscast earlier in the day stating that a woman's body had been discovered in a gym bag beside a Dumpster at 40 East Hastings—a social housing complex. The following day, Al and Toby went to the morgue, but the body was so badly decomposed that they were unable to identify it as April's. Tests later concluded that the body in the morgue was, in fact, that of April Reoch.

On New Year's Day, 2001, the Odd Squad, led by a Vancouver Police Department piper, led a crowd of people assembled at the Carnegie Centre, a library and community centre located in the heart of the Downtown Eastside, to First United Church, a block away, to attend April's funeral. Odd Squad members and a few other Vancouver police officers attended, wearing dress uniforms. Al Arsenault gave a touching eulogy on April's short and tragic life. He described her as a selfless, compassionate individual who shared her story so that others wouldn't have to suffer as she did. Over two hundred people attended April's funeral, and the event was covered by society columnist Malcolm Parry in the *Vancouver Sun*.

On or around the day April was murdered, Al Arsenault and Toby Hinton had seen her and had taken notes about their conversation. April told the two officers she was staying with a man at 40 East Hastings. The man, she told them, was Ian Matheson Rowe. Once it was established that the body in the morgue belonged to April Reoch, homicide detectives began questioning Rowe about April's death. Rowe told police he hadn't seen April in several weeks. Al and Toby knew he was lying—and they had their notes to prove it. Rowe became the prime suspect in April's murder investigation. It took almost nine months and an elaborate police sting operation, but Rowe was eventually charged and later convicted of murdering April Reoch. In the end, Rowe confessed to choking to April to death in a violent rage after she stole his rent money and spent it on drugs. Rowe hid April's body in his apartment for several days before leaving it beside a Dumpster, concealed in a gym bag. Had he been able to lift her body into the Dumpster, April, too, might have been declared a missing woman, and the man who murdered her likely would not have been brought to justice. But April's situation was different. She knew Al and Toby.

Not surprisingly, I've never met a woman who aspired from an early age to be an addicted sex trade worker. Women constantly asked for my help in accessing housing, detox beds and treatment programs. I did my best, but for the most part my efforts were futile. I had trouble finding recovery houses and detox beds for these women, let alone safe, affordable housing in Vancouver's expensive real estate market. The need far exceeds the services available—it is as simple as that.

Overcoming an addiction is a difficult challenge under ideal circumstances. Being homeless, without a phone and without an advocate, most Downtown Eastside women find it impossible to access treatment. There are only six detox beds for women in that community, and no longer-term treatment beds. Even outside the neighbourhood there are few resources that women can access. The good, licensed facilities scattered throughout the greater Vancouver area have waiting lists that preclude most poor women ever accessing their programs. Without question, treatment services for both men and women are important, but for women the need is beyond urgent, and we can no longer afford to be idle.

Over the last several decades we've watched governments cut back on services for the most vulnerable people in our communities. This includes the closing of mental health beds and women's centres and reduced funding for foster care programs that house defenceless children. Most of us would be horrified to learn that mental health institutions in the greater Vancouver area routinely place mentally ill women in the drug-infested, crime-ridden hotel rooms that line the Hastings strip—a veritable chemical gulag. They do this because it is difficult to find housing for mentally ill women given the meagre shelter allowance provided by welfare (recently increased from $325 to $375 a month). Mentally ill women are easy targets for pimps and drug dealers and fall victim to violence, exploitation and addiction once they are placed in this neighbourhood.

We can't fix problems if we don't acknowledge that they exist. We need more, many more, licensed treatment facilities for women and youth. The costs are enormous when those who become addicted have to wait years to access treatment services, if they can access them at all. Providing these services early in an addiction cycle will ultimately save a lot of tax-payer money on expenditures such as court costs, health care, policing and insurance premiums. The human cost is also grave—in suffering and in the tragic loss of human potential. In the lead-up to the 2010 Olympic Games, which Vancouver will be hosting, our city needs to become proactive in providing safe, affordable housing for our vulnerable citizens and addiction treatment services for our addicted populations.

There are some who believe that addicted women made lifestyle choices that relieve the public of any responsibility or obligation to help them. Most addicted women I've known were abused as children and/or suffer from mental illness. Children who are exploited and are forced to live in unsafe domestic situations don't get a vote on how tax dollars are spent. If these children could talk, they would tell you they need safe, secure housing and adults in their lives who are healthy enough to love and nurture them. They would also tell you that if they don't get the help they need when they are young they stand a strong chance of maturing into addicted adults who will live in poverty and interact with the criminal justice system throughout their lives.

The Pickton trial will cost Canadians millions of dollars. The police investigation alone will cost close to $70 million, 70 percent of which will be paid for by B.C. taxpayers. The questions most people ask are: How did so many women go missing? and Why did it take so long to stop it? Stevie Cameron's investigative work will help to shed light on these questions, and more citizens will thereby understand the need for us to prevent anything like this from ever happening again. I take comfort in knowing that these issues are being brought to the public's attention so they can be discussed and acted upon by people not only in Vancouver, but throughout British Columbia and the rest of Canada.

Elaine Allan
Vancouver
March 2007

PROLOGUE

"No! Oh no—no!"

With a shriek of grief and shock, Charlotte Frey tore herself out of her seat in the courtroom and fled, followed by her adult son, Ricky Frey. They had been sitting quietly in the families' section, listening to Crown prosecutor Derrill Prevett's opening statement on the first day of the trial, when Charlotte suddenly realized that it was her Marnie he was describing. Or rather, what was left of Marnie—a jawbone with three teeth, recovered from a pile of sifted dirt.

As the day progressed, we learned that a few of Georgina Papin's hand bones had been uncovered under the floor of the slaughterhouse, that Brenda Wolfe's jawbone had turned up in a cistern beside the slaughterhouse, and that the severed heads, hands and feet of Andrea Joesbury and Sereena Abotsway had been discovered in plastic buckets in a workshop garage near Pickton's trailer. For hours on end, police officers took the stand to describe blood and body parts, smells and filth and decay, dying pigs and one horror after another. The public recoiled and protested; newspapers and television backed off. Every media outlet warned about the unpleasant content of their stories; most buried them on back pages or cut them back to a few minutes on the nightly news.

The *Toronto Star*'s Rosie DiManno protested strongly.

THE PICKTON FILE   XXV

"This strikes me as unworthy," she wrote at the end of the trial's first week. "While newspaper editors make decisions of taste and merit every day, it is not the media's job to protect the public—or victims' families—from painful revelations, especially those exposed in open court as evidence.

"I made the same argument against evidentiary self-censorship to my own paper during the Paul Bernardo trial, which altered the journalism landscape on trial reporting. His victims lived and died with the horrors; the least we could do was not avert our eyes, or filter out repugnant details. We are not entitled, in my view, to an amelioration of wickedness, massaging facts for decency.

"Murder is always indecent. Some murders may be more grotesque in their execution than others. But a child starved to death, a teenager dismembered, an old woman raped and stabbed—these are no less hideous than prostitutes butchered and fed to the hogs. I won't accept a hierarchy of evil in the slaying of human beings."

I agreed with every word she wrote.

But she wasn't running the newsrooms of the country; nor was I. Two weeks after the trial began, it was a back-page story and only the *Vancouver Sun,* the *Vancouver Province,* the *Globe and Mail* and the Canadian Press were covering it on a daily basis. Most broadcasters and other media reported only when a story was too sensational to pass up. Even then, I often had to hunt to find them. But the row of white tents that went up in Begbie Square for the television and radio broadcasters is still there, waiting for the reporters to come back each time a big story breaks in this case. The tents won't come down until a verdict is reached.

There is still plenty to learn. The forensic evidence alone—how it was collected and handled, and what it revealed—has been riveting. The size of the investigation and how the farm became Canada's largest crime scene is just as interesting. We have learned that the police originally arrested three other people in February 2002, all of whom were Willie Pickton's friends. They included Pat Casanova, a friend who helped him for many years with the butchering of pigs; Lynn Ellingsen, a woman who had lived at the farm with him for a short time; and Dinah Taylor, another woman who had been a close friend. They were arrested before he was, but were eventually let go, and it is expected that they could be key witnesses in the trial. We have heard that some police officers had suspected Willie Pickton in the missing women case since 1997, the year thirteen women disappeared from Vancouver's Downtown Eastside. Twenty-seven others disappeared between 1998 and his arrest in 2002.

Over these early weeks, we watched the defence try to show that their client is slow. That he is easily manipulated. That others could have been involved. This last thrust is especially fascinating. It has become clear that part of the defence strategy is to look for the other guy—and the other guy they seem to have in mind is Dave Pickton. By late March, the defence lawyers had raised Dave's name many times. They got the task force officers to admit that Dave had been a suspect, and that he had been followed; indeed, they suggested, he is *still* a suspect. The witnesses agreed: yes, he is. One officer testified that in March 2005—three years after Willie's arrest—the police had Dave under surveillance for almost two weeks. We still haven't heard exactly why, but most people following the case can't understand how Dave could live and work on the same property as his brother for so many years and not be involved. Or at least, not know what his brother might have been up to. A few days later, however, this was corrected: Dave Pickton is no longer a suspect.

The parade of witnesses, most of them police officers, continues. They explain their work taking blood samples, testing fingerprints and matching DNA, interviewing people, trying to get to the bottom of this terrible story.

Back in 2003, I attended almost every day of the months-long preliminary hearing, which is held to determine if there is enough evidence to proceed to trial. That is where much of the evidence we are now hearing was first brought to the court's attention, but a strict publication ban meant we couldn't share anything we'd learned. The first of two trials is now well under way, but there are still legal restrictions on reporters. We cannot report any information that could influence the jury during the trial; to do so would risk a charge of criminal contempt of court. And we cannot report anything that is still under one of the many publication bans issued in this case. All we can report is the evidence the lawyers have put before the jury in this trial.

Given these restrictions, what I've tried to do in *The Pickton File* is tell you how I went about trying to capture the back story—from speaking to people on the Downtown Eastside to watching the investigation at the pig farm in Port Coquitlam. I took pictures wherever I went. *The Pickton File* is about how this story began, and how it developed into the largest criminal investigation in Canadian history.

ONE **GETTING STARTED**

It was early April 2002 and Linda McKnight, my literary agent, was on the phone with the news that the publisher of Knopf Canada wanted to know if I'd be interested in writing a book on the sensational Pickton serial murder case in British Columbia.

"Yes," I said.

"Not so fast," Linda said. She pointed out that it would mean a move from my usual areas—politics and white-collar crime—and that it was a story unfolding in Vancouver, not in Toronto, where I lived, which would mean moving to the west or frequent commutes.

Neither agent nor publisher could have known that the story of Robert William Pickton, a fifty-two-year-old pig farmer from Port Coquitlam, had been on my mind since his arrest two months earlier, on February 22, 2002, for the murders of Mona Wilson and Sereena Abotsway, two drug-addicted prostitutes from Vancouver's Downtown Eastside. Not only were three subsequent charges laid on April 3, 2002, for the murders of Jacqueline McDonell, Diane Rock and Heather Bottomley, but Pickton was also the prime suspect in the disappearance of dozens of other women from the same area. Every day since the arrest, I had been following

1

the story in the *Vancouver Sun*'s online edition, and I knew this was not just a deeply disturbing case, but a fascinating and complex one.

My interest in the missing women went back further, to 1998, when I had begun to see the occasional newspaper story about the families and friends of the women, who were agitating for an investigation—and being ignored by police and politicians. At that time I was the editor of *Elm Street,* a national magazine I'd started in 1996, and in 1999 I asked Daniel Wood, a feature writer from Vancouver, to investigate the situation. Several weeks later, he turned in a brilliant piece—the first comprehensive national story on the missing women of Vancouver's Downtown Eastside, which concluded that the police appeared to be doing nothing about the disappearances of more than sixty women.

When Linda called, I knew right away that this was a book I had to do, more than anything because it was an astonishing and powerful story. I had worked with homeless and poor people for many years at my church's Out of the Cold shelter program in Toronto, an experience that gave me the confidence to think I might be able to win the trust of the Downtown Eastside community. Then there was Vancouver itself. I had lived in the city for years, and had gone to the University of British Columbia. (In fact, I'd met my future husband, David Cameron, in a political science class at UBC in the early 1960s.) I knew the city well, and still had many relatives and friends there.

And though I knew people would ask why I was moving away from politics and white-collar crime, I was quite frankly sick of the same old frauds, the same corrupt politicians trying the same old scams, almost always successfully—and when they were caught and charged, they almost always emerged with very few penalties because of political interference and incompetent policing. What particularly concerned me was the bland assumption that there was a big difference between white-collar and blue-collar crime and that a slap on the wrist—a couple of months in jail or a big fine—would be enough for a crook in a suit, regardless of how much he had stolen or how many lives he'd ruined. For a long time, I have believed that the criminal mind is the same whether the perpetrator is a politician or another well-educated professional, or a drug smuggler, gang member or killer. In both groups, there are psychopaths with no regard for the law. In fact, both white-collar criminals and violent criminals delight in breaking the law. Getting away with it is half the thrill.

Partly because white-collar criminals have powerful friends and allies to make the police and prosecutors think twice about the dangers to their own careers, and partly because they lawyer up right away with influential counsel, police officers prefer hunting down violent criminals. And it's not entirely about self-preservation. Most cops believe white-collar crime is boring; the action, for them, is on the homicide team—the elite in any police force. And none of them would disagree that the Pickton case was the most challenging murder case under way in North America. For me, the opportunity felt like a gift. So why did the Vancouver Police Department take so long to get around to a serious investigation of the fates of the missing women? One good reason was that there were no bodies, and therefore no physical evidence to work with. Another reason was cost: an investigation into a serial killer can be incredibly expensive. A third was expertise: few homicide detectives have the training to deal with full-blown serial offenders. And then there was the status of the missing women themselves: junkies, sex-trade workers. *Good riddance,* some said. *They brought it on themselves.*

By coincidence, when Linda called I was just starting work on a new story for the *Globe and Mail* on Canada's elite team of violent crime investigators in the Behavioural Science Section—or BSS, as it is known—of the Ontario Provincial Police (OPP). Led by Chief Superintendent Kate Lines, one of the best-known homicide investigators in the world, the seventy-person BSS team is tucked away in the OPP's headquarters in Orillia, a small Ontario town 130 kilometres northwest of Toronto. She had agreed to let me talk to the seven groups of specialists who provide an array of cutting-edge police services: criminal profiling, geographic profiling, threat assessment, lie-detector testing, a sexual assault registry, forensic psychiatry and a sophisticated computer system called the Violent Crime Linking Analysis System, or ViCLAS, which tracks and compares criminal activity to find links that point to certain offenders. With a staff of forty-one, the OPP's ViCLAS centre is by far the largest in Canada; by comparison, the RCMP has a total of seventy-two ViCLAS officers in all its offices across the country, including its Ottawa headquarters.

The BSS works not just within the OPP, but with police forces across the country, trying to solve old homicides for which the clues have run out, or cases requiring expertise that most small forces don't have, with a focus on crimes by violent serial predators, including rapists, child molesters, arsonists, killers, and even serial bombers like Theodore Kaczynski, the American better known as the Unabomber, who was caught in 1996 after an eighteen-year crime spree. Aside from a similar section at FBI headquarters in Quantico,

Virginia, there was nothing quite like the BSS anywhere else in North America. Kate Lines, a Quantico-trained Criminal Investigative Analyst (better known as a "psychological profiler") and one of only two Canadian police officers who had taken the ten-month FBI course, had been assisting other Canadian police forces for many years on difficult cases. Former Quantico profilers I talked to—men such as Greg McCrary, who now works as an international profiler and homicide expert—told me the OPP's section was as good as or better than the FBI's.

Because the Pickton story had broken just a few weeks earlier, I had pitched the feature to the *Globe,* sure that the people in Orillia would have some insights into the case and might even be working on it. If they did, they weren't saying. But years later, completely by accident, I discovered that, indeed, they were all over the Pickton case—and had been for a long time.

In June 2002, when I signed the contract with Knopf Canada, we had no idea how massive the investigation would be. We had no notion that the police would sift every inch of dirt on the Pickton farm, a process that lasted from the spring of 2002 to late 2004. We did not foresee the broad publication ban imposed on two court hearings—at the seven-month-long preliminary hearing held in 2003 that would, unless it began to come out at the trial, prevent any word of what was being said in court from being printed or broadcast, lest it influence a potential juror. (Even after the trial began in late January 2007, only what was said each day could be made public.) We couldn't know that by 2006 there would be twenty-seven charges of first-degree murder against Pickton—one charge was later quashed—and that the police would continue to investigate him on suspicion of many other deaths. And we didn't know that the police and other personnel involved in the case, under threat of ruined careers, were forbidden to talk to reporters. In blissful ignorance, all I could do was begin.

—

For me, every new book starts the same way. I take whatever time I need to do three things: gather all the available information about the case; build what I call a "names" list; and prepare a detailed chronology of events. The names list includes every single person connected to the case, whether they be victims, suspects, family members, police officers, lawyers, neighbours, experts, reporters, witnesses, court watchers . . . everyone. I add to their entry in my list everything I know about them, and usually, by the time my book is done, the list contains hundreds of entries. The chronology becomes the spine of my book; I update it constantly, up to and beyond the date of publication. (I am still updating my chronology and names list for my previous book, *The Last Amigo: Karlheinz Schreiber and the Anatomy of a Scandal*, published in 2001; my latest entry concerns Schreiber's recent lawsuit launched against former prime minister Brian Mulroney claiming Mulroney had failed to do any work for $300,000 cash Schreiber paid him to help him with business deals.) Because I was starting from scratch, the whole process took about four months.

At the beginning, I pored over news stories, many of them by Lindsay Kines, a police reporter at the *Vancouver Sun* who had been writing about the missing women for four years before Pickton was finally arrested. It became evident that the families of the missing women trusted Kines because he knew so many details about the lives and the disappearances of their loved ones. But I also realized that he had some good inside information from the Vancouver police, information that made it clear that some of the officers were frustrated with the force's indifference to and lack of action on these cases. A few months before Pickton's arrest, the *Vancouver Sun* added Kim Bolan and Lori Culbert to the story, and between September and November 2001, they produced an eleven-part series on the missing women. Their accounts of police negligence were shocking. Among many other things, they found that the police had accomplished far less than they had claimed, that the investigations were flawed, that there was no compatible system of checking DNA between the Vancouver police and the RCMP, and that there were far more women missing than the police had admitted to. Instead of twenty-seven missing women, there were at least forty-five. The series, later nominated for a Governor General's Award for meritorious reporting, shamed the police into adding more resources to the investigation.

Another valuable source of background information was Wayne Leng, an automobile mechanic who had been first a client and then a close friend of Sarah de Vries, a prostitute who went missing from the Downtown Eastside in April 1998. Leng never gave up hassling the Vancouver Police over Sarah's disappearance, and he set up a website, www.missingpeople.net, devoted to all the missing women, with every relevant news story archived, as well as photographs and a message board on which grieving families and friends could post notes looking for, or offering, information. To this day, it remains the most useful source of information and news stories about the missing women. Leng moved to a new job in California a few years ago, but the website remains his obsession; it is the clearing house for most of the public information about the case.

Along with Daniel Wood's story for *Elm Street,* there was good information in community newspapers and the *Vancouver Courier.* But the national media— the *Globe and Mail, National Post,* and *Maclean's* magazine, for example, as well as broadcasters including the CBC and CTV—had very little on the missing women. One rare television feature was done in the United States: a six-minute item about the missing women broadcast on *America's Most Wanted* on July 31, 1999, and updated on July 22, 2000. But soon after February 5, 2002, when the police first arrested Pickton on an illegal firearms charge, it became clear to the media, both local and national, that he was the prime suspect in the missing women case. From that point until he was charged with two counts of murder on February 22, 2002, coverage in the Canadian media was intense; after the first charges and then later ones, it blew into an international sensation, with major news organizations such as the BBC, the *Washington Post,* the *New York Times* and the *Los Angeles Times* running lengthy pieces.

The stories I collected allowed me to build a timeline—what I call my chronology—as well as a list of potential contacts: the family members of the missing women; Pickton neighbours, friends and family members; community workers; and local politicians. I made an alphabetical list, making sure to attach as much information as I could find about each person. As I called them, I would add more to their files: Would they agree to an interview? Did they know others who could help? What about phone numbers, email addresses and home addresses? I use a number of simple codes that allow me to see at a glance what kind of progress I have made with each name. Almost everyone I called suggested other people I could talk to.

Lindsay Kines at the *Sun* agreed to meet me as soon as I came to Vancouver. And Wayne Leng called many people on my behalf. The police officers working on the case and the scientists working on the property, however, refused to see me or return my calls. Even officers who had nothing to do with the investigation were not allowed to talk about it. The exceptions, fortunately, were retired officers and those who had moved on to new jobs. One of these was Kim Rossmo.

Rossmo is an unusual cat, and a controversial one in Vancouver. He served on the Vancouver police force for almost twenty-three years, many of them in the Downtown Eastside, and during that time he worked his way through a doctoral program in criminology at Simon Fraser University. His thesis project was a computer program he'd designed that helped identify the prime suspect in cases of serial crimes such as rape, murder, bombing and arson. At its simplest, the idea behind it was that offenders tend to kill in the area where they are most comfortable—usually their own neighbourhood. Once all the information is entered that describes the areas where the crimes took place, as well as the suspects and their addresses, the computer almost always pinpoints the prime suspect as the person who lives closest to the places where the crimes happened. Calling it geographic profiling, Rossmo patented the system under the company name of Rigel and very quickly was in demand by police forces all over the world. In fact, he trained Detective Sergeant Brad Moore, the geographic profiler working for the BSS in Orillia.

In 1995, Rossmo was promoted several ranks to a new position of detective inspector, but as his celebrity grew, his popularity in the Vancouver Police Department plummeted. An old boys' club of senior officers who had come up through the ranks the old way—without higher degrees and without any interest in modern technology—hated Rossmo, resented his success and his unusual promotion, and made his life a nightmare. In late 1998, when he suggested that a serial killer was almost certainly responsible for the disappearances of women in the Downtown Eastside, his colleagues became even more hostile. After Ray Canuel, the chief who had promoted him, retired in 2000, Rossmo was left without any protection. He was fired from his senior rank and told that, if he wished, he could return to his old job as a constable on the street. He did not go quietly. He sued for wrongful dismissal, and when the case went to court in 2001, all the VPD's dirty laundry was aired by Lindsay Kines and other journalists, who described not only the bullying and dirty tricks, but also the failure of Rossmo's colleagues to take the missing women's situation seriously. Rossmo lost his case in court; the judge decided that the contract he'd signed allowed the force to remove him from the job and return him to his old rank. But despite the decision and subsequent failed appeals, the reputation of the VPD had been permanently stained by this fiasco.

When I called him in May 2002, Kim Rossmo was working in Washington, D.C., as director of research for the Police Foundation. As we talked, he realized I had done a great deal of homework on the case and he would not have to spoonfeed me the story, something that always irritates the hell out of him. Nor did I have to spoon-feed him: he was up to date on Willie Pickton and knew that the Crown prosecutor had just laid, on May 2, another first-degree murder charge against Pickton for the death of Brenda Wolfe.

Rossmo was patient and courteous, enjoying the play of ideas and steering me away from conspiracy theories and assumptions. He brought me up short with a comment

I have never forgotten: "Serial killers are rare animals. There are not nearly as many around as people think." A simple line, but it has helped me keep my eye on the ball more than once, in that I stopped paying much attention to the inevitable conspiracy theories that were blossoming out of this case.

Rossmo agreed to meet with me, and in late May I flew to Washington.

I liked Kim Rossmo. He was wary at first and radiated all the bustle of a busy man who was giving me a little of his valuable time, but it wasn't long before he revealed himself as a charming, extremely smart guy. His work is fascinating, and he knows it, so he doesn't mind a lot of talk about it. Nor does he mind talking about his last painful years with the Vancouver police. What upset him most at this stage— because it was clear even then that he was moving on well past the sordid world of the Vancouver police's dirty tricks department—were the hundreds of thousands of dollars in legal fees he'd acquired in his struggle. Still, he owns the Rigel software, so eventually he may make some money with it. Kim talked then—and later—about his experiences as a beat cop in the Downtown Eastside and about earlier investigations into missing and murdered women from the area, investigations that predated the one that resulted in Pickton's arrest. And he took me through his failed efforts to persuade his colleagues in the Vancouver police that a serial killer was working in the Downtown Eastside.

I went to see another profiler that summer. Kate Lines had been the second Canadian police officer to go through the Criminal Investigative Analyst training program at Quantico; the first was an RCMP officer, Inspector Ron MacKay. I'd recently reviewed *Dark Paths, Cold Trails,* an interesting biography of MacKay written by Doug Clark, an Ottawa-area journalist. MacKay had originally been an old-school homicide detective with a strong bias against profiling and technology. His 1989–1990 Quantico training made him a believer. In addition to his work as a homicide expert for the Mounties, MacKay had taken on the task of reforming the inadequate databases police used to record violent crimes and look for facts that could show links between these crimes. He wanted a database that would work as well as or better than the FBI's Violent Criminal Apprehension Program, known as ViCAP. ViCAP had two major flaws: not all American police forces were using it, and it didn't track sexual assaults. Under MacKay, the RCMP started designing a new system they called ViCLAS, for Violent Crime Linkage Analysis Systems. What they developed, with help from Dr. Peter Collins, the forensic psychiatrist in Orillia's BSS section, was a booklet with 262 questions to be filled out each time a Canadian police officer investigated the following types of crimes:

- solved or unsolved homicides and attempted homicides;
- solved or unsolved sexual assaults;
- missing persons cases in which the circumstances indicate a strong possibility of foul play and the victim is still missing;
- unidentified bodies for which the manner of death is known or suspected to be homicide; and
- non-parental abductions and attempted abductions.

It took a few years and a lot of persuasion—reluctant police officers in many jurisdictions hated the thought of the time it would take to fill in the booklets—but MacKay eventually established a national database capable of linking the crimes of serial offenders in relation to homicides, sexual assaults, missing persons and unidentified bodies. And MacKay himself became Canada's leading expert on serial killers.

Having learned that he was now retired and running his own consulting business, I decided to grab him before another enterprising reporter discovered him. We arranged to meet for lunch in Ottawa, and discovered that we knew many of the same people, including Kim Rossmo, Peter Collins and Kate Lines, and shared similar interests. He agreed to act as my consultant on the book, telling me he had checked me out carefully before making the decision. I liked Ron MacKay as much as I had Kim Rossmo; they are good guys: serious, committed and knowledgeable.

As I was gathering the information I needed to start work, I decided to buy my first digital camera. It was a good decision—my camera was always with me, and I shot thousands of pictures. My main interest lay in documenting the progress of the investigators at the Pickton farm in Port Coquitlam, where the scene changed week by week. None of my pictures and short video clips are works of art, but they have helped me remember places, people and events better than any notes I ever took, and I began sliding them into my manuscript drafts, my chronology and my names list. The only problem I ever had was losing the camera: two were stolen and I misplaced one, so I am now on my fourth. A digital camera has become as much a part of my working day as my tape recorder or notebook.

The last big issue I needed to resolve before I could begin work in B.C. was a car. We had only one, and it was a beat-up 1996 Jeep Cherokee that leaked so badly around the windshield that it soaked the headliner and the carpet. The car smelled as if a badger had died in it. I shipped it out west for $700; reeking or not, it was cheaper than renting a car for the same period.

By early August, I was in Vancouver, ensconced in a tiny guest suite—outfitted with a desk, a futon and an armchair—at St. Andrew's Hall, the Presbyterian college at UBC where I'd attended services with my family for many years. (David and I had also been married in its chapel.) The college was great. The people were pleasant, but I was almost completely anonymous; the students had no interest in me. I worked there when I wasn't out doing interviews, and the view was superb: I looked out across the campus, past the stunning Chan Centre, to the ocean, with a view of the mountains of Vancouver Island in the distance.

I'm sure many Presbyterian parsons had endured the thin mattress on the futon, but I am not of such hardy stock, and my first purchase was a feather mattress to put on top. I then slept happily in my little college room for many weeks, hearing the distant horns of the tugboats out in the harbour and waking each morning to my view and to that old familiar smell of laurel, damp grass and fir that took me back to my youth on this beautiful campus.

TWO VANCOUVER

Once I arrived, all I wanted to do was get out to the pig farm and look around. Kim Rossmo was in town, and Lindsay Kines had offered to take us both out to Port Coquitlam, a thirty-minute drive east of Vancouver; it would be my first visit to the property, and Kim's as well. By this time, it was early August and the police had laid another charge against Pickton, for the murder of Andrea Joesbury, making a total of seven. We all thought that more were coming.

Kim and I agreed to meet at the Starbucks on Main Street in East Vancouver because it was close to the highway to Port Coquitlam. Right on time, Lindsay pulled in to pick us up. Although this was the first time we'd met, he and Kim knew each other well from Lindsay's detailed stories about Kim's struggle to keep his job and rank in the Vancouver police. Lindsay is a quiet man who listens carefully; I soon found that he has a fierce passion for his work and an encyclopedic knowledge of the missing women's case.

Kim had lived in this neighbourhood before he moved to Washington, and as we drove through it was clear he was still a bit homesick for it.

"I had a great place there," he said, pointing up to a handsome old house carefully transformed into a couple of large apartments. His war with the VPD brass had cost him not only his job, but the home he had bought a few years earlier. He shrugged his shoulders and changed the subject.

We had a fine day for our outing. The day was clear and sunny, with the North Shore Mountains and Washington's Mount Baker to the south standing out in high relief against the blue sky. Port Coquitlam—an old working-class town sustained by the railway, logging, fishing and farming—looked prosperous, with sprawling housing developments covering every hill and valley in sight. But when we got to the farm itself, everything about it surprised me. To reach it, we had turned north off the Lougheed Highway and driven through the middle of a large shopping centre on the eastern outskirts of the town. Lindsay took us through an appealing new subdivision built on curving streets and cul-de-sacs named after great rivers: the Nile, Tigris, Euphrates, Po, Thames and Tiber. Most of the houses, whether they were detached or town-houses, were a good size, two and three storeys high, with nicely landscaped yards. All of this, Lindsay explained, was on former Pickton farmland. So was the new Blakeburn Elementary School. I found out later that the Coquitlam School District had paid the Picktons $2.3 million for that land, while the city of Port Coquitlam had bought a chunk for Blakeburn Park for $1.2 million. Another piece, sold in 1994 to a company called Eternal Holdings, which built townhouses, brought the Picktons more than $1.7 million. I kept wondering where the farm was in all this well-tended suburbia.

Lindsay turned into Nile Gate, which was just a block long, and took us past a small group of unfinished houses that ended beside the Pickton farm property line. These houses, all of which sported FOR SALE signs, had just been framed. Sheets of plywood and scrap lumber were lying around, and the street itself was still just dirt and gravel. At the end, a steel gate guarded by two police officers and a fence stretching around the farm in both directions, threaded with yellow crime scene tape, prevented the curious, like us, from setting foot on the property. This gate appeared to be the main entrance for the police and evidence technicians, and dozens of their cars were parked just beyond the fence, beside a tall wooden pole, jammed into the ground, that held a floodlight and two security cameras. Behind this area were several large white and yellow ATCO trailers that seemed to be used either as lunchrooms and restrooms or as mobile labs and offices. A couple, with large evaporators at the back, appeared to be refrigerated trucks.

The people working here reported to senior officers at the Missing Women Task Force, a joint operation of the RCMP and the Vancouver Police Department formed in April 2001, although the Mounties vastly outnumbered the city cops—in part because the RCMP were responsible for policing in Port Coquitlam. (In most parts of British Columbia, police services are provided under contract to local municipalities by the RCMP, though nearby Port Moody, New Westminster and West Vancouver all have their own police forces.) The task force was also known as Project Evenhanded. That's because the British Columbia RCMP division is called E Division, and all of its special operations, like this missing persons' investigation, are given names that begin with the letter E. At this time, about all I knew about Project Evenhanded was that it had been set up in February 2001, had an office somewhere in Surrey and was run by a staff sergeant called Don Adam.

Lindsay Kines (left) and Kim Rossmo at the Pickton farm, August 2002.

We watched a couple of large yellow backhoes, their buckets rearing back into the sky before falling down on the earth and clawing up soil, swivelling with it and dropping it into huge dump trucks. At least fifty or sixty people were walking around, looking busy, some disappearing from time to time behind vast mounds of dirt that were covered with plastic tarps or with wild grass and shrubs. The place was a mess. Wrecked cars, rusty farm equipment and derelict sheds were scattered all over the place. It didn't appear to be a farm at all, and yet the property, owned by Robert Pickton, his brother, David Pickton, and their sister, Linda Wright, had recently been valued at $3 million. (It wasn't unencumbered, however; in April 2002, Karin Joesbury, the mother of Andrea Joesbury, one of the women Pickton had been accused of murdering, had filed a lien against the property and launched a civil suit against Pickton. And there was a further $1.3-million mortgage on it from the Delta Credit

Union.) Behind all the dirt, trucks and mess, we could see the prim rooftops of new houses.

We left and drove around to the north end of the farm, passing an undeveloped corner that sported a large sign announcing a rezoning application by David Pickton, Robert William Pickton and Linda Wright to change a portion of their agricultural land to residential land and create what seemed to be about nine or ten building lots.

—

Lindsay turned in to another new subdivision called Heritage Meadows, down a street called Elbow Place—by this time, they'd run out of river names. The Picktons had sold it to developers in March 2002, a month after Willie Pickton's arrest, for $769,469; now, only a year later, it was crammed

Backhoes move piles of dirt to the screeners.

with attractive townhouses, all newly occupied. Elbow Place dead-ended at a turning circle with a high berm of grassy dirt beyond the fence. This was the northern portion of the farm and was just a few yards from where Willie Pickton's trailer stood. Lindsay told us this was where the police had entered on February 5, 2002, when they raided the place with a search warrant to look for illegal weapons. We couldn't see anything here of the farm except for the berm.

The east side of the property bordered on the Carnoustie Golf Club, so we drove back around to the front of the property at 953 Dominion Avenue, the real main entrance, at least as far as the Picktons had been concerned. The old family farmhouse, a two-storey building with grubby white stucco siding, sat only twenty feet back from the edge of Dominion; an old dirt lane beside it ran back past sheds and a hip-roofed Dutch barn to more outbuildings and, we learned later, Willie Pickton's trailer. In all, there were only about sixteen acres left of the original Pickton farm. We could see into the window of the kitchen and make out a quart of orange juice sitting on the windowsill; someone told me later that that same quart of orange juice had been sitting there since police swarmed onto the farm on February 5, 2002.

I'd heard a lot about Piggy's Palace, a huge shed where the Pickton brothers had held raucous parties for the local community, as well as for bikers; I'd heard that there were sometimes up to seventeen hundred people at these events, and that the local fire officials finally closed the place down. From behind the fence, I looked around the farm to see if I could spot the Palace, but Lindsay told us it wasn't on farm property. In fact, it was about a mile east of here on Burns Road, which begins where Dominion Avenue dead-ends at the Pitt River. What had gone on here at the farm a few years ago, I later learned, was an early version of the Piggy's Palace parties; cockfights were held in the slaughterhouse, near the back of the farm. Most of the clientele were Filipinos who paid to get in, gambled on the fights and bought drinks and barbecued food from the brothers, but plenty of others came as well. Once Dave Pickton had finished building the Palace, the cockfights on the farm ended.

To the south, and right across the street from the Pickton farm, facing the front of the farmhouse and the barn, was a vast parking lot owned by Home Depot, one of the anchor tenants in the shopping centre we'd come through an hour earlier. This lot was where the police held their first press conference after Pickton's arrest. Just to the east of the parking lot was a large blue clapboard farmhouse, set back about fifty feet from the road; this was the local Hells Angels clubhouse.

While Lindsay drove us around the property, he told us what had happened on Wednesday, February 6, 2002, the night after the police raided the farm and took it over. Lindsay had met a man peering through the closed gate at the entrance to the farm who claimed he knew Willie Pickton. The man was Ross Contois, who turned out to be a criminal with a long and colourful rap sheet of drug and theft charges. He was also a friend of Willie Pickton's. He told Lindsay that the police had interviewed Pickton much earlier about the missing women. "These guys are totally on the wrong trail," Contois said, adding that Pickton was the victim of rumour-mongering. "It's been going on for years."

Later, Lindsay sent me a note describing his encounter with Contois more fully.

"There aren't many funny stories in this case," he wrote. "But did I tell you how I came to meet Contois? I got a tip that police were searching the Pickton farm about 5 p.m. I was actually out strolling with Molly [his daughter] when my pager went off. So I called [Kim] Bolan at work, waited until Sara [his wife] got home, then picked up Bolan and we headed out to the farm. It was pissing rain and we were the first people out there.

"For two hours, we hovered around the entrance to the farm. Then this guy walks up to the gate, asks to see Willie and gets turned away by the police. They ask his name, of course. And he says, 'Oh, you guys know me, Ross Edward Contois.' (It's funny how career criminals, when asked their name, always provide all three, isn't it?)

"Anyway, as he's walking away from the gate, Kim and I approach him, and he asks us what's going on, and we tell him our suspicions, and he goes into this rant about how his girlfriend, Gina, knows all about this, and how it's all lies, and just somebody out to get Willie. We ask if we can talk to Gina, and he says sure, if we'll give him a ride home.

"By this time, it's about seven or so, our deadline is looming, and the last thing I want to be doing is providing a taxi service for Ross Edward Contois. But he's quite insistent that this is the only way we're going to meet Gina, so I leave Kim at the farm and take Contois in my car. He's got a bag with him, and we're less than a block from the farm when he says how he's relieved to get away from there, because he's got a bag full of stolen hammers that he was going to fence to Willie. Now I start wondering what the hell I'm doing with this guy in my car. But he's true to his word. We find Gina. She goes into a long rant. I let the tape run, and then I head back to meet Bolan.

"So that's how I first met Ross and Gina. Is Gina a suspect? I've heard from the cops that there are going to be other charges, likely women who helped lure the missing women out to the farm for him. I've also heard from cops that Pickton, when he was stopped in red-light districts, often had another woman with him. So it's possible that was Gina or someone else. Now, I heard all this months ago, and nobody's been charged yet, so who knows?"

Ross Contois and Gina Houston were two of the more interesting characters that would pop up in the Pickton saga over the next few years. Gina Houston, a former Downtown Eastside addict and prostitute who now rented a small house in Port Coquitlam, was Contois's common-law wife and had been one of Willie Pickton's closest friends for years. It wasn't long before the police zeroed in on Houston as a key witness in their investigation. As Houston herself told people, the police suspected her of procuring for Pickton and taking some of the missing women out to the farm.

By Wednesday, February 6, 2002, the day after the raid, the property was sealed and guarded at every point, with police swarming all over it, a sure signal to reporters that this was much more than just a flap over a few unregistered or prohibited guns. Police cars from Burnaby, Coquitlam and Vancouver were parked every which way around the farm. Rumours raced through the community, and locals began gathering by the Dominion Avenue entrance; the word was that Willie was looking good for the missing women investigation and what might really be happening here was a serial killer investigation.

"I can tell you a search is being conducted on that property and the search is being executed by the Missing Women Task Force," police constable Catherine Galliford confirmed to the crowd of reporters. Another officer told them that Willie Pickton, who had been arrested and charged with possession of illegal firearms, was a "person of interest" in the missing women case. They learned that the police had put in a trailer as a mobile command centre near the barn, and that officers had been there all night.

—

All of this had happened seven months before Lindsay, Kim and I came out to see the place. On February 7, 2002, the police had released Pickton but they told him he could not return to the farm. He moved in with his brother, Dave, who was living in a handsome ranch-style house about a mile away on Burns Road, just two driveways north of Piggy's Palace. Willie was upset that he wasn't allowed back on the property, but Dave Pickton wasn't inconvenienced; he'd moved out of the family farmhouse about a year earlier. I'd learned that he owned at least two companies; one hauled and delivered fill from construction sites, dumping much of it at the farm— hence the mountains of dirt. He also did demolition of small buildings and some construction work. During those weeks of waiting, Willie Pickton spent his days working at one of Dave's job sites. Less than three weeks later, on February 22, 2002, the police arrested Pickton again, this time on two counts of first-degree murder. Ever since that day—and it's been over five years now—he has been held under tight security at the North Fraser Pretrial Centre, in the middle of a large industrial park in Port Coquitlam. He is transported by sheriffs to court whenever pretrial hearings are required.

We didn't drive around Port Coquitlam much longer that day, but as we left I realized it was the first time I had visited the town, despite all the years I'd lived in Vancouver. I'd never even been to Coquitlam, Maple Ridge or Mission, other towns that were to become central to my story. Today, I know them all as well as I know my own neighbourhood in Toronto.

Willie Pickton has been held here at the North Fraser Pretrial Centre in Port Coquitlam, a mile from his farm, since February 22, 2002.

We drove back downtown along the Barnet Highway, which runs along the shore of Burrard Inlet, and Lindsay took us to West Coast Reduction, a massive rendering plant on the inlet, close to where East Hastings Street begins. Over the past seven months, we'd read news articles containing horrific details about the murders of missing women; among the worst were unverified stories about Pickton dumping human remains at the rendering plant. The stories didn't come from the police— not officially, anyway—and by this time in August, there was such a code of silence among the cops and the other investigators, pathologists, evidence technicians, forensic anthropologists and the like, that we were learning nothing. But in the early weeks, leaks from the Missing Women Task Force were common, and that's how we'd heard about the rendering plant. It was no secret, anyway; Pickton's neighbours talked freely about how he had often taken dead animals there.

I stared at the plant. Could this enormous operation, one that stewed carcasses into fats for cosmetics and protein for animal feed and fertilizer and shipped the products all over the world in huge tankers, be the last resting place of these tragic women? It seemed unthinkable.

Even though Kim had been a beat cop in the Downtown Eastside for years, and knew the area well, he seemed just as interested in Lindsay's tour as I was. We drove around the infamous "Kiddie Stroll," centred on Franklin Street, just a few blocks from West Coast Reduction, where underage girls had walked the streets, selling themselves for a few dollars or some heroin or cocaine. Now, it was gradually turning into a stroll for transsexual prostitutes. Finally, Lindsay drove us along East Hastings, in the heart of the Downtown Eastside. This was an area I remembered; as a university student, I had shopped at Woodward's and the Army & Navy Store, both mainstays of this poor community for generations. I remembered the raffish nature of the street, with its little coffee shops, shabby hotels, second-hand stores, churches and drop-in centres; what I didn't remember was a garbage-strewn street packed with addicts and prostitutes and cops. A jostling crowd of eighty or ninety men shuffled around on the sidewalk near the Carnegie Centre, at the corner of Main Street and East Hastings. Kim and Lindsay informed me that this was the area's open-air drug market, which the police seemed powerless to shut down. There seemed to be very few stores open; many places had windows boarded over. The department stores had closed long ago. I looked out the car windows and thought about how happy I'd be to get the hell out of there.

Not long after this, Lindsay and I met for coffee. Why wasn't he doing a book himself? I asked him. Maybe he'd consider working with me? After all, he'd spent four years working on the missing women's story; he had the contacts, the knowledge and the passion for it. But Lindsay told me he'd been taking calls from the families of the missing women for years, many of them late at night while he was at home, sometimes several times a night. He'd spent untold hours with them and had written countless stories. He'd also covered the reaction to the tragedy of the missing women, including the evolving responses from the police, from politicians and from the public. Now it was time to turn the story over to someone new, he told me, someone with a fresh eye. It was time for him to move on to new stories himself. In addition, there was a personal issue at play. Lindsay and his wife, Sara Darling, a CBC reporter, were the new parents of a little girl, and the best way to pay tribute to the women who had died, he said, was to raise his own child with as much love and care as possible. Lindsay and Sara accepted new assignments with the *Sun* and the CBC in Victoria and left Vancouver for good.

THREE **EXPLORING PICKTONLAND**

On July 25, 2002, just before I arrived in Vancouver, the police added another nine names to the missing women's list, bringing the total up to sixty-three. The list had been climbing steadily—from the forty-five they'd admitted to after the *Vancouver Sun*'s investigation less than a year before, to fifty-four on May 27, 2002 and finally to this new total of sixty three. The province's attorney general, Rich Coleman, announced that the cost of the investigation had topped $10 million, with no end in sight; the B.C. government was going to have to ask the federal government for help in paying the bills. Fifty-one anthropologists from five Canadian universities had joined the army of investigators on the farm; they were there to identify human bone fragments. And amid stinging public criticism of police negligence, Terry Blythe, who was still the chief constable of the Vancouver Police Department, announced that he'd ordered an internal review to see how the force had managed the missing women's file. He sounded pretty upbeat. "So far," he said, "I believe we're looking very good in this."

What wasn't happening was any kind of court process, and that was fine by me. It now looked as if the preliminary hearing—where the Crown prosecutors would present their evidence against Pickton before a judge, whose job it would be to decide if the evidence was strong enough to commit Pickton to trial—wouldn't start until November. That meant I had more than two months to complete the dozens of interviews I wanted to do.

The first person on my list was a young woman called Elaine Allan. All I knew about her was what I'd read in the papers: she had run a drop-in centre for sex-trade workers in the Downtown Eastside and knew many of the women who had disappeared.

"Sure," she said when I reached her. "I'd be happy to help."

We arranged to meet for dinner, and I spent the rest of the day making other appointments. I decided to leave my little bed-sitter at St. Andrew's early so I could explore the Downtown Eastside by myself—a little homework before I met Elaine. It was dark by the time I got there, and if it had looked grimy and sinister on my first pass with Kim and Lindsay in bright sunshine, it was terrifying at night. I snapped the door locks on the Jeep and crawled up and down side streets and along East Hastings, trying to absorb it all: the open-air drug market, thick with muttering dealers and customers; the prostitutes waiting on corners, as drivers inched along in their cars, looking them over; emaciated women lurching along the sidewalks, stooping and hunting in vain for the tiniest crumbs of crack cocaine—a process I later learned was called "tweaking." Bodies were slumped in doorways or against garbage cans in alleys.

Just when I'd decided I'd had enough, the phone rang. It was Elaine.

"Where are you?"

"Oh, just driving along East Hastings, looking around."

"You're very brave," she said. If she only knew.

As I ate dinner at Elaine's cheerful West End home, I felt like I had known her all my life. In her thirties, I guessed. Thin as a rake and very pretty, she seemed blessed with a quick wit and a compassionate heart. She had grown up in Coquitlam, the city next door to Port Coquitlam, and had been a communications student at Carleton University, in Ottawa, during some of the years I had been writing about politics for the *Ottawa Citizen* and then the *Globe and Mail*. She knew who I was. In the summers, she had worked in the offices of a couple of Tory cabinet ministers, doing media relations, and she remembered, with a smile, the consternation and rage that had erupted after some of my stories.

In 1997, she'd been working in a corporate job in Vancouver when a friend invited her to volunteer at the Women's Information Safe House (WISH), a drop-in for prostitutes at First United Church, at East Hastings and Gore. Only for sex-trade workers, WISH offered hot meals, showers, clean used clothing and donated makeup. It was small but comfortable, with sofas and armchairs and a television set; the women felt safe and at home there. Street nurses—women like Bonnie Fournier, who ran a health van in the community—would come in, set up a table and take care of various problems. Among the most serious were the abscesses they dressed. These were deeply infected areas of inflamed skin and tissue caused by heroin injections with shared or dirty needles. There were also wounds to stitch up and flu shots to give, along with medical advice and referrals to other agencies that could help. After the nurses left, the women would eat their suppers, watch a little TV, shower, curl their hair, try out the makeup, get dressed and, finally, get back to work out on the street.

WISH was run by a volunteer board and had only one paid staff member, the coordinator. Elaine was working there as a volunteer, but when the coordinator suddenly quit, the board offered her the job, which paid just over $900 a month.

"I can't live on that," Elaine told Cathy Campbell, the Anglican priest who chaired the board. Campbell begged her to fill in for a few weeks. Elaine finally agreed, and the next three years, with her monthly stipend rolling in from the Anglican Diocese of New Westminster, and a bit of outside contract work to keep her in groceries, were among the happiest and most fulfilling of her life. She grew close to the women who came in, listened to their stories, looked at pictures of their children, tried (almost always in vain) to help them find detox and rehabilitation centres, hunted through piles of donated clothes to find them something nice to wear and drove them home when they were too dope-sick to go out on the street.

Food was important at WISH, and the women were lucky to have a volunteer chef, a man known only as Woody, who came from Nova Scotia and made delicious, healthy food with a budget of $26 a day, plus donations and groceries he obtained from the local food bank.

"He played golden oldies as he cooked, including a lot of old Elvis hits, and he always sang along," Elaine remembered. "But he was never there in the church kitchen when the girls started coming in. It was a male-free zone after six p.m." Instead, he left instructions for Elaine and the volunteers on how to heat up and serve the meals to about a hundred women a night.

"He made fantastic pasta. He always wanted them to have fresh vegetables, and there was always a fresh salad. They would eat anything with fish, except tuna casserole.

Their favourite food was shepherd's pie and Rice Krispies squares."

If Elaine was ever a little late getting there herself, she'd find about a dozen women pounding on the door. "They were actually being friendly," she smiled. "It was their way of razzing me. They were always so appreciative of anything I did for them." And each woman had her own routine, she told me. "Some would run to the TV and pick their favourite program or get the best spot on one of the couches. Others would grab stuff for the shower." Donations of soap, shampoo, conditioner, towels and makeup came in; these were the best treats after the dinners.

One of the reasons I needed to talk to Elaine was that she was working at WISH at the time that the general public began to learn that women were disappearing from the Downtown Eastside. In 1997, the year before she began working there, thirteen women vanished. In 1998, the year she became executive director, eleven women disappeared. In 1999, just two disappeared, but the numbers spiked to ten in 2000. Thirty-six in four years, and Elaine knew most of them. One was Tiffany Drew, a tiny woman, cute and blond, who would meet her best friend, a Fijian woman called Aschu, every day for lunch at the Women's Centre and for dinner at WISH. She disappeared at the end of December 1999. According to Aschu, she and Tiffany had a long-standing deal: they always let the other know when they were leaving and when they got home again, and if one girl didn't call, the other was to report her missing immediately. The only problem was that the police refused to take Aschu seriously or file a Missing Persons report—even when Elaine went with her.

Another was Dawn Crey, a pretty, gentle woman from a well-known Sto:lo Nation family; Ernie Crey, one of her three brothers, is among the most visible spokespersons for the victims' families. A man once threw acid over Dawn's head and face, leaving her badly burned and scarred. The showers, shampoo and makeup were a godsend to Dawn, who worked hard to cover her disfigurement so she could attract dates. She disappeared at the beginning of November 2000.

One by one, Elaine went through the list of the women she had known, and told me how she had felt when they disappeared. And what it was like to go to the police, only to be ignored, turned away or lied to. "Oh, she's probably in Las Vegas with a guy," she'd be told. Or "She's probably on holiday."

As we sat over dinner, I noticed that Elaine never talked about the women she cared for as "women;" she called them "girls." For a while, this made me uncomfortable. Gradually, though, the term "girl" started to work for me. That's what the women themselves called their friends. It was a term of endearment, of friendship, of acceptance. I not only stopped noticing the word, it wasn't long before I started using it myself.

Because she'd grown up in Coquitlam, Elaine knew the area around the Pickton farm—in fact, she'd been a rider as a teenager and had often ridden her horse around there—but she'd never seen Piggy's Palace. We decided to go out together and explore.

—

A day or two later, we drove out to PoCo, as everyone calls Port Coquitlam, stopping by the farm for a while to watch the investigators from the side of the road and get some pictures, then continuing along Dominion Avenue for about a mile until it dead-ended at the Pitt River. There was dense bush to our right, part of an old farm; straight ahead was a dyke, beyond which was the river. Immediately to our left, meeting Dominion Avenue at a right angle, was Burns Road. We turned left on Burns Road, passing a clapboard one-and-a-half-storey bungalow on the left side of the road that I'd heard belonged to Bill Malone, a long-time Pickton friend who was fiercely loyal to the brothers. Obese, reclusive and suspicious, he'd lived there for many years and was known to do odd jobs such as cleaning or guarding the property for Dave Pickton. What I didn't notice at the time but spotted later was a surveillance camera Malone had mounted at the corner of his house, just where the roof met the eaves, pointing at the road. We drove slowly for another hundred feet or so until we came to the Palace on our right. It was no more than a quarter of a mile from the junction of Dominion and Burns, and just past a couple of hobby farms. These lots were all about ten acres; each was narrow—perhaps 150 feet wide— and long, stretching back to the dyke and the river.

Piggy's Palace had a semi-circular drive in front, with plenty of room for parking. A two-storey wooden house that looked as if it hadn't been painted in twenty years was set at the side of the lot, about fifty feet from the road; behind it on the left, at least a hundred feet back from the road, was a large silver shed made of corrugated steel. It looked like a barn for battery chickens. I learned later that this property, once called Shiloh Nursery, had sold garden plants. The police say now that it covers about eleven acres. And though most people assumed this was Dave Pickton's place, it was co-owned by the three siblings—Willie, Dave and Linda. After they started selling off large chunks of their family farm for subdivisions, the Picktons looked for another place in the neighbourhood, and the Shiloh property seemed right; it was about the same size as the farm. After setting up a corporation in 1996 called the Good Times Society, which would own the Palace and "raise money at fundraisers for good causes," the Pickton brothers turned the big metal shed into a reception and party hall, equipping it with a bar, kitchen and dance floor that Dave had retrieved from demolitions.

"We had 1,800 people at one of my parties, and my parties were cleaner than any bar downtown," Dave Pickton would tell reporters. He may have been talking about New Year's Eve in 1998, when dozens of police officers arrived to bust up a crowd of at least 1,700 people. That was the last big party held at the Palace.

Today, the place looked abandoned.

My camera was in my purse. My plan was to stop, snoop around as long as I could and get some pictures of the place. But there wasn't time to get out of the car. As we turned into the driveway, a small car appeared out of nowhere and tailgated my Jeep, almost touching my rear bumper and forcing me to keep going until I'd gone around the drive and returned to the road. Glancing back, I saw that the man behind the wheel looked like everything I had heard about Bill Malone. Satisfied that he'd got rid of us; he turned and went back to his own house.

I had been there long enough, though, to figure out that the place was abandoned. Dave Pickton wasn't living at Piggy's Palace; in fact, he never had lived there. For a while, he had lived in a two-storey house on the adjoining lot north of the Palace, but he'd sold it to move next door, two lots past the Palace on the same side. The new house was an attractive brown bungalow, what local people call a rancher, with a well-kept garden, a surprise given the infamous state of the farm when he lived there. Here, the grass was clipped and there were plenty of trees and shrubs hiding a large parking area at the back that held many of his trucks, bulldozers and backhoes. Like the other lots on the right side of Burns Road, this one ran back to the dyke and Pitt River. The dyke had a wide path on the top, and Elaine and I hiked along it to see the backs of these properties. The Palace seemed to have a jumble of buildings; the biggest by far was the party shed.

Police took over the Palace site in April 2002, but although there were seventeen investigators working on it, no one was there that Saturday. It was desolate, grim, abandoned. During our quick circuit of the driveway, we hadn't even seen any equipment like the diggers and trailers that littered the farm on Dominion. From the back, though, there were a few pieces of equipment visible.

Just as they were doing at the pig farm, investigators had divided the land into grids. There were seven buildings on the property to search, besides the Palace itself and the derelict house. Each one, the police said later in a statement, was "subject to a search pattern that at times called for hundreds of grid patterns of only a few inches square to be established . . . and an extensive surface search was conducted." Two excavators were used to move large piles of debris, including heavy aluminum roofing sheets, timber and steel beams, so that investigators could search under the mess.

In one of their press releases, the Missing Women Task Force made an interesting disclosure: "In order to conduct as thorough an examination as possible of a priority area, a makeshift house on the property had to be torn down in order for investigators to sift through the soil beneath it." A number of people had already told me that, at the time of his arrest,

Willie Pickton was building a house for himself behind the Palace. He, Dave and Linda had agreed that the farm should be sold for more subdivisions—in fact, that was what the zoning notice was all about. Another whack off the remaining land. Willie Pickton was preparing for the move by building a home of his own on the Palace land, right behind the Palace itself so that it was hidden from curious people driving by. What one man remembers best about this project was that Willie was building the walls with deep spaces between the exterior walls and the inside ones, "spaces large enough to store stuff, to hide stuff," he told me. "It was weird."

The police dismantled other parts of buildings on the site, and then had to replace the wiring and the lighting. Sometimes they had to begin with a major cleanup. On one occasion, they drained a small outdoor fish pond, secured the fish, searched the pond, put back clean water and returned the fish. But what the investigators found there, if anything, we weren't told.

Having been bullied off the Palace property by Bill Malone reminded us that there was another place nearby that was almost as famous: the Hells Angels clubhouse on Dominion, almost directly across the road from the main entrance to the Pickton farm. I assumed that their clubhouse would be like the others I'd seen: there would be surveillance cameras mounted around the building, and probably one or two in the trees. I didn't want to linger, but a slow drive-by in each direction showed us a driveway with room for several cars, protected by a steel gate, as well as a deep yard with nothing behind the house but grass and scrub. I learned later that there was enough room at the back to park one hundred cars and that this space was often full.

The house itself was a large blue clapboard two-storey building with a gabled front; it lacked some of the customary protective work I'd seen at other biker clubhouses. There was no concrete wall in front of the entrance, for example, nor was there a protected concrete porch at the front door. There was no barbed wire fencing and I couldn't see a surveillance camera although I knew there had to be one. It looked just like a normal family home, but it wasn't, of course; it was a popular after-hours party house, a booze can for bikers and their friends, a place to go when the Palace had finally shut down for the night or the local bars had closed their doors. It was well known to the local RCMP officers who patrolled the town. It was also well known to the Picktons. Not only were the bikers among their closest neighbours, but they often rented the Palace for private parties and would include Dave, a friend of the Hells Angels, when the parties continued into the early morning hours back at their clubhouse. Dave would also ride along with the Hells Angels on their annual toy run, a public relations ploy designed to make the bikers, driving their Harley Davidsons loaded with toys, look like good guys. Carrying one wrapped toy each, they join thousands of other motorcycle riders for the biggest toy run in B.C.; it starts at a large mall, the Coquitlam Centre, and heads west into Vancouver to the Pacific National Exhibition grounds. Not all of the riders with the Hells Angels are full patch members, but many are, and they ride with their patches—their insignia—stitched onto their jackets. The rest are associates, wannabes and friends like Dave Pickton.

The Angels' clubhouse was near the edge of the large parcel of land owned by Home Depot. Beyond the trees and wet grass that bordered the Home Depot property was a laneway and then the store's large parking lot. In the laneway, down a dirt ramp from Dominion Avenue, sat a small white tent, pitched on space donated by Home Depot. The tent, a gift from Hazco Environmental, the company whose backhoes were tearing up the soil on the farm, was dubbed the Healing Tent. It was a place for family members of the missing women to gather in private. Around the outside, they placed cards, notes, stuffed animals, photographs and flowers. The rain would fall on all of it, and the ink would run, the flowers would wilt, and the teddy bears and stuffed kittens would get wet and muddy. Yet it remained somehow a dignified little place.

Inside, there were a few tables and chairs and sometimes some quilting or beading supplies used by female relatives to make small gifts, a tiny suede pouch, perhaps, to hold sweet-grass or a small, round beaded brooch quartered into four sections to represent the four races of the missing women: white,

A view from the Pickton farm across the road to the Hells Angels clubhouse (back, behind the trees), the families' Healing Tent (front) and the Home Depot parking lot (right).

black, red and yellow. This would also become the place where many of the mothers, sisters and daughters met each other for the first time, shared their stories and wept together.

It was all such an odd scene, out there by the vast suburban mall: a small, shabby farm crawling with police and backhoes and men and women dressed in white coveralls and booties; a bedraggled tent offering comfort to bereaved families, nestled up next to a biker club; all those crisp new houses bouncing up out of the muck on two sides of the property. And behind all of this, to the north, the beautiful North Shore Mountains.

The more I explored Port Coquitlam, the more I wanted to know about it. One day, Justin Beddall, a young reporter who had worked for three years for the *Tri-City News* (the three cities being the neighbouring communities of Port Coquitlam, Coquitlam and Port Moody) and had moved on to a reporting job in North Vancouver, called me, offering help. We'd never met, but he knew about the book I was working on. Right away, I said yes. Justin knew the community and had interesting contacts. A good place to start, he said, would be with Albert and Vera Harvey, blueberry farmers who had been friends of Louise and Leonard Pickton, Willie Pickton's parents. They agreed to see us, even though Vera was dying of lung cancer, because she had been close to Louise Pickton for many years and was fond of all the Pickton children.

The Harveys' farm was on Devon Road, north of Piggy's Palace. To get there, we drove north past the Palace on Burns Road, until it ended at Prairie Avenue, where we turned left and then north again after a few hundred feet. The Harveys owned about fourteen acres, with nearly four of them covered in blueberries. The bushes were high, maybe six to seven feet each, some touching each other, but most with a foot or two of air around them. They didn't look anything like the low, skinny bushes I was used to around our cottage in the Laurentians, the ones that cling to the rocks near the lakeshore, where I'd have to work hard to fill an old berry pan with the tiny wild berries. Here in British Columbia, the bushes were larded with clumps of fat blueberries the size of marbles, and there were clouds of birds clacking overhead, figuring out the best place to dive down and help themselves. It was early morning, and a little dew dampened the grass around the bushes.

Albert wasn't in his office, a rickety-looking unpainted wooden shed, low and full of junk. We walked to his house, at the end of a long driveway bordered by blueberry bushes. A few smaller sheds were scattered around the house, one holding a couple of cords of firewood, another serving as a garage. Tools and car parts were lying around. The house, a brown fifties two-storey building in need of paint and a little shoring up, looked like almost every other house I'd seen around here. It still had icicle lights dangling from the porch eaves, and it seemed as if everyone used a back door that opened into the basement level.

As we approached, Albert appeared from between two blueberry bushes on the other side of the driveway, a battered coffee can hung on a string around his neck. It was nearly full of berries. He pulled it carefully over his head and invited us to walk back to the blueberry shed so he could dump it. As we walked, he chattered cheerfully about the business. Blueberry season lasts about two weeks, and they were right in the middle of it; any day now, a big rain could end it, so they were picking fast, while the weather was good. Inside the shed, in the main room, his office, there were three old chairs and shallow wooden boxes stacked in the corners; there were also shelves, a sink and a tea kettle, along with a few mugs. Beyond this room lay a storage room with three freezers; another room held pails, cans with strings and an old iron scale.

Albert had white hair, a deeply lined face, and arms tanned a deep brown. He was in his late seventies and limped from a bad knee. His boots were the kind they used to call Romeos, with elastic sides and steel toes; his jeans, though worn, were clean. You couldn't call him fat, but he was solid. Getting him to talk was no trick: he was happy for the chance to stick up for his friend and neighbour Willie Pickton. Like Willie, he'd worked hard all his life doing what came along—cutting timber, fixing cars, growing blueberries. Like Willie, he was working class and looked poor; like Willie, he was land rich. You could cram a few dozen Craftsman-style houses side by side on these fourteen acres, or a whole subdivision of condominiums. His property was no more than a mile away from the new subdivisions, many of them built on Pickton land, that were chewing up the farmland all around them.

"They weren't a rich family," Albert said of the Picktons. "They started out in Coquitlam; they had a little pig farm there about forty years ago. Then they moved to Port Coquitlam, to the Dominion Avenue property. They butchered pigs and sold them. They even had a meat outlet for a while; it was where the municipal swimming pool is now. They butchered and cut meat and sold it out of a cold room.

"They were hardworking people. I didn't associate with them much, although Vera associated with Mrs. Pickton; she was the cornerstone of the family for money. At one time, when Jack Campbell was mayor of Port Coquitlam, he tried to scare her off her property. He was offering her about $700 an acre. Vera was mad. She called Mrs. Pickton and said,

'Don't you take that offer. The price is too cheap.' So she didn't. Think what it's worth now."

The Pickton sons were mostly in the demolition business, Albert told us, but he had worked for Dave felling trees for a new subdivision after Dave won a contract to clear the land. Willie, he said, was in the topsoil business, and he was always involved in cars. He went to car auctions for old cars and trucks and would then separate the copper, brass and aluminum to sell for a good profit. He'd sell the rest for scrap. Willie also went to animal auctions, where he'd buy weanling pigs for pig roasts. He kept the pigs at the farm, along with some goats.

"He wouldn't raise them till they were big," Albert said. "They were just for roasting on a spit, for parties at Piggy's Palace, like. He was brought up with it; it was a way of life." Everything with Willie was barter, Albert added. Willie would give him topsoil and truck parts; in return, Albert would fix the brothers' large cutter saws, the ones they used for cutting metal.

He thought better of what he'd just told us: "Don't write that down!" he said. "I'll have all the cops in here diggin' everything up!" Harvey was eager to praise the Pickton brothers. "They were always helpful. Willie would do anything for you. If you needed money, if you were broke." Sure, he admitted, Willie took hookers to the farm, and sure, he picked them up in the Downtown Eastside, but he never killed anyone. All the evidence the cops had found on the property, he said, all the clothes and purses and identification and blood, had to have come from the cars Willie had picked up for scrap at auctions.

I told Albert that all the stories I'd read, everything I'd heard, suggested that Willie was a loner, very quiet, overwhelmed by his voluble, profane brother and almost certainly a bit slow mentally. Albert was quick to contradict that impression.

"No, he's chatty, he talks fast. He's very intelligent, I would say. One time I was with this group of guys; he acted simple but was very smart. Yes, he's smart. Remember, Einstein had the emotions of a seven-year-old. He's not stupid; that's just people's judgment. If you had a joke, he'd laugh."

—

We left Albert to deal with an influx of Vietnamese berry pickers. As he handed out the tin cans to them, helping them pull the strings over their heads, he told us Vera was expecting us up at the house.

Vera was nothing like her amiable husband. We found her sitting in a chair in a ground-floor bedroom, wrapped in a shawl and hooked up to an oxygen tank, gasping for breath. Lung cancer had whittled away at the seventy-eight-year-old woman, leaving her gaunt and white, but her eyes were fierce and she had lots to say.

"I know goddamn well he didn't do it," she rasped. "The kids worked really hard. But the Pickton brothers were picked on their whole life. They'd do anything for anybody; they'd help a perfect stranger."

As far as Vera was concerned, Willie had been framed by the cops. And the way he was being treated in jail was a scandal. Dave had called the Harveys not long after Willie's arrest and asked if it would be okay for Willie to phone them from time to time to talk, because he didn't have a lot of people he could call. Sure, Vera said. So Willie had phoned about three times since his arrest. He had also tried to write, but he told her the jail wouldn't forward his letters.

Eventually, Albert began visiting him. Willie said someone was trying to poison him. One time, someone gave him a can of orange juice that had two little holes in it, he said, and he wouldn't touch it. Another time, he was sure he had food poisoning; it lasted three days, and he told the Harveys the guards wouldn't let him see a doctor.

As for all the publicity about the Hells Angels and the wild parties at Piggy's Palace, Vera said, it was all nonsense; she and Albert had gone to almost all the parties, and they were good clean fun. "There was a ten-dollar cover for all the food you could eat—it was always pig on a spit—and booze was two drinks for five dollars," she said. "They had more goddamn security than the airport. There were never any fights, just good times." Why, Port Coquitlam's mayor, Len Traboulay, and his wife used to be regulars there, she added. "And Mayor Traboulay wrote a letter to the Picktons thanking them for a party."

Sick as she was, Vera's eyes gleamed as she remembered one special occasion—the night the police raided Piggy's Palace.

"We were dancing as the cops were taking out the booze."

FOUR **THE LAWYERS**

One day, as I was working at my desk at St. Andrew's, I received an email from another reporter, a woman called Trude Huebner. She had been working for the *National Post* but had recently lost her job in the first round of that paper's layoffs, the first since it started up with such a lavish bang in October 1998. Trude started lining up freelance work right away, and I was fortunate to be on her list of people to contact. She came from Port Coquitlam, knew how to search court records, was a good interviewer and, best of all, had gone to school with the Picktons. Trude even remembered Louise Pickton; she also knew many of their neighbours.

Over the next few weeks, we spent hours driving around the community. This was when it first registered with me that the tri-city area has produced more than one serial offender. Clifford Olson, convicted in 1988 of murdering eleven children—and, unless Pickton surpasses him, the holder of the Canadian title as the country's worst serial killer—lived here; so did John Oughton, the so-called Paper Bag Rapist, the son of a PoCo city councillor and a serial rapist famous for covering his victims' heads with a paper bag. (His lawyer, Glen Orris, is a now a member of the Pickton defence team.) But until Pickton came along, the good citizens of Port Coquitlam claimed Terry Fox as their city's most famous resident. A statue of the valiant young athlete, who ran his Marathon of Hope in 1980 to raise money for the fight against cancer—the disease that interrupted his run and took his life shortly afterwards—stands on the grounds of the new public library, just a block from the courthouse where I would soon be spending several months listening to evidence in Pickton's preliminary hearing.

Trude started by showing me where Willie Pickton's parents, Leonard and Louise, had their first farm, one inherited from Leonard's family, who had homesteaded there more than a hundred years ago. The original farm, now buried under blocks of tract housing, was on Dawes Hill, beside a large parcel of undeveloped land. In 1905, that parcel, about a thousand acres where the Coquitlam River met the Fraser River, was purchased for the new Coquitlam Hospital for the Insane. The name has changed twice since then, first to Essondale, after Dr. Esson Young, the first provincial official responsible for the site, then to Riverview. It is still a psychiatric hospital for people with severe mental illnesses. Part of the sprawling hospital complex was built on the sloping contours of Dawes Hill; the rest was constructed on the flat land below, where the government built a successful farm, called Colony Farm, to supply most of the meat, dairy and fresh produce for the hospital. Farming stopped there in 1983, but some of the old farm buildings have been restored, and the property is being developed as a wildlife sanctuary. At the heart of it are three beautiful old buildings that look a little like barns and house 190 psychiatric patients ordered there by the courts and transferred by sheriffs. It includes nine clinical units, five of them secure, three closed and one open. Formally, it's called the Forensic Psychiatric Hospital, but police and folks around PoCo simply call it Colony Farm and know it as the place for the criminally insane.

Willie and Dave Pickton, along with their sister, Linda, grew up playing on the grounds of Essondale and Colony Farm and going to local public schools with the children of the doctors and other hospital staff. Louise and Leonard Pickton would sometimes hire Essondale and Colony Farm patients to do chores at their place. Trude remembers that Dave and Willie never fit in with the other kids at school; they were dirty, smelled of pig manure and stayed home a lot to help with chores. They did poorly in school, especially Willie. But Linda managed to get through public school successfully. Soon after her family moved to the new farm on Dominion Avenue in 1963, she left home, where she was unhappy, to live with relatives in Vancouver and go to high school there. Linda did well, went on to UBC and eventually went into real estate. She married and had two sons, but later divorced. Most people in Port Coquitlam consider her the brains behind the family's subdivision plans for the farm on Dominion Avenue.

Trude introduced me to people who had known the Pickton kids in those years, people whose memories of the neglect, the dirt and the terrible mess around the farm were sharp and sad. In her own way, many insisted, Louise Pickton had tried to do her best by her kids, but mothering was not a skill she ever mastered. Instead, she was a shrewd business-woman who saw her boys as a useful workforce, and she set them to work slopping pigs and doing other chores, rather than encouraging them to acquire an education. Leonard, who was born in 1896 and was already an old man by the time the children were teenagers, was not involved in raising them at all, recall neighbours and friends, although Linda has told reporters she was close to him.

The Picktons' new property on Dominion was probably once a small part of the large Blakeburn cattle ranch, which covered about eight hundred acres in this northeastern part of Port Coquitlam. According to local historian Chuck Davis, the author of *Port Coquitlam: Where Rails Meet Rivers,* a useful book of local history, the ranch changed its name to the Minnekhada Ranch; today, the only part that remains an agricultural area is the small section around the Harveys' blueberry farm on Devon.

I also learned about many of the local landmarks, places such as the Wild Duck Inn, which was built in 1912 as a bunkhouse for railroad workers and was the oldest saloon in the community; by 2000 it was considered a Hells Angels hangout. As Chuck Davis delicately puts it, "The entertainment has changed . . . with naked dancing ladies the featured attraction." It wasn't the only biker bar in the neighbourhood; just as notorious was the Golden Ears Hotel on Shaughnessy, Port Coquitlam's main street. Once, when I was looking for a place to buy some beer for Russell MacKay, a keen court watcher who had befriended me during the preliminary hearing, I saw a sign painted on the wall of the Golden Ears: COLD BEER. I went in, and they sent me next door, to another part of the hotel. There I found no beer at all, just a naked dancing lady turning around on a tabletop, with three bearded, burly men standing around it watching her. Then they watched me. I arrived at Russell's house empty-handed. He thought it was all very funny, and we had a cup of tea and some of his wife's cookies instead.

—

Trude began pulling court and property records for me, both in Port Coquitlam and in Vancouver, so that I had accurate details about any possible criminal activities of the Pickton brothers and their associates, as well as an idea of what they owned. In the meantime, I continued interviewing people. A friend who had worked on the television series *Da Vinci's Inquest* for two years knew Larry Campbell, the ex-RCMP officer who had recently retired as chief coroner of British Columbia. The show was based on Campbell's career as coroner, which meant he was around a lot as an advisor and also wrote the occasional script. "You have to meet him," she told me. "He knows everything."

Larry Campbell proved to be exactly as promised. When we first met, he was, as they say, considering his options. The *Da Vinci* work was fun, but it wasn't full-time, and he likes to keep busy. He is a serious fly fisherman and golfer, and he always helps his brother-in-law in Saskatchewan with the fall harvest, but it wasn't enough. When we met at Starbucks on Tenth Avenue near UBC—he lives close by—he told me he was thinking about politics, perhaps running for mayor of Vancouver. COPE, the left-wing civic party, was courting him to be their candidate. What about it? I asked.

"Naw, I don't think so . . ." he smiled. It seemed preposterous: Him? A politician? Running with a bunch of dysfunctional left-wingers?

"Naw."

Still, as the television series showed us, and this wasn't fiction, Campbell spent years working on cases in the Downtown Eastside. He was on the board of Triage, a Downtown Eastside organization that provides a variety of good programs to support homeless people, including emergency residential care. He knew the community well: he knew its politics, its people, its issues. And he loved it. As far as he was concerned, the missing women's case had been a travesty from start to finish, and police neglect was a big part of the story. One of the reasons he was thinking of running was to make sure it never happened again.

"I told people years ago that whoever was doing this had to have access to a crematorium, a rendering plant or a pig farm," he said. "Turns out Pickton had access to two out of the three." Nobody paid any attention to his comment.

Over the next few weeks, we met a few more times and he showed me around Triage and introduced me to the staff, who explained their services for addicts who were sick and homeless. Campbell even listened to the noises in my leaky Jeep one day and told me about an inexpensive garage on Main Street run by a father-son team of car repair geniuses. In addition, he gave me a list of good people to call for my book.

One day, looking a little sheepish, he mentioned that he'd agreed to run for mayor under the COPE banner. I wasn't surprised; Campbell may not consider himself left-wing, but he does care about social justice, and COPE's tent was big enough for him. I didn't see much of him after that.

—

October brought one of the rare court hearings in the case so far, and it was all about money. Back in February, when he was first arrested, Willie Pickton had hired a lawyer called Peter Ritchie to act for him. I was surprised. Ritchie was a major player among Vancouver's defence lawyers, and his clients were often high-profile people. One of the most memorable was Gillian Guess, a flamboyant woman who had

Peter Ritchie, Pickton's lead defence lawyer, in a scrum outside the Port Coquitlam Provincial Courthouse in 2003.

been a juror on a murder trial, wore sexy short leopard print skirts and plenty of makeup, and wound up having an affair with the accused man during the trial. Charged with obstruction of justice, Guess was tried in 1998 and convicted.

Ritchie had moved to B.C. from Ontario after law school. During his early career, he had worked as a prosecutor, but he'd been a defence lawyer for many years, and many of his biggest cases were civil, not criminal. And he had done well. At that time, he lived near Larry Campbell in West Point Grey, a well-to-do neighbourhood; his thirteenth-floor practice, Ritchie Sandford, was in the Marine Building, at the foot of Burrard Street, right on the water. He was well known as a good skier, as a talented folk musician with a passion for bluegrass music—he frequented a few places where he did a little picking with other banjo players—and for his elegant appearance. He wore expensive suits, fine silk ties and good shirts, his shoes looked handmade, and on chilly days he wore a navy beret tipped over his short, thick white hair.

How had Willie Pickton known of him? How could he afford him? It turned out this was not the first time Pickton had hired Peter Ritchie. In March 1997, Pickton had been charged with attacking a Downtown Eastside addicted prostitute named Wendy Lynn Eistetter. He had taken her out to his farm late one night; a few hours later, each of them ended up in a New Westminster hospital, suffering from deep, serious stab wounds. Who started it? Who was the victim? The police determined that Pickton was the aggressor, and he called Peter Ritchie for help. Later, the charges against Pickton were stayed when Eistetter failed to show up for the trial. Pickton told friends later that the private investigator hired by his lawyers to look into Eistetter's history had cost him $10,000; he also told a friend that Ritchie's bill for legal work was $80,000. An expensive lawyer for a PoCo pig man. But the family had made millions, Ritchie told reporters, from selling their land for housing developments, so Pickton could afford him.

What I wanted to know was how Pickton knew enough to hire Ritchie instead of someone working over a store in a PoCo or Coquitlam strip mall. I soon learned that the Pickton brothers were plugged in to Vancouver's top layers of legal talent. Dave Pickton's lawyer was Ian Donaldson of Donaldson Jetté, one of the best-known criminal lawyers in the province and a bencher—a member of the board of directors—of the Law Society of B.C. Not long after Willie was charged, Donaldson told a CBC reporter that there hadn't been a trial and there was no proof of guilt.

"I mean, this fellow's presumed innocent, but candlelight vigils and camps and so on can tip the public into thinking this fellow is a criminal," Donaldson said. "He's nothing of the sort." According to the CBC, Donaldson also objected to news that one witness claimed women were injected with antifreeze and that the person had led police to an alleged murder weapon at the farm. "Donaldson said any information like that is suspect," the report stated, "and the source should be checked out to make sure this person isn't gaining anything by pointing the finger at somebody else."

Vera Harvey was right to warn me that it would be unwise to underestimate the Pickton brothers.

On Wednesday, October 2, 2002, the news broke that the police had charged Willie Pickton with four more counts of first-degree murder, for the deaths of Heather Chinnock, Inga Hall, Tanya Holyk and Sherry Irving. This brought the total up to fifteen, four more than Clifford Olson's record. If Pickton were convicted on all fifteen counts, he would be Canada's most prolific serial killer.

Suddenly, Peter Ritchie began a public debate about two issues. First, he said he wanted the general public, including reporters, banned from the preliminary hearing, scheduled to begin in November in Port Coquitlam under provincial court judge David Stone. No, said Stone. This will be held in open court. Anyone could attend, including victims' family members, the general public and journalists. Second, though Ritchie already had a $375,000 lien against the farm property, he revealed that Pickton was almost broke, couldn't afford to pay for his own defence and had offered to turn over his share of the farm to the government if he could get legal aid. The problem Ritchie had with this idea was simple: he couldn't afford to work for legal aid rates, set at

$150 an hour, with a cap of 37.5 hours a week. And he felt it was inadequate to have only two junior lawyers, paid $72 an hour, to help him. Ritchie countered with a request for six lawyers at an hourly rate of $200 each. This suggestion was unacceptable to the Legal Services Society. Then we heard that Willie Pickton was so anxious for the preliminary hearing to begin that he'd told Ritchie he'd represent himself. No one, including Ritchie, thought this was a good idea. On October 4, Ritchie told Judge Stone that he was planning to quit because he had had no response to his request for more money and four lawyers to help him; he added that he had advised Pickton that he would regret it if he tried to defend himself. The judge's reaction was a concern that a delay would cost the taxpayer more money; in fact, Stone was determined to have the hearing start on November 4, despite Ritchie's bluster. Ritchie repeated his belief that Willie Pickton would come to regret it if he tried to defend himself, and outside the court, he explained Pickton's frustration to reporters:

"He's not used to being in jail. He's in jail and has been in jail a long time and on these counts, because they're so serious, he's going to remain in jail until they're dealt with, it appears," Ritchie said.

By this time, Ritchie and his law partner, Marilyn Sandford, who had been working on Pickton's case for eight months, made a bold move. We quit, he informed the Port Coquitlam court registry on October 11. It was brinksmanship at its best.

On November 4, 2002, I arrived at the provincial courthouse in Port Coquitlam in good time; it had taken just thirty-five minutes to drive out from the end of Point Grey, most of the way on the Trans-Canada Highway. Parking was simple: it was below the modern, red-brick courthouse, and it was free. Inside, there were several uniformed men and women wearing bulletproof vests and carrying guns at their hips. I assumed they were members of the RCMP, which had the contract for policing in Port Coquitlam. I was wrong. They were sheriffs, responsible for security in all the Lower Mainland's courthouses and for transporting prisoners to and from court from local jails, including PoCo's Pretrial Centre, just a few miles away.

To enter the area of the courtrooms, we had to pass through new security desks, built just for the Pickton preliminary hearing, where the sheriffs searched our bags and wallets, flipped through the pages of our notebooks to make sure no possible weapons were hidden there and passed wands over us. Then they patted us down before letting us through, taking no chances that some family member or friend of one of the missing women, or some deranged and outraged citizen, would storm in with a weapon. There was also, I learned, a real concern that criminals might want to intimidate or harm Pickton or other witnesses. In other words, he could have enemies on two fronts: relatives or friends of the victims who might try to take revenge, and people suspected of taking women to the farm or being involved with Pickton as accomplices. Would they do anything as drastic as trying to kill him? Maybe not, but the sheriffs were taking no chances—not from angry family members, not from possible accomplices.

We walked into a large open area with a few benches and a small canteen in the centre where a couple of women served coffee, made toast and sold gum and muffins to the people stopping by. Beyond the canteen was an area filled with tables and chairs; people waited here to be called into court, or just had some breakfast and gossiped with their colleagues. Along a long wall to my left I could see double doors leading into courtrooms. It all felt casual; people were relaxed.

Just before ten a.m., a sheriff opened the doors to Courtroom 3. We filed in and down a centre aisle, the press taking their designated seats in the front two rows on either side, members of the victims' families sitting with support workers in the centre on the left, the general public sitting in the centre on the right. The room held about one hundred people, but attendance that day was small; no more than a handful of reporters were there.

Straight ahead of us, beyond the bar separating us from what is known as the well of the court, were comfortable high-backed blue chairs for the prosecutors on the right, the defence on the left. In front of them were the court clerk and court reporter; above them, on a raised platform, was Judge David Stone's desk. But all eyes were on the glass box, about six feet square, in the far corner of the room, beside the judge's seat, to our left. A small door at the back led into a corridor behind the courtroom.

Kerry McIntyre, the sheriff in charge, stood up and told us the protocol: please, no chewing gum, no eating, no drinking. Still, everything seemed pretty informal. The lawyers were already ambling around in front, waiting for the judge and the prisoner to arrive. Peter Ritchie and Marilyn Sandford were standing by their chairs on the left. Sandford is a tall, thin woman who on this occasion looked distracted and worried. She rarely smiled, and one of her arms was in a sling; we heard later that she had recently broken it. To the right were Michael Petrie, the Crown prosecutor, and his second, Derrill Prevett, who was based in Nanaimo. I wondered why he was there; someone told me later it was because he is an expert on DNA evidence, had written a book on it and would probably be the prosecutor who dealt with any DNA evidence that might be raised during the trial. Prevett had a high profile among the reporters in the courtroom; he was the prosecutor in Victoria for the trial of Kelly Ellard, the high school student eventually convicted of the murder of another teenager, Reena Virk. Petrie and Prevett looked a bit alike: stocky, broad in the back, balding. Petrie had a small goatee; Prevett had glasses. They seemed very relaxed.

Judge Stone arrived, and we all stood up. After we sat down again, Pickton came through the small door at the back of the glass box, followed by a guard, who sat behind him. Pickton looked calm. He was wearing a grey sweater, and his stringy, greasy, grey-blond hair hung over the sides of his face and down the back of his neck. He followed the procedures and discussion with interest, but he made no eye contact with anyone in the room and never even glanced towards the gallery—all of us. The only movement he made was a slow, swinging back and forth in his chair, so slow it was easy to miss it.

Stone seemed young, in his early forties, perhaps. His dark brown hair was neatly cut and flowed back in waves on each side of his high forehead. His face was so serious it was hard to tell if he was a handsome man; only once in the next eight months would I see him smile.

Ritchie started things off by telling Stone he was appearing as a "friend of the court" and not in any official capacity because he had withdrawn as Pickton's lawyer, as had Sandford. He said he had written the court registry to say they were withdrawing weeks earlier, on October 11. He explained that there was a Rowbotham application on the issue of funding, and it should be dealt with that week. A Rowbotham application, named after a 1988 decision in the

Ontario Court of Appeal, allows a lawyer to apply to have charges stayed against an accused when the government will not give financial assistance. The decision said that even if an accused person isn't eligible for legal aid, he or she can ask the government for financial help. If the help doesn't come, the charges can be stayed. Ritchie told Stone that he had advised his client to find another lawyer. Pickton listened sleepily, with some self-confidence, but upon hearing this he shook his head slowly. But, Ritchie said, the Rowbotham application had been made only three weeks ago, and if Pickton was to have a new lawyer, he or she would need at least three months to get up to speed. That meant the preliminary hearing couldn't start until February.

Stone wasn't having any of this. He wanted the hearing to begin the following Monday.

Crown prosecutor Mike Petrie scrummed by reporters at the Port Coquitlam courthouse in 2003. The *Vancouver Sun*'s Lori Culbert is behind him.

Crown prosecutor Derrill Prevett is an expert on DNA evidence; John Ahern, another member of the prosecution team, is right behind him.

The next day, the whole circus—with Pickton present by video link from outside his cell at the North Fraser Pretrial Centre—moved to the B.C. Supreme Court to present the dilemma to Associate Chief Justice Patrick Dohm. Ritchie and Sandford were back, as were Petrie and Prevett, along with a third Crown prosecutor, John Ahern.

It was my first visit to this court, and I had trouble finding my way to the right courtroom, not much of a surprise given that there are thirty-five of them. I was so flustered that I forgot to be impressed by the courthouse itself. Arthur Erickson's stunning Vancouver Law Courts building on Burrard Street, covered with an acre of slanted glass and decorated with ivy and waterfalls, was a building I had long wanted to visit. I kept wondering if this feeling of being an outsider would ever wear off.

It was also my first chance to talk to some of the other reporters on the case, partly because I had a hard time understanding the legal issues being discussed. Still, sitting in the courtroom, watching Pickton on the video in his red prisoner's coverall, I knew the agenda remained the same: money. This I could understand.

A few days later, Judge Dohm ruled in favour of the Rowbotham application. The government, through the Legal Services Society, would now pay far more than its normal rate; the actual amount would remain a secret, at least for now. Once again, Ritchie was on board as Willie Pickton's lawyer. And the preliminary hearing would not be starting the following week, as Judge Stone had insisted it would. It wouldn't begin until January 13, 2003, more than two months later.

FIVE **A NUMBERS GAME**

I n some ways it was a relief that the preliminary hearing
had been postponed for three months: it gave me time to
work my way through the long list of interviews I had
scheduled. It also gave me a chance to look through the numbers, statistics and Missing Women Task Force announce-
ments to see where the investigation was at this stage—at
least, where it was according to the police.

It was early November 2002; the police had seized the
Pickton farm on February 5, 2002, and had now been there
exactly ten months. They'd seized Piggy's Palace in April
2002 and moved out seven months later, on October 27.

So far, Willie Pickton had been charged on fifteen counts of
first-degree murder. In order of the date in 2002 on which he
was charged, the victims included Sereena Abotsway and
Mona Wilson (February 22), Heather Bottomley, Diane Rock
and Jacqueline McDonell (April 2), Andrea Joesbury (April 9),
Brenda Wolfe (May 22), Helen Hallmark, Patricia Johnson,
Jennifer Furminger and Georgina Papin (September 19), and
Sherry Irving, Heather Chinnock, Inga Hall and Tanya Holyk
(October 2). The police had also found DNA from two other
missing women, Sarah de Vries and Marnie Frey, on the farm,
but so far had not laid charges against Pickton in these cases.

An official list of the missing women, prepared by the Missing Women Task Force, now had sixty-three names on it. The police were still investigating the rest of these disappearances, as well as following up on 4,300 tips from the public and other possible witnesses.

New people arrived at the Task Force all the time, and by late October 2002, there were about two hundred people working on the Pickton investigation, 130 of them on the farm itself. In fact, there were so many people involved on the farm that the group was designated an on-site police detachment. Seventeen of these workers were the investigators who had been working on the Piggy's Palace site; they had moved to the farm once the search was completed at Piggy's Palace.

Aside from police officers and technicians, this crowd of workers now included a large number of senior university

This metal shed, sitting in the middle of the Picktons' Burns Road property, is the infamous Piggy's Palace. *(Photo courtesy GlobalBC)*

students, who began work on June 3, 2002. Twenty-six of them were osteologists (specialists in bones and skeletal structures); another twenty-five were forensic anthropologists. What's the difference? The forensic anthropologists were trained to look for the criminal causes of death. The American Board of Forensic Anthropology defines the term in the following way: "Forensic anthropology is the application of the science of physical anthropology to the legal process. The identification of skeletal, badly decomposed, or otherwise unidentified human remains is important for both legal and humanitarian reasons. Forensic anthropologists apply standard scientific techniques developed in physical anthropology to identify human remains, and to assist in the detection of crime. Forensic anthropologists frequently work in conjunction with forensic pathologists, odontologists, and homicide investigators to identify a decedent, discover evidence of foul play, and/or the postmortem interval. In addition to assisting in locating and recovering suspicious remains, forensic anthropologists work to suggest the age, sex, ancestry, stature, and unique features of a decedent from the skeleton." Probably the most famous forensic anthropologist in North America is Kathy Reichs, who works in both Montreal and North Carolina, and has written bestselling novels about her fictional heroine, Tempe Brennan, a thinly disguised version of Reichs herself. The current hit televison series, *Bones,* is another spinoff of Reichs's work. Although a fan of Reichs, I also found two non-fiction books helpful on this subject. One, by Emily Craig, called *Teasing Secrets from the Dead,* is about her experience at some of the United States' most famous crime scenes; another is *The Bone Woman,* by Clea Koff, a young American woman who worked on mass grave sites in both Rwanda and Srebenica.

—

All of these people enlisted to help on the Pickton property were senior undergraduate or postgraduate students from the University of Toronto, the University of Manitoba, the University of Saskatchewan, the University of Alberta and Simon Fraser University. The students, who signed non-disclosure agreements and agreed to criminal background checks before they started, were working under the direction of Dr. Tracy Rogers, an experienced forensic anthropologist from the University of Toronto. Other experts were brought in, including Bob Stair, a retired RCMP officer and former B.C. coroner who had managed the province's forensic identification unit. Stair had recently completed a tour of duty working on mass grave sites in Kosovo and had assisted in identifying remains at the World Trade Center in New York after the September 11, 2001, attacks. Chico Newell, another B.C. coroner, had also been consulted.

The process had begun months earlier when an RCMP officer, surveying the property soon after Pickton's February 5 arrest, decided that the entire sixteen acres should be declared a crime scene, the largest in Canadian history. Experts divided the property into 216 grids, each twenty by twenty metres. These grids were further divided into four sections each, making it possible to define which exhibit came from which part of the farm. The osteologists were chosen, the police told reporters, "for their ability to recognize bones in diverse states of decay that have been exposed to factors ranging from fire to water." The forensic anthropologists were there to distinguish animal bone from human bone; they were also, the police said, "providing a biological profile of human skeletal remains (age, sex, ancestry), and analyzing trauma to bone."

The way it worked was that two dump trucks would bring soil to two screeners set up at the back of the property, covered by a huge new open structure that provided shelter from the rain. The soil would pass through the screeners, which would remove large stones and pieces of debris, and the remaining soil would fall onto four conveyor belts. Team members stood on each side of these belts, picking out objects that might be bone or have some other significance—they could be buttons or shreds of cloth, bits of jewellery or hair barrettes, teeth, fingernails or clumps of hair. Finding these items took intense concentration, and it was slow work; between June 3 and October 26, 2002, only twelve-and-a-half grids of the 216 had been examined.

"Geologists estimate that there are 165,000 cubic metres of surface soil above ground that must be sifted and

Osteology and forensic anthropology students, seen here in the distance to the left of the white tent, take their empty buckets back to the screeners for the next shift.

searched," the police told reporters at the briefing. "This does not include the soil below the surface, whose volume of interest cannot be estimated at this point."

The osteologists would take the bone fragments to Tracy Rogers or other senior forensic anthropologists for further study. The students worked in shifts, and from the road I could see them, every hour or so, carrying large buckets from the screeners at the back of the farm to the white tents erected nearby.

How much was all this costing the B.C. taxpayer? A lot. By August 2002, the investigation had cost $10 million, and the expenses were escalating at an alarming rate. The task force found that it was quicker and less expensive, for example, to buy some of the trailers and bulldozers instead of leasing them. The five RCMP labs and a number of other city and provincial labs across the country were backed up with work from the Pickton case, so the task force was sending DNA samples to commercial labs for testing. They were bringing in experts on mass grave sites from a number of countries to advise them on the macabre issues around the recovery and handling of body parts and bones. They were paying to upgrade the security at the Port Coquitlam courthouse so that it would be ready for the preliminary hearing. They had a team of Victim Services personnel, led by Freda Ens, working with the families of the missing women to bring them to the hearing if they wanted to come—and to help the police break the news when another identity was confirmed on the farm. And that was just the tip of the iceberg.

On October 27, 2002, the members of Project Evenhanded spent three hours in a meeting with the victims' families, who were asked to try to identify clothing, purses, identification and other items found on the farm site and at Piggy's Palace. The police also gave the families a nine-page briefing note about the progress of the investigation. So far, the investigators had searched only twenty to twenty-five percent of the grids. They'd gathered 11,200 exhibits, 8,600 of them from "above and below ground" at the pig farm. The rest came from the eight-month search of the Piggy's Palace property. All the exhibits were now undergoing testing for DNA. The note also told the families that the Crown prosecutors had delivered 35,000 pages of evidence to Peter Ritchie's team. And the police tried to reassure the families that they were trying to find out what had happened to forty-five women who were still missing, women whose remains had not yet been identified on the farm.

.   —

All of this information was useful and interesting. It was good to know that so many qualified people were examining evidence on the farm. I was relieved that no expense was being spared, that nothing was too much trouble. But I began to feel as if we were being choked with numbers, statistics and little fact nuggets. I wouldn't say, exactly, that the information was spin, but it was so far from so many important issues that it began to worry me. All the public relations bustle, the steady torrent of numbers, couldn't stop people from asking how this had happened in the first place. Why had the police ignored, for years, the anguished efforts of family members and friends to have their loved ones listed as missing persons? Why didn't the police look for them? When Kim Rossmo told his colleagues in the Vancouver police in 1998 that he was convinced a serial killer was working in the Downtown Eastside, why was the official response a humiliating demotion—essentially a public dismissal? And if Pickton was taking women out of the Downtown Eastside to kill on his farm, why hadn't the RCMP, whose jurisdiction included the farm, picked up on the rumours that he might be involved? Especially when he was "known to the police," as the expression goes, a man who had once been caught by the RCMP running a chop shop (an illegal bit of entrepreneurial activity where he helped take apart stolen cars for their parts) on the farm for the Hells Angels.

I asked Kim Rossmo all of these questions, and his answer was chilling: "I don't think anyone knew what to do. Or how to do it."

In other words, the police, particularly the Vancouver police, didn't know how to run a major serial murder investigation. No one wanted to admit that, even to themselves. Besides, it would be expensive. Better to deny it was happening.

Now both police forces were scrambling, doing massive damage control. The Vancouver force had responded to the catastrophe by hiring Jamie Graham to replace outgoing police chief Terry Blythe, Rossmo's nemesis. Graham was an outsider, which was necessary, but he was also a recognized and respected leader and an RCMP chief superintendent in Surrey. He was untouched by any part of this case when he won the chief constable's job in July 2002, beating out Larry Campbell, who had also applied for the job.

As soon as it was announced, Jamie Graham's appointment was a big issue for me—he is my cousin and someone I admire and care for. I decided the only way to deal with the potential conflict of interest and possible damage to his career and my book was to tell everyone I dealt with, as I went along, about the relationship, and not to call or visit Jamie or discuss the case when we saw each other at occasional family gatherings.

—

As the outrage over the missing women grew, the RCMP had responded by setting up Project Evenhanded in February 2001, and despite the risk of jurisdictional friction and jealousy, the Vancouver police couldn't complain. Lying behind them was a failed investigation of their own, one they had called Project Amelia. Set up in the fall of 1998, it too had been created to staunch the never-ending flow of criticism about their failure to catch or even look for the person responsible for so many missing women, but it never had any real support from the top officers in the VPD, and it collapsed in 1999 after only a few meetings.

After Pickton's arrest in February 2002, part of the damage control was a complete clampdown on information. Project Evenhanded allowed no leaks, no gossip, no speculation. Police officers working on the case were not allowed to tell even their friends in the force what they were doing or what they had found. Their press releases were full of statistics and technical information but very little more; no one ever mentioned responsibility, culpability, mistakes. Everything was a secret. When I stayed for a few days in Port Coquitlam at the Best Western Hotel, a temporary headquarters months ago for some of the police who had been brought together soon after Pickton's arrest, the staff told me they had been told not to talk to anyone about the police having been there. My husband works at the University of Toronto, and one day he brought home the university magazine, which featured a profile of one of the university's anthropology students who was working on the farm. I wondered if her police supervisors went berserk when they saw it, even though the story was both positive and discreet. Maybe it never surfaced in B.C.

For me, one of the most interesting things about Project Evenhanded was where the task force was headquartered.

No one seemed to know where the office was; in fact, I rarely heard anyone even mention it. The office is not listed in the RCMP's website, which shows five different district headquarters offices in Surrey. But one day a former RCMP officer told me where the office is. I got out a map and drove over to 7485 130 Street in Surrey, a large office building of the sort one sees in suburbs all the time. It is located on a dead-end street, and nothing on the outside indicates that the RCMP has a major presence there. Inside, a list of tenants appears on a board in the lobby. If you didn't know, you might never guess that the Major Case Management Operational Service Centre, which takes up the second floor of this building, is the headquarters of Project Evenhanded. And it was only by accident, when I ran the names of the other tenants through some databases, that I learned that IMPACT—which occupies the third floor—is another RCMP office: the Integrated Municipal Provincial Auto Crime Team. Although I could get into the building, I couldn't go upstairs to look around; I quickly discovered I would need a magnetic card to open the door to the stairs or to enter the elevator.

I might not have been so quick to notice the obsessive secrecy if it hadn't been brought to my attention by others. I soon found out that I needed to be very careful. Kim Rossmo had given me a list of former VPD colleagues who might be helpful, warning me at the same time that many of them would not be friendly if his name was mentioned. I started calling the names on his list. A couple hung up on me. One man said "yes" when I dialled and asked if he was so-and-so; when I said who I was and why I was calling, he swore and hung up. These men were among Rossmo's former enemies in the Vancouver police. Many were impossible to find;

The tenants at 7485 130 Street: the Major Case Management Operational Service Centre, a.k.a. Project Evenhanded, and IMPACT, the Integrated Municipal Provincial Auto Crime Team.

their numbers weren't listed anywhere. But some did talk to me, including one retired VPD officer. He was nervous when I called him at his new job. He didn't want to talk on the phone at all; he said he'd meet me at a White Spot restaurant for coffee and could give me only thirty minutes.

When we met, he was less concerned with telling me about the VPD's failed effort to investigate the missing women than he was with warning me to be careful. Former colleagues of his, he said, would stop at nothing to make sure they didn't get blamed. And they weren't the only ones—the RCMP was just as worried. "The RCMP would not participate in a 1998 request for a surreptitious entry into the Pickton farm," he told me. "And they wouldn't take cases. The attitude of the RCMP is that the VPD will do it."

So why should I worry? I asked him.

The police, whether they are VPD or RCMP, will want to know what you're doing, he said. You may be followed. "And for sure someone will try to clone your cellphone."

Clone my cellphone? What was he talking about? At this point, he was anxious to leave. He glanced at his watch and got up, leaving his coffee untouched. "Look," he told me, "one of these days you'll find your cellphone is missing. It won't be for long. Someone will find it and give it back to you. But it will have been cloned, and they will be listening to all your calls after that. They'll want to know who you are talking to and what people are saying. So watch your cellphone." Who were "they?" He shrugged and walked away.

Cellphone cloning, or copying the identity of one cellphone to another, isn't common, but it can be done without too much trouble by experts. They simply put a new chip in the phone to allow them to configure an electronic serial number and a mobile identification number that are the same as those in the stolen phone. There are an enormous number of Internet sites with advice on this, including ones dealing with specific makes and models. The main reason people clone phones is to make long-distance calls that will be charged to the owner, but another reason is that cloning allows a third party to eavesdrop on the owner's calls.

I thought a lot about this conversation. At the time, I believed he was warning me about individual officers who were afraid of being brought down by the fiasco, not about the Vancouver police or the RCMP in general. Much later, I realized how naive I was.

As I drove away, I remembered a conversation I'd had in Toronto at the end of September with Darrow MacIntyre, a CBC Television reporter based in Vancouver, and his Toronto producer, Lynn Burgess. They had worked with CBC Radio reporter Yvette Brend on a documentary about Gina Houston that aired on March 23, 2002, just one month after Pickton was charged with two counts of first-degree murder.

An addict and prostitute, as well as a close friend of Willie Pickton's, Houston is a key witness in this case. At the time, she was living in a small house in Port Coquitlam with her kids and Ross Contois—the man with the bag of stolen hammers who had hitched a ride with Lindsay Kines the day after Pickton's arrest. Aside from Lindsay Kines, MacIntyre might be the only journalist to interview her. He found her almost by accident. He and his crew had been hanging around the North Fraser Pretrial Centre, looking for people who might be visiting Pickton. She was one of the few, and she agreed to talk, but not on camera. They met several times.

"Just dealing with Gina was incredible," says Lynn Burgess. Houston told them she'd been on the street since she was fourteen, and had hung around with many of the women who had disappeared. She also revealed that she had been under police investigation for four years. Houston seemed to like talking to Burgess and MacIntyre and told them a lot about life on the street and about being one of Willie Pickton's friends. She was so close to him that her third child, she said, thought his last name was Pickton.

"During that time, we were followed by police," Lynn Burgess said. "They knew we were meeting her, so they followed us to see what she was telling us, and they'd sit next to us at Starbucks."

Houston had a bit of a crush on MacIntyre, but the last time they met, two days before his piece went to air, she was angry.

"She said to me, 'You are a fucking cop,'" MacIntyre remembered.

"What we heard was that she had gone to the jail to visit Willie and he said to her, 'What the fuck are you doing?' He handed her a list of calls she had made to me. This was the last time she was able to get in to see Willie in prison. After that, he refused to see her."

The police must have given Pickton the list of calls Houston made to MacIntyre to convince Pickton that Houston had ratted him out. They may have told Pickton that MacIntyre wasn't a CBC reporter at all, but an undercover cop. Who knows what they told him. What was certain was that they had a record of his conversations on the phone with her.

A few days later, MacIntyre and Burgess were filming in the Downtown Eastside late at night.

"My phone went missing," said MacIntyre. "We were in a crowd of junkies and other street people. My phone, which was clipped to my belt, was knocked off in the jostling with my cameraman, and I went three or four steps forward before I realized it was gone. I looked around me, at the whole crowd of junkies and hookers, and said, 'My phone's gone—anyone seen it?' and they just looked at me. It was a silver phone.

"The next day I got a call from a guy—he didn't tell me who it was—and he said, 'I found a phone that belongs to you.' I went and got it and didn't think any more about it."

This happened in March. I talked to MacIntyre and Burgess in late September. In late November, a few weeks after my brief, cautionary interview with the ex–Vancouver police officer in the White Spot, I was leaving St. Andrew's Hall one evening to do another interview over dinner. It was about seven in the evening; outside, it was dark and rainy. I put all my stuff in my Jeep and then realized I'd forgotten my tape recorder. I locked the car, went back inside the residence—using my outdoor key—and then took the elevator up three flights to the corridor my room was on. I opened my door with a second key, retrieved my recorder and returned to the car.

Almost right away, even before I left the parking lot, I realized my cellphone was missing. I had promised to call the person I was interviewing to confirm that I was on my way, and I couldn't find my phone. I tore my purse apart, the car apart, my coat inside out. I locked the car again, went back inside and searched every inch of the space in the reception area, the corridors, the elevator and my room. My phone was gone. I never got it back.

I bought a new one and wondered about changing the number. It might have been wise to do so, but I didn't, and for all I know someone was able to hear my conversations for years.

By this time I had learned that this investigation was far broader and much more complex than I had imagined. Reputations and careers were on the line. Criminal charges could be coming. Two police forces were coping with a catastrophic failure, one that was now costing millions of dollars, one that had the world watching it, one that would certainly end in a judicial inquiry to determine how it had happened and who was responsible. In the meantime, however, the coping strategy was working: keep a lid on everything but hold regular press conferences and feed the press a whole lot of facts and figures.

SIX **FAMILIES**

One day in mid-November, when I was walking to the Student Union Building to have lunch with my brother, Chris, I ran into Larry Campbell and his assistant, Stephen Leary, stumping across the quadrangle in front, both looking grim. The mayoralty race was in full boil, with the voting taking place the next day, November 14, 2002, and Campbell had been giving a last-minute campaign talk to students during which, if I read the body language of these two men correctly, Campbell had said something that Leary thought was stupid and Leary was now telling him not to do it again. My appearance may have stopped a fight. I sided with Campbell when I heard about the problem, and he beamed at me. "I want you to come and watch the election returns with us tomorrow night," he said. "We've got a suite at a hotel, and it's just the family and a few close friends." I wasn't sure he meant it, but when he phoned later and repeated the invitation, I accepted.

The best part of the evening was meeting Campbell's family, a funny, friendly group that welcomed a stranger right away. His wife, Enid Edwards, was the senior pathologist for St. Paul's Hospital and the other Catholic hospitals in the area. Her sister and brother-in-law were there from

Saskatchewan—this was the brother-in-law Larry helped with the harvest every fall. Larry's son was there, as was Enid's. There were a few kids running around the small suite, and a few friends smoked nervously on the balcony, including Chris Haddock. Almost no one was watching the television returns. It wasn't because they expected he would win, I thought; it was because Campbell was too nervous to look and the rest were too busy catching up on family news or trying to decide whether Campbell should wear his kilt or his suit when he walked out of the hotel and across the street to Library Square after the decision was announced. The results racing across the television screen—the biggest mayoralty victory in the city's history—went almost unnoticed.

Enid told me it was time to walk across the street.

"You go ahead with Larry and your family," I said. "I'll come on my own in a few minutes."

They left, and I went and stood in another part of the vast throng there to celebrate Larry's victory. It was a wild crowd: addicts and sex trade workers from the Downtown Eastside, lefties from the hard-core COPE crowd, well-to-do professionals from Shaughnessy and West Point Grey, hip young urbanites from the West End, grey-haired retirees from Fairview Slopes. The noise was so loud that it was hard to hear his speech, but no one missed and no one ever forgot one line: "In *this* city—*no one* is disposable." A full-throated bellow of joy erupted from the crowd.

And that is why he won, with 80,772 votes over NPA candidate Jennifer Clarke's 41,936, and why COPE vanquished the ruling NPA, winning twelve of the fourteen seats on city council and most of the seats for school trustees and parks commissioners. The old city council had been wearing much of the disgrace of the missing women's tragedy. The pathetic remnants of shattered bodies scattered in the dirt of a filthy farm were a rebuke to the city of Vancouver as much as they were to the police. It was one of the lessons I was learning about this story: there is no way to separate the fact of sixty-five missing women from the fact of the city's neglect. Mind you, the province also bears responsibility, as does the federal government. Still, the city seems most culpable.

For decades, the Downtown Eastside had been a remarkably convenient place for city council. Through zoning, bylaws and policing, the council had tried to protect middle-class and wealthy residential areas from low-income housing, including rooming houses and single-room occupancy hotels—the appalling SROs that fill the streets of the Downtown Eastside and have made it, as is often stated, the poorest postal code in the country. Prostitutes, drug dealers, panhandlers, the mentally ill, the impoverished and the hopelessly alcoholic have been squeezed into the Downtown Eastside whenever possible. Of course, there are prostitutes and drug dealers all over town—the high-end ones, who can afford nice apartments and good cars. But tourism, property values and common decency have been cited for years as the reasons to, as much as possible, keep the unsightly in one area. The Downtown Eastside is one of the few places in the city where they can find a room. But a room even in the squalid hotels available to them costs $325 a month, money that usually goes directly to the landlord from welfare; the most a single person receives beyond their rent subsidy is $185 a month to live on. To survive, they must do the rounds of all the food banks, drop-ins, shelters, used clothing bins, church feeding programs, medical drop-ins and all the other patchwork programs that can never replace the most basic human needs, the need for a home and enough money to buy the necessities of life.

There are three ways for most of the addicted women to make enough money to buy their drugs. Stealing, or "boosting," as they call it, is one: they steal from drugstores, grocery stores, department stores, you name it. Then they sell the goods to their fence, often just a guy at the end of the hallway in their SRO. They can also deal drugs themselves. Most of these girls have grim little records in the provincial courthouse computers on Main Street listing convictions for shoplifting and dealing drugs. The third way is to sell sex.

As Elaine Allan said to me almost as soon as I met her, "These girls work hard. There's a reason they are called 'working girls.' They have to blow a lot of latex to get enough money to buy their drugs and pay their pimps and get food." Well, I think I'm not shockable, but I discover I am, actually, quite shocked. "Blow a lot of latex," indeed. It was just the first of many street expressions I would learn here; it means, of course, giving blow jobs hour after hour to dates, as the girls call them, who, with any luck, wear condoms.

The average citizen might well not be impressed with these lifestyles and might have more sympathy with people who get mugged in their garages. But what is surprising about Vancouver is that the average citizen *does* get it—they get the neglect of the city and the police, they get the poverty, they understand the abuse and bad luck that drove these girls to the Downtown Eastside. And they often think, "There, but for the grace of God, go I." The average citizen doesn't use the line I had heard already from more than one police officer: "These girls made their choices." The average citizen is smarter than that.

"Yeah," Elaine says with irony. "In school, when the teacher asks them about what they want to be, a thirteen- or fourteen-year-old girl is going to say, 'When I grow up, I want to be an addict and a hooker.'"

One former defence lawyer in Vancouver, whom I got to know well, had worked with hundreds of prostitutes over the years and told me she couldn't think of one client who hadn't suffered horrible abuse, often as a child, often from family members or friends, often from boyfriends who got them hooked on drugs as teenagers, then put them to work as prostitutes to pay for the drugs. And as I started to listen to their stories—thanks to introductions from Elaine, who took me to find them in parks, on street corners, in soup kitchens and often in their own rooms in the hotels—stories told with humour, clarity and chilling recall, I began to understand what my lawyer friend had been telling me. I am sure that not all of these missing women, nor all of the women I met who were still working the streets of the Downtown Eastside or selling dope on the SkyTrain or boosting cans of Ensure from Shoppers Drug Mart, were abused, but if they weren't, the odds were pretty good that they were suffering from fetal alcohol syndrome or schizophrenia. If they ever have a chance to get better or to live what we like to think of as normal lives, it won't be while they are living in the Downtown Eastside. It's a floating population, but the core consists of about 16,000 people, many of whom live in the welfare hotels, many of whom are addicted. Almost all the addicted people are dealing with an alphabet of related diseases—Hepatitis A, B and C, as well as HIV—that they contracted by sharing filthy needles; some have tuberculosis, and only the newcomers are likely to have all their teeth. Any addict who has been there for a few years is almost certain to have sores from infected needle tracks and painful, swollen feet from old, ill-fitting shoes they found in a pile of second-hand clothing.

The addicted women I met there, every one of them, wanted a different life. They wanted to be well, to be part of their children's lives, to have a little place of their own, to eat good food, to have enough money to go to a movie. They certainly wanted to stop selling blow jobs in parks and alleys.

What's stopping them? While there is no simple answer, one of the biggest problems is getting clean. To get into rehab, an addict must first go through three or four days of detox. There are only two places in Vancouver with detox beds. One is the Salvation Army's Harbour Light mission in the Downtown Eastside, where there are six detox beds for women and twenty-three for men. The Sally Ann detox is "medically assisted," which means there are doctors and nurses there every day, but not around the clock, and it's not a separate facility from the rest of the mission. In fact, calling it a facility is lending it more status than it deserves. It's just a separate corridor, not far from the main bustle of poor men and women lining up for a free meal or waiting in rows in the chapel for space to open up in the cafeteria. The corridor, which is narrow and turns a corner, has faded blue cotton curtains hanging in front of tiny rooms just big enough for two to four narrow cots with about eighteen inches between them. Each bed has a sheet and a cotton blanket and a pillow. There is almost no privacy. Men wearing cotton hospital gowns tied at the back, or T-shirts and shorts, wander around or curl up on their beds. Some sit in a common room nearby. At the end of the same corridor, with no separation from the men's area, a cotton curtain pulls back to reveal a room with four cots. These are for women. Behind it is a large closet that can just hold two more women's beds.

The actual detox process has to take into account the drugs being used by the patient. Whether it is heroin, cocaine, crack, crystal meth, alcohol or pills such as Percocet or OxyContin, or a combination of these, as it so often is in the Downtown Eastside, the doctors and nurses expect to deal with such problems as panic, paranoia, tremors, nausea and diarrhea, cramps, chills, runny noses, fevers and desperate cravings. Once the drugs are out of their systems, addicts can move into the first stage of rehab, which lasts about six weeks; after that, with luck, they can manage with regular counselling and medical supervision.

The second place is Vancouver Detox, near the corner of Main and Second Avenue, out of the Downtown Eastside but straight south just a few blocks. It's slightly more upscale than the Sally Ann facility, but there are still only six beds for women. (There are twenty-four for men.) This place is "medically supervised," as opposed to "assisted," which means doctors and nurses are in attendance twenty-four hours a day. When Elaine went to visit the facility, she found six women on gurneys in a hallway; she doesn't know if these were the six beds the facility says it has, or six extra spaces where women wait until a regular bed becomes available.

"Every single night, when I was at WISH, there were women begging me to help them," Elaine told me. "They'd say, 'Elaine, help me, help me. I'll do whatever it takes.' It's rare that I meet anyone in the Downtown Eastside who doesn't want to work and get off the streets."

But it can be months before a detox space is available. "And at Vancouver Detox, a woman from the Downtown Eastside has to compete for a bed with a woman like myself," Elaine explained. "I might be a weekend junkie, and my alcohol or cocaine use is getting out of control. Often, this demand for detox is driven by my job; my employers might say, 'Do it or we will fire you.' I might have a boss, friends and so on to help. I have a phone; I have a place to live. But a poor woman might not have a phone and has no access to one; she won't have help from work or from friends. She may not have a place to live. How does she compete with the other addict to get a bed?"

Some people can go home to a family who will get them through a few days; some might have the money to pay for a private centre. But not the addicted sex trade worker, and especially not when her boyfriend/pimp needs her to keep working to buy his drugs too. Elaine used to call detox centres all the time for women in WISH, and she was always turned down. No beds, no room.

Once a woman does go through detox, she may be able to get into a good rehab centre, where a stay might be a few weeks. But many of these are private businesses run by rapacious owners in filthy houses with staff who have little or no training. I heard of several that were nothing more than business centres for drug dealers, and others where women were sexually molested or forced to have sex with the managers. And none of this is a secret in Vancouver. People read about it in the papers; radio and television shows talk about it.

Larry Campbell can credit his success that November night to many things. But the events that ignited Vancouver citizens' anger against Philip Owen's city hall happened in 1999, a year after the police had been tipped off about Willie Pickton as a possible suspect in the missing women case. The city and the Police Board had shared the cost of substantial rewards—$100,000 each—for help in solving thirty serious home invasions against the elderly, as well as a rash of armed robberies against people in their garages. But there was no reward for information leading to the arrest and conviction of the person or persons taking the women. That is, there was no reward until the families of the missing women persuaded John Walsh, the host of the television show *America's Most Wanted,* to do an item on his show. Thanks to all the publicity the show stirred up before it aired in July 1999, Walsh included an announcement that the province, the city of Vancouver and the Police Board were joining together to offer a $100,000 reward.

"Once we became aware, as did the community, that there was clearly something wrong here, something that we should be concerned about, we started to kick in additional resources," said the Vancouver police spokesperson, Constable Anne Drennan, the same day the reward was offered.

"Once we became aware"? Drennan's statement infuriated anyone who had tried to report a woman as missing or who had tried to get the police to do something, anything, for years; the first woman on the Missing Women Task Force official list is Lillian Jean O'Dare, who vanished in 1978, twenty-three years before the task force was even founded.

Families, friends and social activists had been raising hell for years over the missing women. Kim Rossmo's firing, clearly linked to the VPD failure to investigate the disappearances, had been a major news story week after week. Mayor Owen and his colleagues on council became so unpopular, especially after Pickton's arrest, that he couldn't do anything right. In fact, he did everything wrong. While he insisted that the city cared about these victims, he refused to support Lynne Kennedy, one of his fellow NPA colleagues on council, when she made a motion to strike a committee to find ways to get addicted prostitutes off the streets. He suggested, instead, that she meet with the missing women's families to get ideas from them. He also voted against a motion from COPE councillor Tim Louis to hold an inquiry into the police failure.

There were good reasons for Owen's decisions, but perception being everything in politics, he simply looked defensive and stubborn.

"The city does care and the evidence is there," Owen said. "The evidence is we do care."

Not according to Tim Louis and Lynne Kennedy. As Lindsay Kines and Kim Bolan reported in the *Vancouver Sun* at the time, Louis had asked why it took fifty missing women to force action on an investigation. "If 50 stockbrokers or accountants had gone missing, we'd have every police force in the nation on it. Because these women were considered at the bottom of the totem pole, the people who should have cared and should have done their job didn't."

Lynne Kennedy was just as direct. "Do you sense I am frustrated?" Kennedy told the *Sun* reporters. "I guess I am just disappointed because I think this is an issue that we could have taken some leadership on."

Family members of the victims were even more eloquent. Helen Hallmark disappeared in 1997, along with twelve other women, more than any other year in this grim story. Owen's comments made her mother, Kathleen, angry. "I feel that not only should there be an investigation into the Vancouver Police Department's non-handling of these disappearances, I feel that there should also be an investigation into Mr. Owen," she said. "There is no doubt in my mind that Mr. Owen would not be in favour of a public inquiry, because I do not feel that the police department nor Mr. Owen acted responsibly or took seriously any of this."

For me, the election was fascinating and the issues compelling, but the fury felt by Vancouver's citizens over what had happened to these women and how the city had failed them was stunning.

Thanks to Elaine Allan and all the introductions she made for me, I began spending more and more time in the Downtown Eastside, and it wasn't long before I was comfortable there. I was no longer afraid, ever. If I walked alone there at night to meet someone, I was cautious but never felt threatened; I didn't dress down or feel I needed to leave my purse at home. I was who I was, and so were they, and it was fine. No one was judging anyone. I had the little parking lot I liked, and never thought twice about hiking down the alley beside it to get to East Hastings. I became a regular in the Ovaltine, the famous coffee shop on that street, which is around the corner from the police station and the courthouse. I met prostitutes for lunch, sometimes took them to appointments here and there—usually for medical or welfare problems—and returned them to their appointed corners or streets when they didn't have time to go home first. Some of them I came to know very well. We talked about their lives, where they'd grown up, their children—which always meant looking at many photographs. We would discuss their health and their plans for kicking drugs. And they told me everything they could remember about their friends who had vanished.

I also spent a lot of time with Ruth Wright, the minister at First United Church at East Hastings and Gore and one of the Downtown Eastside's most interesting women. Ruth has two doctorates, one in education and one in theology. She teaches at the Vancouver School of Theology, preaches at any church that will have her, and does high-level management consulting for the business community, all to raise money for First United's mission. This work, in a church so plain that I fell in love with it first out of pity and then out of a passion for what it does, is extraordinary.

"First," as most people call it, has been looking after the poor in Vancouver's Downtown Eastside for a century, but I suspect it has never before dealt with challenges like the ones it faces now. It's not just that about seven thousand people are registered for programs and assistance there, it's what happens every day. Dozens of people sleep in pews all day long. Hundreds drop in for coffee, breakfast and other meals, pick up mail and a few cans from the food bank, fish through used clothing and piles of shoes for something that is clean and looks okay, and for help getting through to social assistance. First is about memorial services for the missing women, and for the old and sick who have no one else to care for them. It's about showers and foot washing. And, for the prostitutes, it's about WISH.

All of this makes for a long day, one that would destroy many people, but Ruth always seems to remain sane and cheerful. She has time for everyone, even me when I am quite suddenly, surprisingly, overwhelmed by everything—the poverty, the grief, the smell, the murders, the shock of seeing a lovely young girl on the porch at First tilting her head to the sky and jamming a needle up her nostril.

This story, I have been finding, has many locations. Not just the Downtown Eastside, not just PoCo, but also Vancouver Island, where nearly two dozen of the missing women grew up. Many others came from the suburbs, the interior and even from out of the province. The common belief is that most of the missing women are Aboriginal; in fact, says Freda Ens, who works with the victims' families and the police, only a third of the women are Aboriginal. Freda is a Native woman herself—she comes from a Haida band in the Queen Charlottes. She not only knew almost all of the women who disappeared, she knew many of their predecessors, other women who were murdered by violent men. Freda was close to Mary Lidguerre, who was driven up Mount Seymour by a date and beaten to death. Her body remained hidden for years, and Freda was one of the people Mary had trusted to look after her child. She also knew Tracy Olajide, one of three women who was murdered in the Fraser Valley by an unknown killer and thrown into the woods. Many people had told me, when I arrived in Vancouver earlier that summer, that Willie Pickton was once suspected of being the killer but DNA tests had ruled him out.

To try to sort out each of the missing women and get to know them, I set up a chart and filled it in day by day, month by month—their names (and their street names as well, because most had an alias), date of birth, date reported missing, where they came from, where they lived and so on. At first, seeing their faces in endless newspaper stories and on websites, especially Wayne Leng's site, www.missingpeople.net, I thought I would never be able to remember who was who. It didn't take long before I remembered everyone. And then I started trying to meet their families.

I didn't meet them all, not by a long shot. But I met a lot of them, sometimes by calling them directly or coming across them at memorial marches and gatherings, sometimes when they called or emailed me. The general public is familiar with a few of these family members—Lynn and Rick Frey, Sandra Gagnon and Ernie Crey—because they have been interviewed so many times, and I spent a lot of time with them too.

Rick Frey, a tall, burly Campbell River fisherman with a cheerful grin and a gentle manner, was Marnie Frey's father; his common-law wife, Lynn, was her stepmother. Long before Marnie disappeared on August 30, 1997, they had

Left: Marnie Frey—a happy teenager in Campbell River.
Right: Marnie Frey shortly before her death.

won custody of Marnie's daughter, Brittney. Like almost all
of the relatives bringing up the child or children of a missing
woman, they had gained custody of the child almost from
birth. The young mothers, painful as the decision must have
been, knew this was the best choice for their children.
Marnie's mother, Charlotte, Rick's first wife, also lived on
Vancouver Island and was herself a former addict.

Sandra Gagnon was born into a large Native family from
the Kwakiutl tribe in north central British Columbia, one of
eleven brothers and sisters. The family has been ravaged by
violent deaths: one of her sisters was raped and murdered by
five men in Nanaimo; another killed herself; her brother was
run down by a police car. Janet Henry, the youngest of the
children, disappeared on June 25, 1997, from the Downtown Eastside. One of the reasons she ended up there,
Sandra believes, is that Janet, in the cruellest of coincidences,
was brutalized by Clifford Olson in her teens. But it wasn't

Left: Janet Henry on her wedding day.
Right: Janet Henry as she appears on the Missing Women Task Force poster.

until 1981, when she was twenty, that the RCMP came to see her at her mother's house in Maple Ridge. They were investigating Olson, whom they suspected of killing children and youths, and said they had found Janet's name in his address book. Janet admitted that she knew him and said that he and another man—"a French guy," Sandra remembers—had taken her in Olson's car, knocked her out with drugs and then let her go when she came to. She had no memory of what happened to her. One of Olson's favourite methods of controlling his victims was to feed them knockout drops of chloral hydrate in drinks, so it is not surprising that she remembered nothing of the assault. Sandra told me that on one occasion, after Olson failed to find Janet at her mother's house, he tracked her to her sister Debbie's house. Fortunately, she wasn't there when he arrived. Olson was arrested in August 1981, and pled guilty to eleven murders in January 1982.

Left: This photo of Dawn Crey was displayed at her memorial service.
Right: Dawn Crey as she appeared on some Missing Women posters.

The task force has not charged Willie Pickton with Janet's murder, but Sandra and other family members remain convinced that she died on the farm.

It was not the last tragedy in this family: Sandra's son Terry took his own life early in 2002, just before I arrived in Vancouver. A beautiful, soft-spoken woman, Sandra has suffered for years from emotional breakdowns and depression, but she is well liked by reporters, who have interviewed her many times. She loves fashion and bright colours; when she shows up in court, she always wears high heels and pretty outfits. She puts the rest of us to shame, I tell her, and she laughs; the twinkle in her eye lets me know she agrees with me.

Janet had a daughter, Debra, who is living with family in the interior. She is a bright and able young woman who is finishing college and hopes to go into police work, perhaps investigating serious crimes.

Ernie Crey, who lives in Chilliwack, a hundred kilometres

east of Vancouver, is as well known as the Freys and Sandra Gagnon. A fisherman and Native activist, he's a member of the Sto:lo Nation and in 1998 published *Stolen from Our Embrace,* a book he wrote with Vancouver journalist Suzanne Fournier about residential schools. His sister, Dawn Crey, a gentle, pretty girl whose face had been almost destroyed when a date threw acid on her, disappeared from the Downtown Eastside on November 1, 2000.

These four people are the family members you see on television most of the time. They are friendly, passionate and accessible—dream interviews for reporters.

Other family members are rarely unfriendly, but they are more reticent. Erin McGrath, whose sister, Leigh Miner, disappeared on December 14, 1993, took me through Leigh's heart-breaking story. It has no ending, because they have never heard what happened to her. So far, there has been no announcement that her DNA has been found on the farm. Erin, her husband, John, and her mother, Doreen Hanna, live in a small community north of Victoria on Vancouver Island, where they are sharing the responsibilities of raising Leigh's child.

Jack and Laila Cummer, whose granddaughter, Andrea Joesbury, vanished on June 6, 2001, lived in Victoria when I interviewed them; not long afterwards, they moved to the countryside to be closer to Erin and John. The horror of what had happened to Leigh and to Andrea brought the two families together.

Mothers raising grandchildren, sisters raising nieces and nephews—these turned out to be common stories as I came to know the families. I drove to Guelph during one of my trips home to Toronto to talk to Sarah de Vries' mother, Pat, and aunt, the famous children's writer Jean Little. Sarah disappeared on April 14, 1998, and Pat and Jean,

Left: Andrea Joesbury was reported missing on June 8, 2001, by her doctor when she failed to show up for an appointment.
Right: Leigh Miner was reported missing on February 24, 1994.

who are sisters, have been raising Sarah's children almost since they were born. The large Victorian brick house, on a tree-lined street in the old part of town, is crammed with books, dogs, parrots, comfortable furniture, green plants and pictures; it's cluttered and cozy, and it wrapped itself around me so thoroughly that I suddenly realized I had removed my shoes and was about to tuck my feet under myself on the sofa.

Like every family who invited me into their home to listen to their story, I found Pat and Jean to be warm, realistic and very direct. I never had to pussyfoot around. They knew what had happened to their girl, and they were angry about the failures of the police, but they focused less on the past than on doing the very best they could for the future of their girl's children. The kids were rambunctious, happy, intense and engrossed in their busy school lives. It looked like a scene in one of Jean's books, and in a way it was—she has written stories about Sarah and the children that explore some of the issues they have all had to deal with.

A good example of the ability to manage tragedy with honesty is the team of Marion Bryson and Laura Tompkins. Marion, who had been a single mother working as a waitress to support her children, must once have been as beautiful as her daughter Patricia Johnson was when she failed to show up for a meeting with her uncle on February 27, 2001. While it's lined and sad, Marion's face has the same classic lines of jaw and nose that made her daughter so spectacular. And when she smiles, it's like looking at pictures of Patti.

Laura Tompkins is an immigration lawyer whose son is the father of Patricia's two children, a boy and a girl. Because Marion is too fragile, Laura is raising them, but the close bond between the two women is readily apparent.

Sarah de Vries, a talented writer whose poetry and journals have touched many Canadians, disappeared on April 14, 1998, leaving behind two children.

Patricia Johnson, who died when she was only 24, seen here at a happy time in her life. (*Photo courtesy Laura Tompkins*)

Laura is protective of Marion, making sure the press doesn't hound her.

But when I interviewed her, Marion didn't hesitate to talk about her daughter's life. "She was very open with us," Marion said, smiling. "Almost too open." Patricia was a wonderful mother: she called on the children's birthdays, on Halloween, on St. Patrick's Day, and she loved planning presents for Christmas and birthdays. And when she was pregnant, Marion said, she was careful and stayed off drugs and alcohol, so the children were not born with fetal alcohol spectrum disorder or drug addictions. "The children are doing well," Marion said, "and I wish I could tell you just how much joy they have added to my life."

Like almost all the other mothers I have met, Marion never shies away from what she believes happened to her daughter. "I can't bear the idea of my daughter being all cut up," she told me. "She didn't deserve any of this. This has torn me apart."

SEVEN **UNDERSTANDING WILLIE**

I stayed in Vancouver for most of November and December 2002, until it was time to go home for Christmas, panicked by the sense that I was running out of time. The preliminary hearing was starting on January 13, 2003, and I had no idea how long it would last, or even if there would be a trial afterwards. Maybe Willie Pickton would simply save everyone a lot of trouble and plead guilty in January. I'd been on this story since April, and I still didn't know very much about what had happened on the farm.

But I had listened to many disturbing stories about things that had happened there when Willie was growing up, and they helped me understand him. People kept asking me if he was a psychopath. Well, I would hedge: Pickton hasn't been tried or convicted yet, so we are not even sure he killed anyone. But the fact is that the first book I bought after taking on this project was Robert Hare's *Without Conscience: The Disturbing World of the Psychopaths Among Us.* In 1980, Hare, now a professor emeritus at the University of British Columbia, developed the famous Psychopathy Checklist, which became the standard international guide for identifying psychopaths. It was revised in 1985 and is now known as PCL-R.

Of course, once you start researching psychopaths, you soon realize that there is no universally accepted definition of one; even the word "psychopath" itself is under attack. Since I am not an academic and am somewhat bewildered by all the arguments, I accept the general idea that psychopaths are people with little or no conscience. They don't feel any guilt or remorse about their actions. They can be very intelligent and very charming; they can also be violent, cunning and manipulative.

"From the scientific perspective, psychopathy is a culmination of characteristics, inferred personality traits and behaviours that hang together," Hare told writer Robert Hercz, in a feature published in *Saturday Night* magazine in September 2001. "Psychopaths can sing the lyrics but they don't respond to the melody, the melody of normal human interactions and emotions. There is something missing. He has no compunctions; he kisses or kills without a thought."

Without Conscience is fascinating. It kept me engaged on a long flight to Vancouver, and I particularly liked the section on white-collar psychopaths, the kind of people I had been writing about for years. The only problem was that everything I had read to this point led me to believe that understanding psychopaths is difficult, even for experts. In this case, for example, three siblings grew up in the same house, with the same influences, and only one has been charged with murder. But experts say not all serial killers are psychopaths; one study told me that only fifteen to twenty-five percent of men and seven to fifteen percent of women in American prisons display psychopathic behaviours.

Thinking about all this those first few months, I realized I would not know whether Pickton was a psychopath until we started hearing evidence in court. As I reminded myself, we still didn't know for sure that he had killed anyone. People like Albert Harvey were convinced of his innocence and blamed bikers who, the theory went, used the farm to dispose of the bodies.

Still, I had heard enough about Willie's family life to make me realize it had been brutal and difficult. His father was not involved in raising the children; his mother, Louise, might have done the best she knew how, but she was eccentric and tough. A workaholic who ran the family meat business in Port Coquitlam, Louise supervised the kids, expecting them to put in long hours slopping pigs and looking after other animals, even on school days. At one point during his boyhood, people told me, when Willie wanted to hide from someone, he would crawl into the gutted carcasses of large hogs. Another story, widely repeated among family friends in Port Coquitlam, told of his grief at the discovery that his parents had slaughtered a pet calf he had raised himself when he was a boy. He never got over it and repeated the story to people he grew close to over the years.

He was slow in school, spent years in special education classes and finally quit partway through high school. He didn't date, perhaps because girls shunned him; his personal hygiene was the stuff of PoCo legend, both in school and afterwards. Even after he grew up, he stank of manure, dead animals and dirt, and his clothes were never clean. He had a visceral fear of showers, which he claimed was because his mother had always insisted he take baths. One friend of his was a self-appointed nag who would tell him when he was too rank to be endured, and he would meekly obey her order to bathe—always in a tub.

Then there was the story of when his younger brother, Dave, was learning to drive, a story that reveals much more about the mother than about the son. On the evening of October 16, 1967, when Dave was sixteen and had recently acquired his driver's licence, he took his father's 1960 red truck from the farm and headed east along Dominion Avenue towards Burns Road. It was about 7:40. Just ahead of him, on the right side, one of the neighbourhood kids, a fourteen-year-old boy named Tim Barrett, was walking down the road. How exactly it happened no one can say now, but Dave slammed right into him.

Dave knew right away that Tim, who was lying crumpled on the road, was badly hurt, and he raced home in a panic to tell his mother what had happened. Louise Pickton stopped what she was doing and hurried over to the place where the injured boy lay. (We don't know if Dave drove to tell his mother or ran on foot. And we don't know if they ran or drove back together.) After looking Tim over, she leaned down and rolled and shoved him to the edge of the deep slough that ran along the side of the road and pushed him in. Then she turned and went home.

Dave was frightened. He drove the truck to a mechanic in Port Coquitlam who handled the Pickton family's vehicles and asked the man to bang out a dent in the front of the hood and replace a broken turn signal. He even wanted him to repaint the area with the same red house paint the Picktons had used for the truck before. The mechanic repaired the dent and the turn signal but refused to do the painting.

In the meantime, the boy's parents, Phillip and Lois Barrett, were frantic. Phillip Barrett phoned neighbours again and again to see if anyone knew where he was. Just before one a.m., he went to the local police station to report his son missing. The next morning, one of the neighbours, a woman whose son had seen Tim the night before, went out to help

Barrett search the road area. Barrett spotted his son's shoe at the side of the road. Looking around this spot, he and his neighbour reached the slough that runs about ten feet from the road. Peering down into the water, they spotted Tim's body.

The police arrived right away and pulled the body out of the murky water. An autopsy showed that the cause of death was drowning, not the injuries he had suffered when the truck hit him—although these were significant. He'd suffered a fractured skull with a subcranial hemorrhage and a fractured, dislocated pelvis, but the pathologist who did the autopsy stated that these injuries would not have killed him.

When he died, Timothy Frederick Barrett, who was born on February 13, 1953, was in grade eight at the local public school. He had lived with his parents around the corner from Dominion Avenue at 2475 Burns Road, in a house now owned by the Picktons' crony and watchdog Bill Malone. The Barretts buried their son on October 20, 1967, in the Port Coquitlam cemetery after a funeral service in the Garden Hill Funeral Chapel. Three days later, on October 23, 1967, New Westminster coroner J.A. Baird filed a report listing the cause of death as drowning but noting the serious injuries caused by the vehicle that hit him. In March 1968, a coroner's jury listened to the evidence of several people, including neighbours, the mechanic who fixed the truck and the police officer who investigated the case. The verdict was accidental death. But at the same time, as the coroner informed the five-man jury, a criminal investigation was under way.

And that investigation, of course, was into Dave's actions that night. He did not get off scot-free: he was sent to juvenile court and was not allowed to drive a car for two years. More details are not available, however, because his record is sealed and the coroner's inquest was not mandated to investigate all the little mysteries that arose on that fair October night. Louise was never charged, but the true story quickly got out among the neighbours. Many years later, in the early 1990s, Willie told the story to one of his closest friends. This friend told me.

While this event would have scarred Dave more than his brother, this chilling portrait of Louise as mother remains. And what about the father, Leonard? He had, according to family friends, very little influence on his children, but Russell MacKay, the court watcher and retired Port Coquitlam welder who had done work on vehicles at the farm, told me he had heard stories of Leonard's violent abuse of Willie. To balance this view, I had also read newspaper interviews with Linda Pickton Wright, who talked about her father with great affection.

I couldn't let go of the belief that it was Louise, not Leonard, who had been the main influence in Willie Pickton's life. Everyone who knew them told me Willie was very close to his mother. Had she supported him? Helped him or his brother and sister set up a business? Did she have any role at all in their working lives, once they were grown up?

—

It has been my experience, in many years of investigative work, that official documents, dry as most people believe them to be, often give us the best clues about why people act in certain ways and what motivates them. Corporate records are almost always a fair guide to the pecking order in a company. Lawsuits and divorce actions, dug up in court filings, lay out hurt, jealousy, rage and grievance, and almost always the financial motivation behind so much of the unfortunate behaviour laid out in grisly detail on the pages. Property records are always fascinating, especially the ownership structure and the records of purchase and sale. In many of these are laid open mortifying sagas of debt, greed and waste.

The records I pored over in the missing women case were scanty compared to those in many other stories I'd worked on, but were interesting nonetheless. The history of the farm property sales to developers showed how much money Willie, Dave and Linda had made over the years. Two other official documents proved especially fascinating. These were Leonard and Louise Pickton's wills. It took me a long time to obtain them because they were in the Royal B.C. Museum's provincial archives. After a couple of days spent stumbling through the Supreme Court's information retrieval systems, where I had been told I could search wills, I gave up and hired a lawyer to locate them for me, asking her to find not just the wills themselves but all information from the pro-bate, which usually includes lists of assets and debts and administrative information.

Leonard Francis Pickton didn't disappoint me. Described as "retired," Leonard, who was born in London, England, on July 19, 1896, died on January 1, 1978, leaving an estate valued at $148,001.13 to his wife, Louise Helen Pickton. His real estate holdings were valued at $143,665.38, and he had owned two small life insurance policies that totalled $4,335.75. Louise got it all. At first I assumed the real estate meant the farm; when I turned the page to the probate details, I learned it meant four separate parcels of land.

The first was a lot in Coquitlam, in the New Westminster District. It was valued at $40,000, but there was a mortgage on it of $22,069.39, held by the Caisse Populaire de Maillardville, leaving equity of $17,930.61. The mention of the Caisse Populaire interested me; turning to Chuck Davis's ever-useful book on Port Coquitlam, I learned that thirty French-Canadian families had left Quebec in 1909 for jobs in the mills in Coquitlam. Led by a priest called Father Edmond Maillard, they settled on the north side of the community, "the other side of the hill," as people called it. More Quebeckers came in stages, and the area had many French Catholic churches and institutions. The Caisse Populaire was just one.

The second property was the farm on Dominion. It was valued at $275,000 but Leonard owned it in equal parts with Louise, so his share was worth $137,500. Two mortgages were registered against the property: one for $7,000 with the Farm Credit Corporation, another with the Bank of Montreal for $21,940.56. What remained for her of his share was $123,029.77.

The last two properties were a surprise: small parcels of land in the northeastern corner of British Columbia known as the Peace River Regional District. One was worth $2,245; the other, $460. And finally, there was a small life insurance policy worth $4,335,75, so his estate was worth a total of $148,001.13.

In his will, dated March 10, 1975, just three years before he died, Leonard stated that if Louise died before him, his two sons, Robert William Pickton and David Francis Pickton, would be the joint trustees of the estate, would inherit everything and could do whatever they wanted with it. The only proviso was that they would have to pay Linda Louise Pickton, their sister, a lump sum of $20,000. But Louise did outlive him, so the money came to her, all of it.

Two years later, on March 18, 1977, Louise drew up her own will. In it, I learned that she was born in Calgary, Alberta, on March 20, 1912. Willie always told people his mother came from Saskatchewan, so this was a surprise. The value of the farm in Port Coquitlam was still $275,000 but the mortgages had shrunk to a total of $9,954.61, so the equity was now $265,045.39. The lot in Coquitlam, after the mortgage was paid off, was worth $18,878.61 while the land in the Peace River District retained a value of $2,705, and Louise owned another two small parcels there valued at $200 each. So the total value of the real estate, after the mortgages were paid off, was $287,029. Louise also had a bit of money in the Westminster Credit Union and the Caisse Populaire de Maillardville, which added up to $2,088.31. The only debts registered against her estate were $1,800 for her funeral costs and another $1,764.50 in legal fees for work in connection with Leonard's estate.

After Louise died on April 1, 1979, Willie, described as a "farmer" in the documents, was shocked to find out that his mother had ordered her trustees—himself and his siblings—to pay him $20,000 cash right away. Sort of like his father's plan for Linda. The rest of the money, $86,633.33 each, was to be paid to Linda (an "accountant,") and to Dave (a "truck driver") immediately, but Willie's share was to remain in trust, controlled by Dave and Linda. Although they were required to pay him the interest on his money on a regular basis, he would have to wait until he was forty to collect his share of the estate.

Ten years. He would have to wait ten years. Linda was living on Osler Street in Shaughnessy, one of the most exclusive areas in Vancouver; it was close to The Crescent, the street that circled Shaughnessy Park. Trained as an accountant, she was now working in real estate and already seemed to have more than enough money to keep her happy. Dave had his demolition business and his soil business; he too was doing well. Willie may have calculated that he was getting $20,000 more than they were, but how much comfort was that when the delay in his cut of the family money—and $86,633.33, which was a good sum back in 1979—meant that he was indentured to the farm for ten more years? It was a terrible blow to him, and he frequently argued with his brother about the injustice of it. He wanted his money, and he told a close friend that Dave refused to let him have it.

"Willie *never* spoke of what his family willed to him," this friend told me. "All he said was he wasn't allowed his share until he was forty. I had asked him why didn't he buy a place of his own and for a while he did have realtors around talking to him. I guess it was around the time he was fighting with Dave all the time about his money."

If Louise's intent was to protect Willie from himself, it backfired. Pickton was devastated and frustrated by his mother's betrayal.

—

The more I thought about Louise Pickton, the more she interested me. I needed a professional opinion on her, but I was also looking for some professional advice on sex offenders, serial killers and psychopaths. If Willie Pickton had killed these women, if he was indeed guilty of the charges that had been laid against him, it seemed to me it was possible he might be all three things—a sex offender, a serial killer and a psychopath. I needed help understanding a person like this. One of the people who agreed to talk to me, on the condition that I not use his name, was a clinical forensic psychologist who specialized in sex offenders and violent criminals and who had many years of experience working in the federal prison system. As he laid out the common qualities shared by most sex offenders, I compared them to what I knew of Pickton's background.

These were people, I learned, who, early in their lives, suffered neglect and emotional abuse as well as physical abuse. As a result, they were unable to form healthy attachments to their primary caregivers. Although Willie Pickton would tell people he was close to his mother—his sister, Linda Wright called him a "mama's boy" in an interview—I also knew he was very angry about his mother's will. He often talked about how hard he had to work as a child and how there had never been time for fun. So his feelings about his mother have to have been ambiguous at best.

"A person will develop a sense that other people are better than they are, that others have value while they do not," the psychologist told me. "That is why they set up dependent relationships. They are looking for someone who will accept them as they are and who can be relied upon." This seemed to describe Pickton very well. He never felt accepted by Dave's friends. He was never really part of that gang, even though he worked with them and attended some of their parties. He remained on the fringe, an observer. He cultivated the persona of a helper, of someone who was generous with his money, who paid for groceries or beer or drugs, who would offer a room in his trailer to someone who needed a place to stay or a job to someone who needed a break. Someone weaker and poorer than he was.

A person like Willie Pickton who received very little affection as a child or a man, the psychologist told me, would try to soothe himself with alcohol, drugs or sex. Willie chose sex. But no normal woman would have anything to do with him; to get sex, he had to pay for it.

"One of the most destructive early experiences in life is to be humiliated," this expert said. Willie Pickton was humiliated all his life: as a boy, he was shunned by other children, was slow in school, was unattractive to girls, had difficulty speaking clearly, and was ignored or made a figure of fun by his brother's friends. At the same time, because he was growing up in an environment where his associates had no regard for the law, it became easier for him to cross the bridge into criminal behaviour himself. As for intimate relationships, the best he could do was to establish dependent relationships with poor women who needed money, food and drugs. Still, these relationships meant he was no longer the hopeless, inadequate one.

As we talked about Pickton that day, the psychologist raised an interesting issue. "What did he see happening to women who got into the clutches of the Hells Angels?" he asked. "Women who were being degraded—was it arousing? Was he attracted? Did it give him a sense of importance?" Modelling can be a very important determinant of behaviour, I learned. In other words, watching the Hells Angels degrading women—or even watching how his brother treated them—could have been a powerful factor in the way Willie Pickton treated them.

If he were diagnosed as a psychopath, the general view is that he would have no attachments, no concern for others, and that people wouldn't mean anything to him; he would see himself as better and smarter, and would think that other people had it coming to them. He would not feel sorry for anyone. He would reason that it was easier to kill people who were causing him trouble than to deal with them.

My problem with fitting Willie into this profile was that I knew, because I talked to many people who were fond of him, that he did like many people, and did feel sorry for them, and did have concern for their well-being. Over the years, for example, several different women had stayed with him. He liked having them around: they were company, they cooked and cleaned and took meat orders for him. The relationships were not sexual, although in one case he certainly wanted it to be. "We used to cuddle together on a couch," one woman told me, "and sometimes I'd sleep with him in his bed. He'd try once in a while to have sex with me, but I'd tell him to go into the bathroom and jack off." Willie never minded, she said. And yes, she admitted, he masturbated a lot. He'd bought an inflatable life-size doll from a sex shop in Port Coquitlam, ostensibly as a surprise for Dave's birthday; when she teased him about it, he'd smile. He never took offence.

But this fact fit the psychologist's view of a man like Willie Pickton. "One area is important," he explained, "and that is the extent to which someone uses sex as a way to cope. Does this person have a pattern of using sex to cope? Is he using pornography or masturbating compulsively? It's not necessarily lethal, nor does it always lead to sexual assaults. But if he has deviant sex interests, recurrent sexual fantasies and, in particular, experiences the sexual, sadistic pull of arousal, it can lead to significant harm."

What interested this expert and others I spoke to was whether Pickton prepared a rape kit before he went out looking for women on the Downtown Eastside. Did he carry duct tape or other restraints such as zap straps, the reusable plastic ties that police often use instead of handcuffs? Did he carry a knife? If Pickton were sexually deviant or sadistic, if he had fantasies of sex with his victims, if he planned ahead to prevent women from escaping, if he threatened them—all of these would suggest a psychopathic personality. But especially if he was generally antisocial. Then, I was told, he would present "the most classic illustration of the psychopathic individual."

Just before Christmas, as I was trying to finish several interviews, I also had to start packing. I'd just learned that my rent at the college would be going up to such an extent that it would be far cheaper to take an apartment someplace. This move would turn out to be the first of many, all a chore: it meant packing up my clothes, books, telephone, computer equipment and printer, and all my research, which was stowed in three-inch-thick three-ring binders. Not to mention groceries, laundry supplies and bits and pieces of crockery I'd bought to see me through. Sometimes I felt like the Ancient Mariner; most of the time, though, I felt like a bag lady living in a dank Jeep as I drifted around town looking at places. A friend finally loaned me her apartment for a week or two, and I found a sublet near the Vancouver General Hospital beginning in mid-February. To begin with, I reserved a room in a bed and breakfast for the last two weeks of January and the first two of February, finished several more interviews and went home for the holidays. I wouldn't be back until the hearing started, and then I'd stay until it ended. Everyone said it would last three or four months.

Just like everything else about the timing of the case, that estimate proved to be wrong.

EIGHT **THE PLAYERS**

I stayed in Toronto as long as I could and flew back to Vancouver on January 12, 2003, the day before the preliminary hearing was due to start. My brother had been storing my Jeep in the outdoor lot beside his apartment building on the UBC campus; once I climbed in and started it up, it seemed to be wetter than ever—my feet were sloshing on the pedals, and water from the headliner dripped into my face. I made a note to get it in to a repair shop right away and was happy to think of putting the car in the underground garage at my new place. And this, a high-rise with small balconies on Twelfth Avenue in the South Granville area, looked as if it would be great, at least for the next month. Twelfth Avenue is a good route for me, running as it does from Tenth, outside the University Gates, and straight through to the Trans-Canada Highway. Once I'd stopped sailing over the Port Mann Bridge into Surrey by mistake and mastered the tricky little United Boulevard exit to the Mary Hill Bypass into PoCo, I found the route fast and simple.

But the moment I walked into the lobby of the bed and breakfast hotel, called Shaughnessy Village, I realized I'd made a mistake. It seemed like a cross between a senior citizens' residence and a hangout for eccentrics, and it sported a vaguely nautical theme, with portholes for windows. The desk clerk was businesslike, but hesitated as he took my credit card.

"I think you should look at the room before you commit to a month here," he said. "You may want to upgrade to a bigger one."

I went to see for myself. He was right. For about $60 a night, the room I'd ordered had a narrow bench along one wall that pulled out into a bed. It had a tiny corner for cooking, with a cook top and a bar fridge, but there were no plates, cups, glasses, forks or spoons. There was a tiny square of a table, with enough room for one person to eat a meal, but not big enough for my laptop and a notebook or a phone. There was also a miniscule bathroom. I thought in horror of the contract that said I'd be there a month.

"You want to upgrade?" the man asked. "The room will be wider, and there is a proper bed."

He tore up my contract and put me in a larger room for two weeks. I had two weeks to find something else. Going back up in the elevator, I stood with a tall black transvestite. She was wearing a tight dress, high heels, an hour's worth of carefully applied makeup and extensions. She was just moving in and told me she couldn't wait to meet people.

"Isn't this place great?" she gushed.

"Sure is," I smiled back.

The new room was only slightly better, but the good news, I thought, as I surveyed my little castle, was that at $91 a night it wasn't outrageously expensive, my car was safe in a locked basement parking garage, the neighbourhood was nice, and I had cut my contract to two weeks.

It was now past ten p.m., and the next day was the start of

the prelim. How could I have thought the Presbyterians charged too much?

—

The next morning, worried that I wouldn't get a seat in the courtroom, I left Shaughnessy Village at about 6:30 a.m., stopping at a Starbucks on my way to the Trans-Canada. My mood lifted as I drove. The rising sun was starting to burn off thick white clouds of hoarfrost on the blackberry bushes that bordered the highway, and the mountains were beginning to emerge from the damp and foggy morning. It was a big day, and I was grateful for the extraordinary opportunity to tell this story. My heart lifted. I sipped my cappuccino and settled into a drive that had already become comfortable.

Even though I. arrived at 7:30, it didn't feel too early. I had no reserved seat in the random draw that determined which media representatives would get the leftover places in the press section once the big local and national outlets got their seats. This meant I would be competing for one of the few seats set aside for the general public. In spite of all the predictions of media frenzy on the first day of evidence in the Pickton preliminary hearing, there was no lineup to get in at this hour. I was alone except for the television trucks that were setting up their positions and satellite systems as I arrived. I got another coffee from the café across the street from the courthouse, which was about to become the unofficial green room for reporters because it allowed us to keep an eye on what was happening on the courthouse steps.

By 8:30, there were plenty of reporters milling around, and we began to shuffle through security barriers at 9:00. Inching forward, we submitted to searches of our bags, purses, wallets and pockets, a procedure that would be repeated every time we left the courtroom area, even to use a pay phone or washroom outside the secure zone. A few minutes before 10:00, the ·sheriffs opened the door to Courtroom 3, and I breathed a sigh of gratitude as I slipped into a seat in the section set aside for the general public, which took up the last two rows on each side of the main aisle.

"There's gonna be a full house today," one sheriff said to another as he watched the rush. There wasn't. By the time the court clerk asked people to rise as Judge David Stone entered, the hundred-seat courtroom was only three-quarters full, and throughout the day, despite all predictions, there were always several empty seats. Four of them had been set aside for the Pickton family and friends—for David and Linda and perhaps Albert and Vera Harvey. None showed up.

Mike Petrie, the lead Crown prosecutor, strode in. Petrie grew up in Vancouver and graduated from UBC law school in 1979. He spent several years as a Crown prosecutor based in Cranbrook, where he worked on cases throughout the towns of the East Kootenays before moving back to the Lower Mainland as a Crown prosecutor based in New Westminster. Today, his balding head was freshly buzzed, his brown suit perfectly matched to a dark gold shirt and figured tie. Looking cheerful and confident, he glanced around to see who was there; this was the day we'd all been waiting for, and it was no different for him.

His colleague, Derrill Prevett, was not far behind. At first glance, he looked like a Petrie clone, but more country club: he was wearing flannels, a navy blazer and a striped silk tie. An experienced homicide prosecutor with nearly twenty-five years of trials behind him, Prevett was in demand for cases in which DNA evidence would be crucial; his new book,

DNA Handbook, written with Cecilia Hageman and Wayne Murray, had just been published.

John Ahern, a seasoned Crown prosecutor from Vancouver, was the third member of the prosecution team and was just as friendly and approachable as the other two. Ahern had been on an auto-theft task force for the Insurance Corporation of British Columbia, and then gone into private practice for a short time. Missing the challenge of prosecutions, he returned to the Crown's office, where he is valued for his precise management style; it seems few lawyers have his ability to keep files and facts well ordered.

As always, Peter Ritchie came in after the Crowns. He looked perfect: slim, his dark wool suit tailored to his figure, his white shirt crisp and neat, his snowy hair freshly barbered. His junior, Patrick McGowan, with his short red hair and narrow face, seemed serious and humourless. We expected to see Marilyn Sandford that morning, but learned that she was working on the case outside the court.

The other senior member of the defence team was Adrian Brooks, a lawyer from Victoria. Brooks likes reporters and is friendlier to us than most of his colleagues are; that may be because he is married to Kim Westad, a senior reporter for *The Times-Colonist* in Victoria. Or maybe it's just because he is a nice man. As he entered, there was an interesting dynamic at work in the room. Three years earlier, in a sensational case that had transfixed Canadians from coast to coast, Brooks had defended Victoria teenager Kelly Ellard when she came to trial for the 1997 murder of teenager Reena Virk. Ellard was one of a gang of seven girls and one boy who attacked Virk in a sickening case of bullying, but it was Ellard, with the help of the boy, who held Virk's head underwater with her foot until she drowned.

Victoria's Adrian Brooks is one of B.C.'s
most experienced defence lawyers.

On April 1, 2000, Ellard was found guilty of second-degree murder and sentenced to life in prison, although she was given eligibility for parole after three years. Prevett was the Crown prosecutor who won the case.

Later, I learned that the defence team had rented an apartment in a building nestled up against a Chinese restaurant across the street from the courthouse. This might explain why we could never find them during the lunch hour. And although it was Petrie and his colleagues who told us the best places to eat in the neighbourhood, we could never find them either. Their offices were in the courthouse itself, and were off limits to the press.

As we sat waiting for the preliminary hearing to begin, we heard strange clanking, moaning noises; it turned out that the court used pneumatic pipes for its message system. After a while, we got used to it.

Once again, I tried to guess who the other journalists in attendance were. Aside from Trude Huebner, the only one I recognized was Kim Bolan, one of the *Vancouver Sun*'s star investigative reporters, who had worked on the paper's missing women series. But I soon got to know the others: Dan Girard, the *Toronto Star*'s Western Canada correspondent; Greg Joyce, with the *Canadian Press*; the *Vancouver Province*'s crime reporter Suzanne Fournier; Ian Bailey of the *National Post*; the *Globe and Mail*'s Jane Armstrong; Allan Dowd of Reuters; Deborah Jones for *Time* magazine; Jeremy Hainsworth, who was stringing for the Associated Press; and a whole host of radio and television people. It took me a while to sort this last group out, but the main players included three regulars from the CBC: CBC Television's Natalie Clancy, CBC Radio's Kelly Ryan, and Pierre Claveau for Radio-Canada, the French-language service. Dave Lefebvre was present for CityTV, Kate Corcoran for CTV and Darlene Heidemann for BCTV, owned by Global Television.

A few newspaper and television reporters from the Seattle stations were also present; their satellite vans were outside. It didn't surprise me that they had made the trip; their city was still reeling from the 2001 arrest of Gary Leon Ridgway for the deaths of four prostitutes in a series of murders known as the Green River killings. A possible link between Pickton and Ridgway had been made not long after Pickton's arrest by Gary Bigg, the boyfriend of one of the missing women, Heather Chinnock. Bigg told reporters that Chinnock said she had partied with Ridgway at the Pickton farm. (Ridgway pled guilty in 2003 to forty-eight murders and was sentenced to life with no parole.)

The courtroom artists, Felicity Don and Jane Wolsak, if not kept in check, could easily take up a couple of seats each, once they jockeyed for the best spot in the front rows and spread their stuff around—coloured pencils, large pads of paper, erasers and opera glasses, which they used to stare at facial features and other details. They were the only ones allowed to bring opera glasses into court. Because we couldn't take photographs, it would be hard to remember later what everyone looked like, even with detailed notes. I'm no artist, but I decided to get a sketchbook and see what I could do myself.

Next, I tried to sort out the Victim Services workers, who sat with the family members of the victims and of the other women who were still missing. They watched over them, helped them get to court and took them to the Terry Fox Library at noon, where a group of volunteers had prepared lunch for them, and where they could talk in private without reporters pestering them for interviews. Freda Ens led this team, and by this time I knew her well. Although she was not a police officer and didn't work for the Vancouver Police Department, she did work out of their Main Street headquarters in the Downtown Eastside as executive director of the Vancouver Police & Native Liaison Society. Working with her was Marilynne Johnny. Both women are Native: Freda is a Haida from the Queen Charlotte Islands, while Marilynne is from Salmon Arm and belongs to the Adams Lake Band.

Elaine Allan had come to bear witness on behalf of all the missing women she cared for at WISH. Her appearances at the courtroom were brief, usually for just an hour or two, and she was almost always by herself. Her office was in New Westminster, not far away, but the route was always clogged with traffic, so she couldn't stay long.

Then there were the victims' families. That day, I had no idea if any of them were present.

Another group that would turn up frequently at the proceedings was the court watchers. On this first day, there were

Freda Ens, a Victim Services worker with the Missing Women Task Force, and Elaine Allan, former executive director of WISH, the drop-in centre for sex-trade workers at First United Church in the Downtown Eastside.

two of them. One was Russell MacKay, the retired welder who had done occasional jobs on the Pickton farm. The other, a woman I had already interviewed, was dismissed as an obsessed eccentric by anyone in the room who knew her. Sylvia Osberg, seventy-two years old at the time, had lived in Port Coquitlam all her life. She and her husband had a large and interesting old clapboard house surrounded by a carefully tended garden bursting with fruit, vegetables and flowers; she was hospitable and had an excellent sense of humour. But she was fixed on the idea that former PoCo mayor Len Traboulay, now deceased, was corrupt and was a key player in the gang of people who kept Piggy's Palace going. There was no mischief, no wrong-doing, that she would not attribute to Mr. Traboulay, who could not now defend himself. But almost everyone had dismissed her beliefs. At first, I liked her and believed her to be intelligent and the best kind of citizen activist. I soon discovered I was pretty well alone in these kind thoughts. And it wasn't long before she turned on me, as well, and accused me of taking part in a criminal cover-up.

The sheriffs were another faction in the strange new club that was coalescing here in Courtroom 3. They were tough as nails and took seriously their job to maintain order and decorum in the courtroom. They were also well-armed, Kevlar-packed and bristling with walkie-talkies. God forbid your cellphone were to ring; they would hoist their thumbs and nod to the door, mouthing, "Out!" They were not kidding and would hold the door open until you slunk out, scarlet with embarrassment. Chewing gum, eating, drinking from a water bottle, hanging onto a fresh cup of coffee—all were forbidden. They watched us like hawks for the slightest infraction.

Two of the final key players in this courtroom were the court clerk and the court reporter. The court clerk was the only one who seemed to have a grip on all the paperwork at the front. The court reporter was Melanie McEachern, who ran her own court reporting business, M. McEachern & Associates, in North Vancouver. She would become extremely important to the reporters as she owned the transcripts of the daily proceedings. I knew I couldn't afford them; word was they would cost between $800 and $1,000 a day.

And then there was David Stone, a provincial court judge who had settled fishery disputes, given advice to warring couples locked in toxic divorce actions, and tried any number of thieves. This case, potentially the largest serial murder case in North American history because of the number of women who had gone missing, would make him a household name.

The lawyers I'd talked to liked him; one, who had gone to university with him, remembered him as a slightly left-wing social activist. Good sense of humour, too. Not much of that showed through in the courtroom, however. He was serious and unsmiling, much as he had been in November, when he was trying to push the case along in the face of the delay caused by Peter Ritchie's request for more money.

Just outside the courtroom were some other people who would very quickly become important to all of us: Irene and Lou, sisters who ran the little snack bar. They could make us a fast breakfast, knew how we liked our toast, remembered our favourite sandwiches and would hold on to our coffee if we had to run back into court. They also made the lunches for the prisoners who came in for court appearances and trials and were held in basement cells during breaks and lunch hours. Lunch for me was always the same: juice or coffee, a sandwich, a cookie and an apple. Irene and Lou were too discreet to tell me what Willie Pickton's lunch preferences were, but I overheard one official saying he hated lettuce or anything green in his sandwiches. "Just meat. Hates coffee too."

I also heard that he was very friendly with the court staff. "*Good* morning!" he would chirp brightly when they arrived at his cell to fetch him to court.

And this man at the centre of the circus, the person who had brought us all together, was the one we were all waiting for now. Finally, we saw the sheriff who was guarding Robert William Pickton peeking through the glass window of the narrow door that opened into the bulletproof glass box in the far left corner of the courtroom, to Judge Stone's right. The sheriff got the nod and opened the door to let the prisoner walk into the room and sit down. The sheriff sat behind him, slightly to his right. Two other sheriffs flanked the well of the court, one on either side; three more took positions at the sides and back of the public gallery.

Pickton was wearing a dirty grey sweater. His greasy hair hung down the back of his neck, but his crown was almost completely bald. He showed no emotion, no curiosity; he was quiet and calm. As the morning progressed, he didn't look at the gallery at all; his attention was fastened on the witnesses, the lawyers and the judge.

As the preliminary hearing started, the ban on publication of evidence was on everyone's mind. We all wondered what the Seattle reporters would do. And what we would do if they went ahead and started reporting what they heard.

We found out on day two. Both Mike Petrie and Peter Ritchie told the judge that the Americans had distributed some of the evidence they'd heard—it was published on websites run by the television stations, in a story by Christine Clarridge on *The Seattle Times* website, and on the Associated Press wire. Ritchie demanded that the hearings be closed to the public. Stone rejected that idea but drafted a tough new ban, which the sheriffs put up in the elevators, on the door into the parking garage, on the doors to the courtroom and on any other door they could think of. He would bar any reporter who broke the ban, Stone warned us, and anyone found guilty of contempt of court could be looking at up to two years in jail. The Americans left for good.

NINE **LISTENING IN COURT**

Prelim or no prelim, I couldn't ignore the problems with my waterlogged car any longer. I'd had to stop offering anyone a ride. Trying to hide a smirk, the service manager at a repair centre in PoCo diagnosed the problem as a major leak all around the top of the windshield, owing to rust, a fact of life for drivers in Toronto. The windshield needed to be taken out, the rust removed, the window put back and sealed—and it would all cost several hundred dollars. I said I'd think about it. After all, the basement garages at the courthouse and the hotel kept the Jeep dry most of the time; maybe it would eventually get dry enough to mend itself.

The following evening, when I got back from court, I parked the car under the hotel, walked to a nearby restaurant to meet a friend and, later on, walked back. I needed to run an errand, so I took the elevator down to the parking garage and headed over to my designated space. The Jeep was gone.

It was an odd moment. I couldn't believe it. I immediately thought I'd made a mistake and left it somewhere else and just forgot all about it. Except that I also remembered driving down the ramp, swiping a pass card through a reader, entering the code the hotel had given me and parking in the place they had assigned to me. I looked around the garage—maybe in a fit of absent-mindedness I had parked in another spot. Except I hadn't. The place had threatening signs for cars parked in the wrong places; they would be towed. Okay. Someone had stolen my car. That meant someone had stolen all the stuff in it as well, including my new digital camera, which I kept in the glove compartment because I couldn't take it into court. Leaky or not, the car had a noisy alarm and, according to the reassuring notices upstairs, the garage was monitored by video cameras.

The men at the counter looked bored. No, no one had reported an alarm going off downstairs. And no, the video cameras didn't record anything; they simply showed what was happening at the time. No, they hadn't noticed anyone leaving in my Jeep. No, there was nothing they could do. Maybe I should call the police. Which I did. All they said was, "Noted. Now you'd better call the Insurance Corporation of British Columbia. Your report number is . . ." ICBC, the provincial government agency responsible for auto insurance in B.C., took the report and told me to call my insurer in Ontario. And that was that. As far as everyone was concerned, the car was gone for good.

This unpleasant and infuriating event confirmed everything I'd suspected about the hotel. Of course their video cameras were useless; I should have known that.

Budget Rent A Car had something they called an Echo Special, a deal on rentals of their smallest cars. I took one right away and renewed it every month until the preliminary hearing ended. It cost me $6,000—just about what I got back from the insurance company. The car kept my feet and head dry, which was a nice change, but I was concerned. Why steal my Jeep? It was old and infirm.

The day after my Jeep disappeared, Elaine Allan called. Someone had just stolen her car, which had been parked at her apartment building in the west end. It turned up a week later on a nearby street. Then, a day or two later at court, Kim Bolan told us someone had stolen her car. We all managed to dismiss these thefts as pure bad luck, but I confess to a few paranoid thoughts nonetheless.

Losing my car wasn't as grim an inconvenience as staying at Shaughnessy Village. One day, looking for the laundry room, I discovered a small room in the basement with a sign on the door: HOME CARE. Just what I suspected. It explained all the old ladies hanging on to their walkers in the elevator. I was having trouble living in these cramped rooms for two weeks; if I had to live there full time, I would go crazy. I imagined life there, day after day, trying to sleep at night on the bench, trying to feed myself in the tiny corner that wasn't big enough to hold more than a few groceries. I felt so sad. I wished I could write a big story about this hotel, but instead I simply moved out at the end of my two weeks. I'd had enough.

My favourite place in PoCo to do interviews was the Pantry, a little restaurant attached to the Best Western Hotel on the city's outskirts, near the Pickton farm. For a while, the hotel had been the informal headquarters for the police who first converged on the farm, with many of the visiting specialists staying there. Sure, the man at the front desk said, sure they could take me. The cost for the room was the same as that at Shaughnessy Village, and no one stole my car. Janice Jones and the other women who worked in the Pantry were always good to me and to the interesting mix of people I brought there. I'd have breakfast alone, getting ready for court or for an interview later. When I brought people in, they'd let me sit there with them for hours, taking notes and asking questions. And they brought us the best turkey clubs we'd ever had.

Two weeks later, I moved to a modest second-floor sublet in an old apartment building on Tenth Avenue and Oak, near the Vancouver General Hospital again. I dreaded each new move, because every time, I had to schlep my computer, printer, phone, suitcases and books, as well as two dozen three-inch binders filled with interviews, court and property records, news clips and other material.

—

By this time, I was receiving court transcripts by email, 100 to 130 pages a day. Getting them had been a major effort. As the days at court settled down and most of the television people disappeared, the rest of us realized we had to have transcripts. What we were hearing day after day was important, and we needed to have the actual words, not just our own notes. And we knew, because it was already happening just days after the preliminary hearing had begun, that editors and producers would start hauling their reporters back to base to cover other stories. Paying for a reporter to sit in a courtroom all day when it was impossible to publish or broadcast any details of the case was a cost they were unwilling to bear.

But some of these reporters didn't want to miss anything. That's why the *Globe and Mail*'s Jane Armstrong volunteered to set up a pool of subscribers to the transcripts, while Michael Skene, the *Globe*'s lawyer in Vancouver, negotiated a group deal with Melanie McEachern, the court reporter. The more of us in the pool, the idea was, the lower the cost to each. It looked as if we had enough, at one point, to bring the price down to about $80 a day, but even that was too much for the *Toronto Star*, CTV and *Maclean's*, who all chose to do without. That meant the price for the rest of us jumped to about $100 to $110 a day.

CTV decided to send an intern every day to take notes, and for many months two young interns alternated on this job. *Maclean's* sent a reporter only a couple of times. The *Star's* Dan Girard was there for many weeks, until his paper decided he was needed elsewhere.

The transcript issue became tricky. Ms. McEachern would send them by email to Michael Skene, along with the invoices, and Michael would forward them to those of us who had agreed to buy them. Part of the agreement was that we could not give copies of them or forward them by email to anyone "outside our organization." In my case, that meant I could share them only with people working for my publisher, Knopf Canada, and its parent, Random House. In the case of an organization like the CBC, where journalists worked in a far more collaborative way than I, as a solitary writer, did, the transcripts might be shared by many people. As it happened, no one at Random House or Knopf felt the need for copies, but many others outside the publishing house did. I always had to refuse, and it was always awkward.

Until the publication ban is lifted, I cannot describe what was happening during those long days in court. I can't tell you what we heard, or even who testified. I can say it was harrowing. The family members who sat through it, buffered by Freda Ens on one side and Marilynne Johnny on the other, impressed me with their courage and stoicism. Some, but not all, were getting professional counselling. A few reporters, too, spoke of the counselling arrangements their news organizations were making for them.

I got to know many of the family members who came to court. If they wanted to talk to me, we'd often go for coffee or a meal at the Pantry, where Janice and the other staff members would gently look after us. What always surprised me about these families was that they would tell their stories of lost mothers, daughters, sisters and grand-daughters without embellishment or excuses. Whatever had caused the double tragedy of addiction and prostitution—because it always started with the first and ended with the second—they were willing to lay it out in a straightforward way. Abuse was almost always present. Sometimes it was sexual, sometimes physical, sometimes emotional. Sometimes all three. Sometimes it was the father or the brother or, very often, a boyfriend who turned the girl on to drugs and then put her to work to pay for them. Sometimes—all too often, in fact—it was the family running a foster home. Neglect was another common cause, and mothers have admitted it to me. Poverty, too, was a factor in many cases, although a number of the missing women came from prosperous, even wealthy, homes.

Many of the family members I talked to knew how they had failed these women. Some parents felt they had been too careless about the kind of people their daughters hung around as teenagers; others felt they had been too strict, and that their "tough love" policies had been the cause of permanent rifts. A few mothers told me they should have left abusive marriages that had harmed their children, or acted with more courage to stop abuse they suspected their daughters might be suffering. Others wished they had sought professional help earlier. Sisters tore themselves apart about not returning phone calls for help. But the saddest family members were those who had seen their girls taken to foster homes by welfare officers because of neglect and addiction in the family. The regrets of these people had no limits and no answers, and most of the people I interviewed will never forgive themselves.

Still, many of these families tried everything. Tough love. Intervention. Counselling. Group homes. Detox, rehab and medical supervision. Forgiveness. Eventually, almost every family came to the same point: acceptance. "We're here for you if you want to get help," many would say. "Until then, we're here for you just as you are."

It was like that for Marilyn Kraft, who flew in from Calgary one week to attend the preliminary hearing. She agreed to talk to me, and because she was staying with friends in Surrey, I drove there later that week and met her at a Red Robin for lunch. She handed me a picture of her step-daughter, Cindy Feliks, who was forty-three when she went missing on November 26, 1997. No matter what was happening in her life, Marilyn said, Cindy always kept in touch with her and other family members. And no matter what was happening, Marilyn always loved Cindy. Marilyn said she tried to report Cindy missing at the time she disappeared, but had no success; it wasn't until January 8, 2001, when the whole city was in an uproar about the number of women who had gone missing, that the Vancouver police finally entered Cindy into their missing persons list. On January 10, 2003, just three days before the preliminary hearing began, the Missing Women Task Force told Marilyn that Cindy's DNA had been found on the farm, but they weren't planning to lay charges at that time.

The story Marilyn shared with me was grim. When she was about twenty-two and recovering from a brief, failed marriage in Detroit, Michigan, Marilyn had met Don Feliks, a cute young man who worked at a gas station, and soon they were living together. She didn't know he was married until his wife

Cindy Feliks with her daughter Theresa.
Cindy was 43 when she disappeared in
November 1997.

turned up at their house to announce that she was putting the four children they'd had together up for adoption; she couldn't cope. Marilyn told Don she'd be happy to have the kids live with them. The youngest was three months, the oldest was seven. Cindy was five. "I never regretted it," Marilyn told me.

But Don soon left them and moved to Florida. Because she was originally from Vancouver, Marilyn moved back there with the children and raised them on her own. She remarried when Cindy was fifteen. Not long afterwards, Cindy decided to try to find her father. When she tracked him down in Florida, he invited her to come visit him for two weeks. A few days after Cindy left, she called Marilyn in hysterics; her father was trying to get her to have sex with him—"that's how a daughter shows love to her father," he had told her—and had threatened her with a gun.

"I told her to get the hell out of there," Marilyn said. "She ran out and went to a neighbour." Marilyn arranged a ticket for her so that she could fly home right away.

But Cindy's shock and disappointment changed her. She started hanging out with a wild gang at school and soon quit school altogether. Within a few months, she was shoplifting, stealing from her friends and experimenting with drugs. Soon she was hooked. Despite marrying and having Theresa, a little girl she loved, the next few years were a nightmare for both Cindy and the people who cared about her: she was working as a prostitute because she couldn't kick her drug habit, and was in and out of prison.

Audrey Feliks, another of Marilyn's adopted daughters, grew up to have the same problems that bedevilled her sister, and Marilyn had to obtain custody of Audrey's child. The good news in all of this is that this child, who still lives with her grandmother, is happy and thriving in school.

Marilyn's trip to the Port Coquitlam courthouse turned into an ugly mess. As soon as she returned to Calgary, she wrote to the Missing Women Task Force and the Vancouver Police Department to complain that they had not adequately prepared her for what she was to hear about her daughter in court, nor offered her counselling to deal with it.

It is true that she was not prepared for what she heard; I witnessed her reaction. Although she remained calm, she was clearly in shock. Her hand flew to her mouth to suppress a gasp, and her eyes widened. Although she was trembling, she sat perfectly still until it was time to leave the room for the break.

Her other complaint was about money. Despite the task force's agreement to pay her travel expenses, which included a rental car and plane tickets for herself and her granddaughter,

Marilyn was told by Rita Buchwitz—a Victim Services worker who was often in court—that she would receive only $74.81 of the $663 she had spent. Each family was eligible to receive up to $3,000 to help them get to court hearings and the trial, but the task force wouldn't cover the cost of Marilyn's grandchild because she was not considered a relative; she was Cindy's niece, and the priority for financial assistance had to be for Cindy's own children. Marilyn felt the Victim Services workers were callous and uncaring.

As soon as Marilyn Kraft made her feelings known about the way she had been treated, other families did so too, in particular Lynn and Rick Frey. They were vociferous in their complaints, especially about the Victim Services workers. They were so angry, in fact, that it became a news story for a short while. All of this made me uncomfortable and sad. I like the Freys. They'd been hospitable, generous with their time and open with their story. At the same time, I have rarely met finer women than Freda Ens and Marilynne Johnny. I know they were devastated by the losses; many of the women whose names were now being heard in court had been close to them. I also know how hard they worked to protect and care for the families who visited the court. And although I knew her less well, Rita Buchwitz always seemed to be a kind and thoughtful person.

Lynn Frey dismissed the efforts of the Victim Services workers as a joke. As she said to *Vancouver Province* reporter Suzanne Fournier, "The Victim Services people don't do any debriefing and after what they did to Marilyn Kraft, none of us believe we'll be reimbursed." Lynn went on to describe her own experience in visiting the court. "I had no idea what I was going to hear because none of those Victim Services workers would tell me anything," she told Fournier. "I stood up in court and my knees almost gave out, but the victims' assistance people all just sat there."

What may not have occurred to the aggrieved family members was the fact that the Victim Services workers answered to Don Adam, the RCMP inspector who headed the Missing Women Task Force. They weren't professional counsellors, and they didn't work for the families. Their job was to be the administrative liaison between the task force and the families, and to help the families make arrangements to get to the courthouse. The workers sat with the relatives in the reserved section of the courtroom, took them out if they needed a break and arranged a private room and food for the lunch break. But they were not allowed to give the families any information about the case or about their loved ones; that job was done by task force police officers.

The fracas sparked by Lynn Frey's complaints was one of the rare times that families showed their frustration at the way they were treated. They felt the task force told them as little as possible. Why they didn't receive more information, I don't know, but the result, for me, was that I had families calling me every night to try to find out what had happened in court that day. I wasn't the only one—other reporters received calls as well. At first, because my heart went out to them, I tried to think of what I could say—but there was very little, and the best I could do was let them vent. One day, I finally decided that this was not my job and I could not spend hours every night, at the end of long days, acting as some kind of counsellor. But as I listened to the phone ring and ring, hour after hour, the determination of these families to get answers made me angry. Not at them. I didn't blame them. I just wished the task force would find a way to give these people the information they craved.

TEN **MORE THAN A YEAR**

At least twice a week during the preliminary hearing in Port Coquitlam, I would drive over to the Pickton farm at noon or at the end of the day to watch the progress of the investigation there. Although the police wouldn't let anyone on the property, a construction crew had been on Dominion Avenue for weeks, putting in a large storm sewer under the road in front of the farm. In fact, supervised by the search team, the workers ran the new pipe under the farm to one of the subdivisions behind it. When they repaved the road afterwards, the level of Dominion had been raised a few feet. Now, when I was on the shoulder, instead of standing level with the property, I was well above it. I could see everything more clearly.

By this time, it was early spring, and the weak sun delivered a little warmth. The leaves were starting to come out, and the fields were covered in pale green fuzz. Spring was showing up everywhere—except on the Pickton farm, which remained a big, wet mess of dirt. But I could see students working at the screeners and evidence technicians working at the Dutch barn. And the task force was getting ready to take apart Dave Pickton's old house.

It had been just over a year since Robert Pickton's arrest.

The Missing Women Task Force now included more than five hundred police officers—most of them Vancouver police or RCMP officers, but some on loan from the New Westminster, West Vancouver and Delta police forces—as well as civilian employees, and the number of anthropology and archaeology students had doubled to 102. There seemed to be more and more people on the farm every day, including visiting police officers there to have a tour around the place. The digging, sifting and sorting looked as if it would go on forever, and it was going to be expensive; we heard that the attorney general's office had budgeted $10 million to pay for the investigation in 2003.

Scientists had identified the DNA of nineteen of the missing women so far, and police laboratories across the country were clogged with hundreds of thousands of samples to test, so many that other investigations were stalled until the pig farm samples were finished.

Despite the farm's notoriety, the BC Assessment Authority noted "improvements" made on the place thanks to the presence of the police and all their trailers. Much to the annoyance of Linda Wright and Dave Pickton, who still hoped to develop the land and would now have to pay higher taxes on it, the tax assessors concluded that the farm was now worth $3.5 million dollars, $500,000 more than the previous assessment.

Vancouver Sun reporter Kim Bolan talked to Linda Wright about the assessment. "How can they charge us for improvements that are not ours, that we have no control over and that are going to be demolished?" she asked. "I don't understand why the assessor is not being logical." Wright complained to Bolan that the authorities had refused to classify the property as a farm, insisting that it be assessed as if it were being used for industrial purposes.

—

By now I had a new digital camera, which I was using to document the changes taking place on the property. Joyce Lachance, who had known Willie Pickton and had visited the farm a few times before the police took it over, suggested one day that we walk down the east side of the property, outside the chain-link fence, to see the trailer, workshop and slaughterhouse where Willie had lived and worked for several years. They were invisible from the road at the front and from the townhouses at the back. Let's do it, I said.

I had met Joyce at the courthouse. Although she wasn't related by blood to one of the missing women, she sat in the section reserved for family members of the victims because she and Lynn Frey had been foster sisters. Joyce was there every day. I like her—everyone does. She has a big heart and a great sense of humour, not to mention an encyclopedic knowledge of PoCo inhabitants.

She also has a funny story about Willie Pickton. In the summer of 1999, Gina Houston, the prostitute who had been a close friend of Pickton's and wound up as a major witness for the trial, lived in Joyce's basement apartment for a while. Houston was expecting her third child, and Joyce decided to have a baby shower for her. Gina gave her a list of about sixteen women to invite, and Joyce was a little worried about having to buy a lot of food.

"Willie will help you," Gina told her.

Sure enough, Pickton called Joyce and asked if he could help her get the food for the shower.

"Yeah, that would be great," she said.

"What should I buy?"

"I don't know. Some cold cuts? Something for dessert? That kind of thing."

"Okay."

Pickton scoured the local Real Canadian Superstore and finally, still unsure of what to choose, asked a clerk to help him. He arrived at Joyce's house with several bags of groceries and cheerfully unloaded them from his truck, tickled to be part of this girly event. He'd bought a lot of sliced meat, bread, cheese and crackers, as well as a cake.

"And a garlic ring," Joyce added. "A garlic ring! Funny thing to bring."

Thankful for all the food, Joyce added it to the dishes she had prepared and waited for the guests to arrive. Only a handful came. There was enough food left over for another party, so Joyce and Gina decided to divide it. Everything remained friendly until they got to the cake, which hadn't been touched. Each wanted it, and the argument grew heated, Joyce remembers with a laugh. Gina got it.

Although she moved out of the basement apartment soon afterwards, Gina kept in touch with Joyce. All Gina talked about was Willie, and how often she was at the farm.

Not long after Pickton's arrest, Joyce had walked along the eastern perimeter of the farm with a friend; no one had stopped them, which is why Joyce and I thought it was worth trying to do it again.

It was pouring when I was ready to pick her up, so I stopped at the building centre just up the street from the PoCo courthouse to get some rain gear. Sure enough, when I asked if they knew Willie, the men who worked there said they certainly did—he had been in there a lot. Dave too. But they made it clear they didn't plan to answer any more questions.

Joyce and I parked on the shoulder of Dominion Avenue, near the side of the farm, and started to slog along the chain-link fence. Men in the guardhouse at the farm entrance watched us, and I saw one of them lift a phone. The ground was soaking wet, and we had to inch our way along the top of a steep bank of grass, grabbing the fence to keep our balance.

After we'd gone about a hundred feet, a car drove up close to us on the other side of the fence and a police officer got out.

"You'll have to go back," he yelled at us.

"We're not on the property," I yelled back. "We can walk along here if we want. I'm a reporter, and I want to see the rest of this place."

"Nope. Turn around and go back. There are sinkholes along there, and if you fall into one you're in trouble. They're dangerous."

February 5, 2003: The new, higher road is going in beside the Pickton farmhouse; the electrified chain-link fence marking the edge of the property is visible at the far right. The screeners are under the canopy at the back on the left.

By February 5, 2003, the Dutch barn behind the farmhouse had not yet been scoured by evidence technicians.

I was sure he was just trying to scare us off and stood my ground. Joyce seemed to find all this rather funny.

"You have to turn around. You're hanging on to the fence, and it's electrified. You're setting off all the alarms on the place. The guardhouse is going nuts."

I knew we were beaten. We turned back. It was a good move—I heard afterwards that there were indeed sinkholes in this area of the property and that they were indeed dangerous.

By early April, only two journalists were attending the preliminary hearing every day. I was one, and the other was the CTV intern, who was still alternating with another intern every couple of weeks. Other journalists came when an important witness was scheduled to appear. Aside from Joyce Lachance, Freda Ens and Marilynne Johnny, the family section was often empty as well. There were only two court watchers now, but they came in almost every day. My pal Russ MacKay, the retired welder who had done work on the farm, and Art Lee, a retired radio and television repairman in Coquitlam who had grown up in the Chinese community beside the Downtown Eastside, followed the case closely and liked to chew over the testimony of various witnesses and speculate about what would happen next. They often picked up on comments I hadn't noticed, so their opinions were valuable to me.

Some days I'd go back to Russell's house in PoCo for a cup of tea with him and his wife, Maxine, who still worked as a bookkeeper in their home office. I always enjoyed being in their comforting home after a rough day in court; their rambling bungalow on Pitt River Road was blessed with a view down over the town and a large garden crammed with trees, flowering shrubs and dozens of species of dahlias. These dahlias, all staked and babied, were Russell's passion, and he would lead me up and down the paths to show me his favourites.

Art Lee told me stories of the old days in Vancouver's Chinatown and the Downtown Eastside, and one day, when I complained that I couldn't find a Chinese restaurant in Vancouver as good as the ones we had in Toronto, he took me to one in Coquitlam to prove that they did exist. He was right.

The hearing had settled into a steady pattern of witnesses arriving and giving testimony, and lawyers dealing with it. Judge Stone pushed the process along efficiently. Although he allowed the participants enough flexibility to cope with unforeseen delays—and these cropped up regularly—he insisted on keeping the hearing moving and would ask for other business in the case to be transacted to make best use of the time.

Adrian Brooks did most of the work for the defence; we rarely saw Peter Ritchie, who cross-examined only one witness during the seven months the hearing lasted. Ritchie did give an unforgettable performance one day when Adrian Brooks was cross-examining a key Crown witness. Ritchie was sitting in one of the large blue chairs used by the defence and the prosecutors at the front. He swivelled away from the judge to look at the gallery and remained that way, his hands folded across his stomach. As we listened to Adrian Brooks wade through his list of questions, we saw Ritchie's head drooping. Before long, he was fast asleep. His nap lasted about fifteen minutes; I think what woke him up was the snickering of the sheriffs. Ritchie snapped back to life, flustered and red-faced, as Brooks wound up his questions in a hurry. Later, Judge Stone was heard to ask one of the sheriffs if it were possible that Mr. Ritchie had been asleep. We all sympathized; it was easy to get sleepy in that courtroom. But we tried not to actually fall asleep—we had been warned that one of the duties of the sheriffs was to eject any members of the public caught dozing in court, and that included reporters. (But not lawyers.)

Marilyn Sandford also put in long hours in the courtroom; she and Adrian Brooks shared most of the duties. Occasionally, Patrick McGowan, the junior member of the defence team, had his chance to cross-examine witnesses, and once in a while a newcomer would arrive with special skills to add to the mix. The most memorable was Richard Brooks, who, we heard, lived with Marilyn Sandford and had a reputation as a ruthless cross-examiner. He more than lived up to his billing.

On the prosecutor's side, Mike Petrie slogged through most of the evidence day by day, but Derrill Prevett and John Ahern took major chunks. So did Geoff Baragar, who started coming to court a few weeks after the others. Tall and red-haired, Baragar is a competitive skier who spends as much time as possible outdoors, skiing, sailing, scuba diving and riding his Harley Davidson. He has his pilot's licence and loves to fly. Like Peter Ritchie, he grew up in Thunder Bay, Ontario, but he went to McGill for his B.A., took his master's in economics at the London School of Economics and got his law degree from UBC. Except for a five-year stint working on insurance fraud for the Attorney General's commercial crime section, he has spent his career working as a prosecutor, and it is what he loves best.

Each side, prosecution and defence, had interesting and skilful lawyers; to my surprise I was never bored in court. There were sometimes informal debriefings during breaks or after the hearing ended for the day. When we were confused, which was often, Petrie was frequently available to explain what was going on. Russ MacKay and Art Lee would often listen in on these sessions. Baragar, Prevett and Ahern were also accessible, but the defence team usually left the court in a hurry at the end of the day and rarely stood around during coffee breaks. As a rule, Ritchie was available only on big news days and seldom spoke to reporters, but Marilyn Sandford and Adrian Brooks were always polite and friendly and tried to explain what was happening when they could. No one on either side of this case, neither the prosecutors nor the defence, would agree to formal interviews.

—

When court emptied for the day, I often drove to towns in the Fraser Valley to talk to people. One of the most interesting was Maggy Gisle, who had been an addict and prostitute in the Downtown Eastside for sixteen years. For the last six years, Maggy had been clean and sober, and she was now living in a pleasant apartment in Langley with her boyfriend and her little girl, Lisa-Marie, a precocious, chatty six-year-old.

Maggy's story was not unusual: she and her twin sister were born to a Native family, but the girls were adopted as babies by a white couple in Powell River. Like her sister, Maggy grew up to be a beautiful teenager, bright and talented; both were superb swimmers and were being groomed to compete nationally. But there was trouble in the family, and Maggy moved out with a boyfriend when she was about fourteen. She dropped out of school and started experimenting with drugs, and it wasn't long before she was hooked. The boyfriend moved with her to Vancouver's Downtown

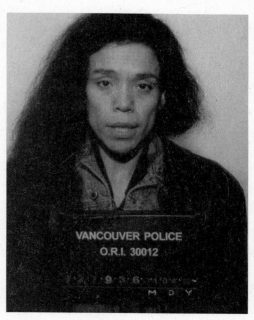

A Vancouver Police department mug shot of Maggy Gisle, who had been an addicted sex-trade worker in the Downtown Eastside for sixteen years.

Eastside, where she went to work as a prostitute so she could buy their drugs and pay the rent.

The next sixteen years were a slow descent into hell. Like all the girls in the Downtown Eastside, she had a street name—hers was Crazy Jackie. She was famous for her beauty, her brains and her daring. She mastered the skill of stringing a trick along for days on toots of cocaine in a hotel room until his bank card was rejected. And she survived violent beatings, including one on Mount Seymour administered by a regular client who, this one time, had brought along a friend. The men got her into a car, raped her repeatedly and beat her to a pulp. Because she was so small and thin, they underestimated her strength; they also had no idea of her will. She escaped by crawling out a car window, and ran naked down the road until another driver picked her up and took her to the hospital. To this day, she is convinced the second man was Gary Leon Ridgway, the Green River Killer.

By the time she hit bottom, Maggy was living in the Vernon Rooms, a rundown hotel on the corner of East Hastings and Vernon, at the eastern border of the Downtown Eastside. It was a small three-storey place with narrow bay windows that evoked a time, many years in the past, when it had had some charm. Now, the sides were covered with peeling clapboard and stained stucco. It was run by Hells Angels who forced their tenants—most of them long-time prostitutes at the end of the road, women who not only had lost their looks but had been ravaged by HIV, Hep C and all the other illnesses and problems brought to them by their addictions and the perils of prostitution—to buy their drugs from the management. Any infraction of the rules meant vicious beatings by the house enforcer.

Despite all of this, the women who lived in this hellhole developed strong friendships. Maggy's best friend in those years was Cara Ellis, who also lived in the Vernon Rooms, or the Ho Den, as they called it. Like many other women on the Downtown Eastside, Cara and Maggy tried to kick their drug habits. Maggy went through detox and rehab thirty-two times, relapsing each time. In 1997, she finally succeeded in quitting for good, and went searching for Cara to try to talk her friend into joining her at the recovery house. Cara, then twenty-five, refused, and Maggy never saw her again. Cara disappeared shortly afterwards but she wasn't reported as missing until October, 2002.

Because she had been on the Downtown Eastside for so many years, Maggy knew almost all of the women who went missing, but losing Cara hurt the most. One morning, I got up early and drove to Langley to pick Maggy up for a day in court. She wanted to see it all for herself. She was waiting when I arrived, dressed in her best: a flowered dress and black shoes with low heels. Her thick black hair was pulled back at the sides, and she had put a little makeup on. Lisa-Marie was happy; she was staying with a neighbouring mom and was excited about a day of fun.

On the way to Port Coquitlam, Maggy was nervous. Tears ran down her face as she talked about Cara and her other missing friends. She was afraid she would say something inappropriate in court and the sheriffs would kick her out. She was stiff with apprehension by the time we parked the car and took the elevator upstairs. Once we were through security, I got her some coffee; Irene and Lou at the little concession stand were nice to Maggy, and she began to relax.

Once we were in court, Maggy sat quietly, her back upright, her hands folded in her lap, following the proceedings intently. Everything was fine for a few hours. Jane Armstrong from the *Globe and Mail* was there that day, and when I introduced Maggy to everyone at the break, Jane started talking to her; the next thing I knew, Maggy had agreed to an interview at her home in Langley. I wasn't happy.

"Jane, Maggy is *my* source," I protested.

"Well, then," Jane said with a grin, "you shouldn't bring her to court." She had a point.

But things changed as soon as we went back into the courtroom. A few minutes after we sat down again, a man entered the courtroom and sat behind us on the left. I paid no attention. Not long afterwards, Maggy started to tremble. I turned and saw tears running down her face. "What's the matter?" I whispered. She just shook her head. But she didn't calm down; instead, she became even more anxious. Finally, she leaned in to me and said, "That guy over there. He's H.A. He collects debts. He used to come into the Ho Den all the time. He's gonna recognize me."

She was terrified. One of the sheriffs looked at me and raised his eyebrows. I nodded to him, and he came right over and took Maggy out. I followed. Maggy told him that the man was a member of the Hells Angels, that she knew him because he used to drop by the hotel she had once lived in. She thought he might be there to intimidate her, to stop her from talking to the Missing Women Task Force. The sheriff moved fast. He grabbed another sheriff, and the two of them went back inside; a third sheriff stayed with us. A minute later, the heavyset man, dressed in jeans and a windbreaker, was hustled out of the courtroom. The sheriffs spoke to him and took his name, and it was clear that the man realized his image had been captured by courthouse cameras. He left in a hurry.

The experience rattled Maggy, and she wasn't able to go back inside. The day was nearly over anyway, so we drove back to Langley. She was silent most of the way. But by the time we arrived, she had worried out a theory. Her live-in boyfriend was a biker, she told me. Reformed, and nice to her, but still a bit of a wannabe, a hang-around. Maybe he had told one of his pals that Maggy was going to be attending court. Maybe this was what she believed it was—a warning to keep quiet.

The next time I saw her, she was in a women's shelter in Chilliwack. She, Lisa-Marie and her boyfriend had moved to a townhouse near Langley, but it was in an isolated area and she was still worried about his biker connections. Their relationship had deteriorated badly and she knew it was time to leave. She had planned her escape carefully. A few people united by the missing women were holding a

After many attempts to achieve sobriety, Maggy Gisle succeeded and had a healthy baby girl, Lisa-Marie. This photograph was taken in 2003; by then Maggy had been clean and sober for six years.

weekend meeting at a house in Chilliwack, and Maggy
made arrangements to get to it with Lisa-Marie. All she
took with her were a few things for Lisa-Marie, which she
stowed in an overnight bag. When the gathering ended, her
host drove Maggy and Lisa-Marie to the shelter. A week
later, they moved to a shelter in Maple Ridge, closer to the
social workers who had been working with her. Almost
everything she and Lisa-Marie owned was still in the townhouse, and she didn't dare go back. After a few weeks went
by, the boyfriend moved out and Maggy moved back in.
Things seemed okay for a while, but she had no money and
eventually she had to take him back. She hoped it would
work out, and she tried to tell herself that the scare at the
courthouse hadn't been serious.

ELEVEN **COMMITTED TO TRIAL**

As the weather grew warmer, I continued to spend many of my weekends driving around the province to talk to people. Most of the time, I went by myself, and I always enjoyed the trips; no matter how often I do it, I think the drive up the Fraser Canyon from Chilliwack through to Kamloops or over to the Okanagan is a gift from God. The same is true of any interview that takes me on a BC Ferry from Horseshoe Bay or Tsawwassen to the islands or the Sunshine Coast. And, as always, I spent a lot of time in the Downtown Eastside, often with Elaine Allan, who introduced me to dozens of women who were living there in hotels. The Downtown Eastside may not be a pretty place, but it is one where I now feel at home.

By this time, I was also interviewing a new category of sources: people who had worked with Willie Pickton or partied with him either on the farm or in the Downtown Eastside. What became clear, as I listened to these people talk, was that Pickton was no loner. This was a sociable guy. He liked to head downtown after a day's work on the farm or at one of Dave's demolition sites.

One of his favourite downtown hangouts was the Astoria Hotel—"his truck was parked in front of the Astoria Hotel for twenty years," is the way one street nurse put it—so Elaine and I went to scout it out. There's a small liquor store at the front of the hotel on the right; on the left is the counter where residents pick up mail and keys. The bar behind is a dark, grubby place with worn captain's chairs and small round tables that are nicked, scarred and stained. A pool table on one side attracts a lot of customers; the rest wander to and from the bar, where they buy their drinks. No waitresses here.

I could picture Willie sitting here as he looked over the women in the room and ordered rounds of beer. He knew everyone and liked being the big spender. Sometimes, women told me, he'd give them twenty dollars and send them out to buy drugs; the idea was that he'd be treating them, but it would be back at the farm, not on their turf in the Downtown Eastside.

—

One Sunday the next summer—it was July 21, 2003—I was in Victoria visiting Jack and Laila Cummer, Andrea Joesbury's grandparents, who lived in a sunny, plant-filled apartment on a street called Dingley Dell. *Only in Victoria,* I thought. Just as we were sitting down in their living room with a cup of tea, the phone rang. Big news. The police were searching a new site in Mission, about sixty kilometres east of Vancouver, and it was on TV right then! We turned on the television to see RCMP Corporal Cate Galliford reading a statement to reporters.

Early that morning, she said, the Missing Women Task Force had begun "sealing off an area located just east of the Ruskin Bridge in Mission, on the south side of the Lougheed

Highway. This land is designated First Nations property, and today the First Nations band responsible for this area was served with the search warrant." Because the case was before the courts, she stated, she couldn't say anything about evidence or how it related to the investigation, but the site itself, a mix of wetland, a slough and groundcover, was about 1,150 feet long and 165 feet wide. A team of eight RCMP divers was on the site. Back at the Pickton farm, the task force had just shut down two of the soil sifters and moved them so that the earth underneath these sifters could be excavated and examined. The fifty-two anthropologists who had been working on those sifters were moving over to help with the Mission site, but the remaining two sifters and the other fifty anthropologists would continue their work at the farm.

Jack, Laila and I watched in silence as the briefing went on. One thing was clear: the task force had done a lot of preparation before they made this announcement. They'd consulted with experts—"the Department of Fisheries and Oceans, the B.C. Conservation Office and a senior biologist from a private environmental consulting firm"—to make sure they weren't damaging the property or harming the fish habitat there. The first order of business was to clear all the groundcover; next, the searchers would rake every inch of the area while the dive team searched the slough itself.

"It's important to point out that we will only be clearing away tall grass and weeds and cutting back bushes in order to search underneath them," Galliford said. "There will be an on-site environmental consultant while the cutting is under way." As for securing the site, they'd installed nearly a mile of chain-link fencing, put in twenty-four-hour security and brought in a Zodiac patrol boat to watch the mouth of the slough and keep out any boats trying to come into the area.

I got to the Mission site the next morning. It was a beautiful sunny day, and Mount Baker shouldered into the blue sky just to the southwest of the site. The police had appropriated the shoulder of the road on the south side and had guards standing at every access point, keeping people out. Within the fencing, dozens of people were hacking away at the brush and placing ready-made wooden staircases so that searchers could easily climb up and down the banks from the road to the slough. Across the slough and along the top of another high bank of earth and groundcover was the main CPR railway track. West of the site, on the same side, the shoulder was wide enough to allow a large tent to go up; this was where the task force stowed their gear and served meals. I counted eight portable toilets and a Dumpster.

Television crews use cherry pickers to get a good view over the highway to the new search site in Mission, B.C. *(Photo courtesy Liz Fox)*

The only place for the media to park (and we had to have accreditation just to get into the lot) was across the highway, on the north side of the Lougheed, where there was a large parking area. Three of the television network satellite trucks there each had cherry pickers to lift camera operators high enough to look down over the bushes and the slough. One cherry picker held a family member of one of the women Pickton had been charged with killing.

North of the media parking lot was a pleasant suburban development planted around Silvermere Lake, a small lake fed by the Stave River. This area, which is owned by the Kwantlen band, is popular with hikers and picnickers.

The Lougheed is a major route through the Fraser Valley, so aside from the curious, there were locals going by, all slowing down to see what they could. I was standing by the side of the road, giving a live interview to CBC Radio reporter Kelly Ryan, who was hosting *As It Happens* that week. As I was describing the scene, a distracted motorist a few feet away from me was craning his neck to see what was going on at the site and slammed into the rear end of the car in front of him. The drivers and passengers of both cars hopped out, much to the fury of the guards, who told them to move along.

Within a few days, the rubbernecks were gone, but the search team stayed at the Mission slough for weeks. While we had no idea what had brought the task force teams here, we did know that, in 1995, a roadside vendor out for a walk in this area had found part of the skull of a young woman, likely between eighteen and twenty-five years old, that might have been here since the 1980s.

The man turned the skull fragment over to the police, but they were never able to determine who the woman was. In

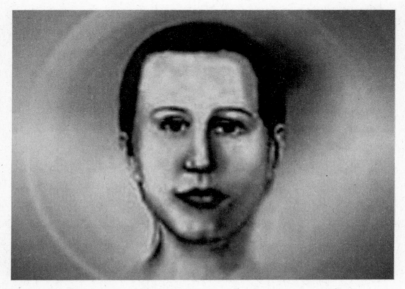

A police artist's picture of Jane Doe, the unknown woman whose skull was found in the Mission slough in 1995. Pickton was charged with her murder after her DNA was later found in bones on the farm, but Judge James Williams quashed the count before the trial started in January 2007.

2000, the RCMP released a Crime Stoppers video re-enactment to try to get information from the public about the victim. One of the bits of information they parted with was that the skull had been cut down the middle by a table saw.

Maybe this search had something to do with the skull, but if it did, no one was saying.

—

The next day—Wednesday, July 23, 2003—was the preliminary hearing's final day. For the first time in months, Courtroom 3 of the Port Coquitlam Provincial Court was full. Several family members of the victims were there, and the reporters' benches were packed. As usual, the courtroom artists jostled each other for space to set out their pads, charcoal and coloured pencils. In the far left corner, Pickton sat as usual in his glass box. On Monday, his hair had been long and stringy; today, he was freshly shaved, his hair was clipped short at the back of his neck, and he wore a clean shirt. As he always did, he made notes in a large black binder he held on his lap; as always, he did not look at the people in the gallery. The sheriffs we had come to know well by now were here in full force, but today they weren't offering any of their usual perceptive, funny quips. Their faces were devoid of any expression at all. The coffee ladies, Irene and Lou, had tiptoed in and sat quietly at the back. A few officials from other courtrooms slipped in as well.

To my shock, after so many months of sitting here calmly listening to evidence, it was hard to keep my composure. My eyes were stinging with tears I tried to hide, there was a big lump in my throat, and my hands were icy. It had been such a long haul. I had entered this story sixteen months earlier knowing nothing; now I lived in this world of horror and pain. Images crowded my memory as I thought of the many witnesses I'd listened to and all the family members who had come in here and talked to me later.

I suspected the process had been as difficult for the lawyers as for the rest of us. At the front, Adrian Brooks sat with his chin in his hand, his eyes closed. Peter Ritchie, his fingers templed, had pushed his chair back and was watching the judge. Patrick McGowan worked on his binder notes, while Marilyn Sandford sat hunched over the table, staring at nothing. The prosecutors, Mike Petrie, Derrill Prevett, Geoff Baragar and John Ahern, who were often as restless as a band of boys—looking to see who was in the room, chatting with

The prosecutors leave the Port Coquitlam provincial courthouse on July 23, 2003, the last day of the preliminary hearing. From left to right, Derrill Prevett, Mike Petrie, John Ahern and Geoff Baragar.

each other—were all in a row, silent, grim-faced and motionless. Everyone was waiting.

Calling this "a very difficult and emotional case," Judge Stone began by thanking both the Crown prosecutors and the defence for their work. "The case is probably unique in Canadian criminal law in its evidentiary scope," he continued. "Not only are there thousands of exhibits involved in this case, but the case is unique in that, while the preliminary inquiry has proceeded, new evidence has been coming forward. This has posed procedural problems for the Crown and defence throughout this proceeding. Without a great deal of cooperation from both sides, the proceeding would have taken a lot longer and it would have cost a great deal more in terms of court resources and money. Without sacrificing the

interests of their clients, both sides have conducted themselves in the highest traditions of the bar in making admis-
sions and agreeing to procedures that would be taken as new
evidence became available. I would just like to personally
thank both teams for their assistance."

Judge Stone went on to summarize the evidence he had
heard and took us through his conclusions.

And then he committed Robert William Pickton to trial
on fifteen counts of first-degree murder. I could almost hear
everyone in the room exhale. He read out the names:
Sereena Abotsway, Mona Wilson, Jacqueline McDonell,
Diane Rock, Heather Bottomley, Andrea Joesbury, Brenda
Ann Wolfe, Jennifer Lynn Furminger, Helen Mae Hallmark,
Patricia Rose Johnson, Georgina Faith Papin, Heather
Chinnock, Tanya Holyk, Sherry Irving and Inga Hall.

Elaine Allan is scrummed by reporters at the end of the preliminary hearing in Port
Coquitlam, while court-watcher Russ MacKay looks on at right.

At the end of the day, court artist Felicity Don waits while television and news cameras capture her work for the evening news and morning papers. The picture shows Judge David Stone speaking while Pickton makes notes on a pad.

But during these months, Judge Stone said, he had also heard evidence on seven other cases that had come in soon after the trial started. If they had been included in the original list, he would have committed Pickton to stand trial on twenty-two charges. The Crown would be able to pursue additional counts against Pickton through a process called direct indictment, which allows prosecutors to skip another preliminary hearing because the accused has already been ordered to stand trial. The names Stone read now were Marnie Frey, Tiffany Drew, Sarah de Vries, Cynthia Feliks, Angela Jardine, Diana Melnick and one Jane Doe, the young woman whose skull had been found in the Mission slough.

It was strange to leave the Port Coquitlam courthouse that lovely summer day. It felt as if school was out, yet I would miss all the people I'd met. They were good people, all of them, and for these few months we had become an odd kind of family.

What I didn't understand then was that we would come together, again and again, as the years went on. I had no idea at all.

TWELVE **CLOSING THE FARM**

It was time to go home. For sixteen months I had been working flat out on the Pickton story. It had turned into the most absorbing and difficult challenge of my working life as a journalist, and I had to accept the fact that it would not end soon.

People invariably asked two questions when they heard what I was doing. The first was, "How can you stand it?" My answer risked sounding sanctimonious, but it was always the first reaction I had: "It's a privilege." This was a rich, complicated, painful and fascinating story, but most people could think only of the grotesque rumours about what had happened on the farm. I thought of the victims and their children and families; of the judge, who managed a horrendous preliminary hearing with extraordinary dignity and compassion, as well as efficiency; of the lawyers, who met Judge Stone's standards of decency; of the sheriffs and witnesses; of the victims' families who had received me into their homes with warm welcomes and honesty. I thought of people like Trude Huebner, who had done such terrific research for me, and journalists Lindsay Kines, Justin Beddall and Ian Bailey, who had been generous from the first day. I thought of Elaine Allan, who always dropped everything to help me, even just to meet me for coffee to decompress, and of all my friends and family in Vancouver, who were so hospitable and kind. And I thought of my family in Toronto, who gave me unstinting support and never complained about my being gone so long. Even though I flew home as often as possible, it was a long time to be away, and I had been in B.C. almost full-time since September.

But part of the privilege, too, was to be in British Columbia. Everything about it delighted me. One day in spring, leaving my last borrowed apartment, I walked down a street with a double row of cherry trees blooming on each side and found myself wading ankle deep in pale pink and white blossoms at every corner. *Life at its best,* I thought, happily kicking them up with every step.

Still, I needed to go home, to my city without views, with no Mount Baker to dazzle me on my drive to PoCo, with no sweet, distant smell of the sea to send me to sleep at night. I needed to think about what I had learned and how to tell the story. And because my flight was due to leave on Saturday morning, I had only two days left to say goodbye to everyone.

The preliminary hearing ended on July 23, 2003, and the following day I went back out to PoCo to see Freda Ens at the Healing Tent. "What can I bring?" I asked. I knew this was where the mothers, sisters, daughters, aunts and grandmothers of many of the missing women would meet to quilt and make the beaded pins and suede pouches stuffed with sweet grass and herbs. They needed sewing supplies, I was told; someone had filched the things that had been there. As a former quilter, I knew what the list would be: I stopped at a sewing centre and picked up quilting needles, needles for leather and suede, scissors, rotary cutters, memory boards, rulers and tape measures and hauled them out to restock their equipment.

I'd never been inside the tent before; it was, as the big sign outside warned, OFF LIMITS TO THE MEDIA. When I arrived, there were about half a dozen women there, of all ages, working on the pouches. Freda and Marilynne Johnny introduced me to everyone.

I thought I had never seen a sadder face in my whole life than that of Dorothy Purcell, the mother of Tanya Holyk, who disappeared on October 29, 1996. Tanya's DNA was found on the farm, and eight years later, on October 2, 2002, Pickton was charged with her murder.

Tanya was only twenty-one when she disappeared. She had lived with her mother, and when Dorothy—known as Dixie to most people—had tried to report her daughter missing, the police had paid no attention. "Dixie's a fighter," Freda told me later. Thanks partly to Dixie's persistence, the

Tanya Holyk was twenty-one when she disappeared; she was last seen on October 29, 1996, and Willie Pickton was later charged with her murder.

Vancouver police finally began taping calls that reported missing people. With other Native women, Dixie began lobbying Native police forces, persuading several of them to push for changes to policies on missing persons across the country.

The statistics spoke for themselves: "Aboriginal women between the ages of 25 and 44 with status under the *Indian Act* are five times more likely than all other women of the same age to die as the result of violence, making them prime targets and the most vulnerable in our society," reported a 1996 federal government study. In March 2003, before I ever met Dixie Purcell, a committee called Policing with Aboriginal Peoples, working with the Ontario First Nations Police Commission, had held a conference they called Responding to Missing Aboriginal Persons. Their conclusion was an important first step in forcing police across the country to overhaul their guidelines in dealing with missing persons reports. After reviewing missing persons policies from several Canadian police services, the groups concluded that "the defining issue was the degree to which bias and stereotyping played a role in the application of the police response to a missing person case involving a person from a marginalized group."

Under the direction of Inspector Glenn Trevett, who had often spoken to Dixie Purcell, the Ontario Provincial Police was the first police force to develop a policy that was culturally relevant and sensitive in its dealing with Native communities. Later, the RCMP changed its policies to match those the OPP had put in place, and finally, the Canadian Association of Chiefs of Police asked all Canadian police services to consider adopting the principles incorporated into the OPP *Lost/Missing Persons Manual*, especially with respect to Aboriginal and marginalized people.

—

When I left the tent, I crossed Dominion Avenue to see what was going on at the farm. The searchers had been inching their way forward to the main road and, the last time I looked, evidence technicians, covered in their white Tyvek suits and booties, had been all over the Dutch barn. Other had been working on the farmhouse—the building known as "Dave's house," even though he hadn't lived there for a few years.

The *Vancouver Sun*'s Lori Culbert had obtained a copy of a report by RCMP Health Services that detailed the "constant health concerns" the searchers needed to deal with, including testing water and soil for contaminants such as animal and bird waste. The RCMP's staff psychologist, Dr. Roland Bowman, was responsible for making sure that workers received counselling if they became distraught as a result of what they were seeing. A special concern was the group of young students working on the farm, but the report noted that they seemed to have done well and that the people who were most upset were the off-site workers. One psychologist, Dr. Brian Johnson, debriefed 126 people who'd worked on the farm and wrote afterwards that "None of the employees interviewed demonstrated signs of being traumatized." He added that most of the people enjoyed working for the task force and "did not look forward to the project ending."

The barn was among the last buildings to be searched. Like all the others—the garage/workshop, Willie's trailer, the slaughterhouse and the piggery, the motorhome—when the technicians were done with the barn, the backhoes rolled in and tore it apart, and trucks carted away the pieces. Soon, all that was left was Dave's house, the old family farmhouse.

That Friday, as the women stitched and talked across the

A team of forensic search technicians work at the Dutch barn in 2003. An evidence tent is on their left; to the right is the canopy over the students working on the screeners.

street, Dave's house sat empty. The searchers were still working hard; with the barn down, they were excavating and sifting the soil under it. They were about to tear down the farmhouse and dig under it, as well. The police told the families that the house was coming down around noon on Saturday, July 26, and invited them to watch. I found out about it, but would be on a flight back to Toronto by then, so Russell MacKay offered to take pictures for me. It didn't take the backhoe more than a few minutes to knock it down, Russ said afterwards.

—

The second question people ask me is, "What about the brother?"

The original Pickton family farmhouse, most recently lived in by Dave Pickton, is covered by tarps in the spring of 2003, as search technicians take apart every room. The police evidence trailer is at the right.

July 26, 2003: A backhoe knocks down Dave Pickton's former house, the last building to come down on the farm property. The Missing Women Task Force invited families to be there for this event. (*Photo courtesy Russ MacKay*)

If Willie Pickton is indeed guilty of murdering many women on the farm over many years, they don't understand how Dave Pickton could have lived and worked with his brother for most of his life and not been a part of this horror.

But I've heard nothing so far to suggest that he was.

That's not to say Dave Pickton is a sweetheart—far from it. Years ago, he was involved with Willie in vehicle insurance fraud. The farm was a great place to dump cars, trucks and other items that had been stolen and cannibalized for parts or claimed for insurance, a common scam pulled on the Insurance Corporation of British Columbia (ICBC). With the equipment they had available, the Picktons were able to dig deep holes to bury stolen goods, even those as big as vehicles and parts. Or they would simply leave a vehicle where it was and let Dave's dump trucks pour tons of dirt over it. When the RCMP came calling, based on evidence that was piling up, they convinced Willie that they knew what he and his brother were doing and persuaded him to show them where the cars were buried.

But in 1992, Dave Pickton faced a far more serious situation when he was convicted of sexually assaulting a woman who worked for him as a flag girl on a construction site in 1991.

"You could smell him before you saw him," the woman told the *Globe and Mail's* Jane Armstrong in an interview, adding that Dave had pinned her to the wall of a trailer on the work site and said he was going to rape her. "The attack ended when another employee walked in," Armstrong wrote. "Dave was found guilty, fined $1,000 and sentenced to a year's probation, while the woman lost her job and eventually left the area, fearing for her safety. Before the trial, she said, bikers appeared at her house and warned that she would end up in concrete if she testified. 'He's got no respect

The Pickton farmhouse: gone.

Dave Pickton. (*Photo courtesy GlobalBC*)

for women,' she said. 'He thought he could get away with what he did.'"

Another woman who knew him well told me she had never met anyone more foul-mouthed around women than Dave Pickton. This woman had been a close friend of his, but she couldn't stomach his attitude towards women. "Dave was rude and obnoxious. If he thought a woman was overweight, he would say, 'You fat cow.' He'd tell women quite openly, 'You're getting fat. You have a big ass.'"

But he had his good side, the woman insisted. He was generous and always paid for everything, picking up the tab in bars, buying meals and paying for groceries. He didn't get drunk, and he didn't do drugs—even though most of the men working for him did. And he worked like a dog. "He was a very good businessman, a workaholic," she remembers. "I stayed at the home many times; Dave would get up at dawn and go out till dark."

Most people preferred to keep their distance from Dave Pickton. Famous for his temper and combativeness, he was just as well known for his ability to skate away from serious consequences, such as jail time. He'd had a number of other brushes with authorities. In 1996, the city of Port Coquitlam had tried to get a court order to stop the brothers and their company, the Good Times Society, from holding parties on the property, stating that it was agricultural land. That attempt failed. In 1998, the Picktons got in trouble for serving liquor at the Palace during a high school graduation celebration; again, nothing happened and they kept their licence. That same year, Dave was ordered to destroy a vicious dog he owned; when he fought back, he was allowed to keep it. On three occasions, he was able to settle damage claims for traffic accidents out of court.

But after a number of complaints and warnings, authorities were finally able to shut down his party palace on Burns Road. The last straw was the 1998 New Year's Eve bash, which has entered Port Coquitlam lore. At least 1,700 people turned up, and while the brothers claimed the event was orderly, others spoke of open drug use, brawls and cars being driven into ditches. This time, after an investigation by Randy Shaw, the local fire chief, the brothers were served with an injunction prohibiting any more parties—although people say they continued in defiance of the injunction. It took the city of Port Coquitlam until 2000 to shut down Piggy's Palace for good, and they succeeded then only because the brothers hadn't filed financial statements and the Good Times Society had lost its status as a non-profit organization.

Since his brother's arrest, Dave had been available to reporters from time to time; get him on a good day and he had no problem talking. But he had never been to court to support Willie—he must have believed the courthouse was full of media folk ready to swarm him. He probably had no idea that, most of the time, the room was almost empty.

———

I spent the rest of the summer of 2003 trying to make sense of what I had heard at the preliminary hearing, reading through transcripts, trying to figure out how to tell this story. It was difficult to talk to anyone about it; most people couldn't believe I was still at it—"What! You haven't finished your book yet?"—and just shook their heads when I explained that the farm was still being searched, that the task force was still interviewing people, and that thousands of exhibits were still waiting for DNA tests in police labs in

Vancouver, Edmonton, Regina, Winnipeg and Ottawa. In fact, the DNA testing process was taking so long that police scientists had developed a new robotics system in the Vancouver lab to speed things up.

All of this was costing a fortune. In mid-September, Greg Joyce, the Canadian Press reporter in Vancouver who was covering the Pickton story, wrote that British Columbia's solicitor general, Rich Coleman, estimated the total cost of investigating Willie Pickton and the missing women at $70 million. "It will no doubt be the most expensive domestic investigation in Canadian history," Coleman said, but added that B.C. taxpayers would be paying only seventy percent of this. The rest of the money would come from Ottawa, under a cost-sharing agreement.

—

One day in mid-October 2003, Joyce Lachance called me with big news. "Rosco's dead," she announced. "He was found in his room at the Golden Ears. They say it was an overdose."

Ross Contois, Gina Houston's boyfriend, had been released from a stint in prison shortly before he died and, with nowhere to go because Gina wouldn't let him back into her place, he moved into a room at the Golden Ears, the biker hangout in Port Coquitlam. When he was found dead, many suspected he'd been hot-capped (murdered with a lethal overdose of drugs). If that's what happened to him, it's not surprising: Contois was a loose cannon with a big mouth; discretion was unknown to him.

Another twist in the case occurred in early November 2003. On November 5, Gary Leon Ridgway, more famous as the Green River Killer, pleaded guilty in a Seattle courtroom to forty-eight murders committed between 1982 and 1984, and told the judge in a prepared statement, "I killed so many women I have a hard time keeping them straight." The following day, November 6, Corporal Cate Galliford, a spokesperson for the Missing Women Task Force, said Ridgway was still a potential suspect in the disappearance of forty of Vancouver's missing women. In fact, we learned that the police had had several meetings with Seattle's Green River Killer investigators to compare notes—women had begun disappearing in Vancouver soon after the murders stopped in Seattle. And then there was Gary Bigg's statement that Heather Chinnock claimed to have partied with both Ridgway and Pickton at the Pickton farm. Willie Pickton had been charged with Chinnock's murder on October 2, 2002.

Twelve days later, on November 18, 2003, the search of the Pickton property ended. The tents were gone, as were the ATCO trailers, the searchers and the forensic technicians. Only the canopy built to protect the screeners remained. The place was still a mess. Piles of rusted machinery and vehicles cluttered the bleak landscape of mud and swampy holes. Dave Pickton and Linda Wright agreed that the land had to be cleaned up, but its future was unclear: would they try to develop it for more housing, as they had planned to do before Willie's arrest? Not even they knew.

Then, on November 20, the task force held a press conference to announce that they were adding four names to the list of missing women: Sharon Anne Goselin, who was fifty-three when she was last seen, in May 2001; Cara Louise Ellis, who was twenty-five when she was last seen, in 1997; Gloria Christine Fedyshyn, who was twenty-seven when she was last seen, in 1990; and Sharon Evelyn Ward, who was twenty-nine when she was last seen, in February 1997.

Maggy Gisle called me right away, crying so hard she could barely talk. "Cara was my best friend," she wailed. "My best, best friend."

Even though the police were not saying that Cara was dead, the announcement that she was now on the task force's list of missing women was a clear indication that she was presumed dead. Maggy was inconsolable and went back, over and over again, to the last time she saw her, that day when she begged Cara to join her at the recovery house where Maggy had finally found sobriety and peace.

But Maggy was not too upset to disagree with the date—January 1997—the police put on Cara's disappearance. "I know I last saw her in the spring of 1997," Maggy said. "I know that for sure."

Almost a month later, a week before Christmas, Geoffrey Gaul, a spokesman for the Attorney General's office, announced that the Crown was proceeding on seven new charges of first-degree murder against Willie Pickton, bringing the total to twenty-two. We had already heard the evidence on these seven charges during the preliminary hearing; they were the ones Judge Stone said he would have sent to trial if they had been included in the original indictment he received when he started the hearing in January 2003. The names of the victims were Tiffany Drew, Sarah de Vries, Marnie Frey, Cindy Feliks, Angela Jardine, Diana Melnick and Jane Doe. A trial began to look a long way away.

I started picking through the blather from the spokespeople on all sides to see what it really meant, and what I finally realized was depressing. This case was going to take another year, at least. Gaul said it could be the fall of 2004—nearly a year away—before pretrial procedures, whatever those were, would begin. And it might be the spring of 2005 before a trial could start. This was going to be a long, quiet period.

But all hell broke loose again in January 2004. On January 28, almost two years after Willie Pickton had first been arrested, the police announced that nine more women had been connected to the farm. Three of these women were Jane Does, women whose DNA was found on the property but didn't match the DNA of any of the sixty-one missing women on the task force's official list. The other six identities were known. The police said they had found the DNA of Yvonne Marie Boen, who disappeared on March 16, 2001; Andrea Fay Borhaven, who disappeared in 1997 and was reported missing in May 1999; Wendy Lynn Crawford, who disappeared on November 27, 1999; Dawn Teresa Crey, who disappeared on November 1, 2000; Cara Louise Ellis, last seen in the spring of 1997 and reported missing in October 2002; and Kerry Koski, last seen on January 7, 1998. This new list brought the total number of women whose DNA had been found at the farm to thirty-one.

It got worse five weeks later, on March 10, 2004, when the RCMP put out an appeal to people who might be storing meat in their freezers. "Specifically, we are looking for any meat that was obtained over the past several years, up to February of 2002, and is still in the possession of individuals—for example, still in their freezer," the police said. "Our chief reason for having people contact us is that the meat in their possession, the meat obtained from the Port Coquitlam farm, may have been exposed to, or is possibly connected to, existing evidence that is related to the murder charges against Mr. Pickton."

It was a careful way of saying the gruesome thing that had been in the back of many minds for a long time: Had human meat, or human meat mixed with pork, been sold to the public? By the end of March, however, no one had contacted the police. (At the end of October 2004, officials at Health Canada issued a report stating that, even if human remains had been fed to Pickton's pigs and even if the remains had been from women who had hepatitis or had contracted HIV and even if those pigs had been sold to the public for human consumption, the risk of anyone contracting a disease was "very low," indeed, "infinitesimally small.")

It's odd now, when I look back on this period of the Pickton case—when investigators were working flat out, although nothing seemed to be happening—to realize how busy I was. The fact that nothing was going to happen for at least eighteen months meant I had plenty of time to do most of the remaining interviews and research the project required. I spent much of the spring of 2004 in British Columbia, visiting families and trying to complete the rest of the interviews on my list. Always in the back of my mind, though, were three possibilities: that Willie Pickton would suddenly decide to make a deal with the Crown prosecutors and plead guilty, as Clifford Olson had done; that someone would kill him; or that he would die of the hepatitis C he'd contracted in 1997. Any of these scenarios would mean a rush to finish my book.

At the time, I would have welcomed such a tough deadline. The end of 2003 and most of 2004 were difficult months for me personally, and the Pickton story was often a welcome escape. In the late fall of 2003, William Kaplan, a Toronto author, had sold the *Globe and Mail* a three-part series adding up to about forty thousand words of invective, much of it about me. He had published an earlier book that went after me for the investigative stories I had published about Brian Mulroney's Conservatives, who'd formed the government in

Canada from 1984 to 1994. But at the heart of his series was the accusation that I had been a confidential informant for the RCMP in their investigation into the sale of several Airbus planes to the Canadian government during the Mulroney years. Kaplan made that the gist of his story, and neatly buried the fact that Mulroney had accepted $300,000, in cash, from Karlheinz Schreiber, allegedly for some work he would do to promote a pasta business of Schreiber's.

I found out about the series the night before the first part ran and woke up to the shock of seeing my face on page one of Canada's biggest national newspaper, a paper where I'd worked happily for many years. With my reputation seriously impugned in this public way, I was forced to begin several months of my own consultations with lawyers. Chief Superintendent Al Matthews, the RCMP officer in charge of the case, finally admitted that almost everything he had said about my role in the Airbus investigation—damaging information he had placed a few weeks earlier in the court in a sworn affidavit—was untrue. This time the *Globe and Mail* ran only a short story on a back page. I filed a formal complaint against the officer and against the RCMP with the Commission for Public Complaints Against the RCMP, but after many months of delays all I ever received was a thick file of legalese essentially stating that because the investigation was still before the courts they could do nothing. In the meantime, however, and what was more important to me, was the tremendous support I received from journalists and the public across the country. When I was able to return to the Pickton file late in 2004, it was with a great sense of renewal and faith: it would take more than a William Kaplan or Brian Mulroney to bring me down.

THIRTEEN **TOO MANY JUDGES**

The fall of 2004 in Toronto was crammed with appointments and obligations I'd put off because I'd spent so much time in B.C. I felt I had neglected the Out of the Cold program at St. Andrew's, and I missed it; I always felt it was one of the things in my life that kept me in balance. I needed to get to know my cats and dog again, see friends and have people over for dinner, something I hadn't done for a long time. Best of all was the time I got to spend with my family, lazy evenings of talk and Chinese food—I still say the Chinese food in Toronto beats Vancouver's any day— and it was good to be back in my own home, sitting by the fire and reading, sleeping in my own bed.

But the Pickton case was rarely out of my mind, and as soon as Christmas was over, I headed back to Vancouver. In February, David and I were moving to Jerusalem, where he would be a visiting professor in the political science faculty at the Hebrew University. We planned to be there for several months, and I hoped to spend my time there finishing a first draft of the manuscript. Before we left, therefore, I needed to wrap up a number of scheduled interviews.

By this time, I could see the shape of my book as a whole, and I was always interested in people's reactions when they found out I was doing research for a book on this case. Discovering what interested them always made me think again about what should be in the book.

Many people assumed it would be a book about the missing women: "You must have interviewed all the families." Of course it is about the missing women, I would reply, but my scope is broader than that. I'd interviewed many family members, but not all of them. Maggie de Vries, a Vancouver writer and editor, had published *Missing Sarah,* a fine book about one of the missing women—her sister—and I couldn't write about any of them in such a personal and therefore knowledgeable way. *Missing Sarah* focused on one person, but her story shared much with so many of the others.

"Well, then, you must be writing about the failure of the police." Partly, I would answer. There is no doubt that both the Vancouver police and the RCMP failed in this case, and that, too, deserves a book of its own. Some day, one may be written from inside the investigation, most likely by a retired cop—now that's a book I'd like to read. I was fascinated by the science of the story, but at this point, writing about the forensic work done by anthropologists, osteologists and other specialists was impossible. Maybe later.

I was also after the story of the hunt for a serial killer who preyed on some of the city's most vulnerable residents. One man had been charged—Robert William Pickton—and I wanted to know more about him. I wanted to learn whether others might have been involved. My job now, as I saw it, was to try to pull together all the stories swirling around the case so that people could understand how this could happen in Vancouver, who all the players were, and what actually had happened. And, as always, I felt my time was running out.

—

By the time we left Canada for Israel, I had packed up my research many times. Instead of trying to cart it with me every time, I'd learned to ship it, praying I didn't lose anything. I never did. Box after box of transcripts, reference books, photographs, clippings and documents would stack up in my front hall in Toronto, waiting to be taken to the local Canada Post outlet, although I always kept my interview notes in my personal luggage. I had become a paranoid duplicator, backing up all my computer files on DVDs and portable hard drives, keeping extra sets wherever I lived.

My main preoccupation, before we arrived in Jerusalem, was ensuring that we had high-speed Internet in our apartment. When we got there, however, I discovered it wasn't hooked up. I was distraught, ignoring the grand piano and fine furniture in our big apartment, and not even taking in our sunny terraces, the flower-filled park across the road, the fact that the Old City was a twenty-minute walk from our place. How was I going to keep up with what was happening in Vancouver? I wailed. How on earth could I manage with dial-up service? I hadn't been able to absorb more than four words of our copy of *Hebrew for Dummies,* so I couldn't begin to negotiate a contract with an Internet service provider. It never occurred to me that almost everyone in Israel speaks English.

I set our computers on the dining-room table and, in despair, flopped down on the bed for a nap. When I woke up, I turned on my laptop to look for the phone numbers of friends I could call for help with this technological nightmare. To my astonishment, emails began racing into my Outlook mailbox faster than they ever did at home. Some had been sent minutes earlier from Canada. A friend who called to see how we were doing enjoyed reminding me that Israel is one of the most technologically advanced countries in the world. Where we lived, in the heart of the city—close to the president's residence, the Old City and the King David Hotel, where most world leaders and celebrities stay—there was a brand-new system of Internet hotspots providing free high-speed service to thousands of people. The project, called Unwire Jerusalem, had been sponsored by the Jerusalem Business Development Corporation to help with the economic renewal of the city. Eventually, it would include the whole city; for now, we were in the centre of it, and we could send and receive with no trouble at all.

I suspected that the technology had a lot more to do with the Israeli intelligence service monitoring the communications of guests at the King David than with keeping people like us happy, but I didn't care. Now, I hoped, nothing that happened in Vancouver or Port Coquitlam would escape my notice. Advancing technologies had made it possible for me to work anywhere. I often thought back to 1993 and 1994, the years when I was writing *On the Take,* my book about the Mulroney years in government. We didn't have email or the World Wide Web. I used a fax machine to keep in touch with people, and I used primitive dial-up services to subscribe to several newspaper databases, as well as crucial company and government databases.

—

Eighteen months had passed since the preliminary hearing ended on July 23, 2003. When investigators had finally left the Pickton farm site on November 18, 2003, and turned it over to the family, many people assumed that no one would ever want to live on that site or use it for any commercial purpose. Those who lived in townhouses built on former Pickton land were distressed to think there might be graves or human remains under their homes, but they couldn't afford to abandon them or take a loss on selling them. It turned out that they didn't need to worry about their property values. Early in 2005, the North Fraser office of BC Assessment released figures showing that the Pickton farm was now worth $5.9 million, $1.6 million more than it had been worth a year earlier. The rise was attributed to the soaring price of real estate in Vancouver and its surrounding suburbs, suburbs that included the three communities of Port Coquitlam, Coquitlam and Port Moody. As each was no more than a half-hour commute to downtown Vancouver, they were exploding with new subdivisions, and the Picktons' seventeen acres, finally free of police interference and cleared of all buildings, were ready to develop. A new road and sidewalks ran past the farm, and a new sewer system and new street lighting had been installed. And right across the street, the mall—already anchored by a Canadian Tire, a Home Depot and a couple of supermarkets—was expanding to include more restaurants, services and stores.

Near the end of March 2005, Associate Chief Justice Patrick Dohm announced that Judge Geoffrey Barrow of Kelowna, B.C., would be presiding over Willie Pickton's trial. A University of Victoria graduate and a former prosecutor in Kamloops, Barrow had been appointed to the Supreme Court in December 2001. His appointment was a surprise: why wasn't a judge based in Vancouver or New Westminster taking the case? There had certainly been some lobbying for the appointment—it was a high-profile case, and for some judges living outside the Lower Mainland a stint in Vancouver would be pleasant. But how Dohm chooses which judge will try a case remains a mystery.

Another mystery was why Dohm insisted that the case be tried in New Westminster's Supreme Court building, when the spacious and specially designed Courtroom 20—constructed at a cost of $7.2 million dollars for the 2003–2004 nineteen-month Air India trial—was available at the Vancouver Law Courts. This courtroom had 137 seats, 30 of them set aside for the media and 80 for the families of the victims (in that case, the 329 people killed in 1985 when a bomb exploded over the coast of Ireland on an Air India flight from Canada to India). Courtroom 20 had been equipped with all the latest technology, including voice-activated video cameras, video monitors, high-speed Internet access so the lawyers could do quick research or contact their offices, digital recording and video conferencing. Simultaneous transcription of proceedings, visible on some of the monitors, also made life easier for the legal teams. An overflow courtroom, with video monitors showing the trial, was nearby.

But Dohm had chosen New Westminster's Courtroom 102, a wee space that would barely hold forty-five people in addition to the judge, lawyers, court officers, sheriffs and jury. It was half the size of David Stone's provincial courtroom in Port Coquitlam, and a fraction the size of Courtroom 20. The overflow courtroom right beside it was just twice its size. Parking in New Westminster would be a problem for everyone except court officials, who could park under the building, and the press was squawking about the thirty- to forty-minute daily commute from downtown Vancouver. None of this mattered; Courtroom 102—called the judge's courtroom—it would be.

My best guess is that Dohm thought a small courtroom would be easier to control. Most of the public and the media would have to sit in overflow courtrooms, watching video monitors, while family members of the victims would have their own room in which to watch the trial in privacy, although a few family seats would be set aside in the judge's courtroom.

The trial was scheduled to begin on May 25, 2005, with a few days for disclosure arguments from both the Crown prosecutors and members of Pickton's defence team. So far, the Crown had disclosed 500,000 pages of documents, but the defence wanted another 1,800 exhibits disclosed. Geoffrey Gaul, a lawyer himself and the spokesperson for B.C. Court Services, explained the reasoning to me. "In any prosecution," he said, "there's information that the prosecution would conclude as either irrelevant or perhaps privileged and, therefore, not subject to disclosure. The defence can actually disagree

Courtroom 102, looking towards the judge's seat. The court clerk and reporter sit at the table directly below the judge's desk; jury seats are at the far right; prosecutors sit on the right, before the judge; the defence team sits on the left. *(Photo courtesy the Attorney General of British Columbia)*

Courtroom 102 from the judge's end of the room. The witness box is in the foreground—Pickton will sit in the black chair, surrounded by a bulletproof glass box. Behind him is a glass wall, and beyond that is the public gallery. The press sits in the front row, victims' families directly behind the press, and the public and court officials at the back. The entrance to the room is at the far right of the picture. *(Photo courtesy the Attorney General of British Columbia)*

with our assessment of that." In other words, the prosecutors don't want to cough up everything they've got, but the defence insists on having every scrap, including all DNA and forensic evidence, the names of informants, the police officers' notes and all wiretap evidence. Even when the prosecutors have concluded that a line of investigation is not relevant—say, a possible suspect is eliminated—and therefore, in their view, the material they have gathered is not relevant, the defence may demand to see it so they can make up their own minds about its usefulness to their client's case.

Dohm predicted that, once the arguments over disclosure were resolved, the pretrial arguments phase—known as the *voir dire*—would begin in September 2005 and last for four months. This stage, before a jury has been chosen, is technically part of the trial itself. Often described as a trial within a trial, the voir dire allows defence lawyers to apply to the judge to remove certain pieces of evidence and witness statements from the trial altogether. These applications are argued by both sides, the defence and the prosecution, both using case law to try to persuade the judge of the righteousness of their arguments. Almost all of this proceeds unnoticed by the general public. Under section 648 of the Criminal Code, all evidence and statements given in court fall under a publication ban when there is no jury present. That ban continues until a jury is sitting there, however long that might take. Once the trial ends and a defendant has been convicted and sentenced or found innocent and released, the publication bans are lifted and reporters can write about what they learned during the preliminary hearing and the voir dire, including the material the judge excluded from the case. These are the interesting tidbits you get later, usually in paragraphs that begin, "What the jurors didn't hear during the trial was the fact that . . ."

Once the voir dire phase was finished, the trial itself, we learned, would begin in January 2006, nearly four years after Pickton's arrest. It would last, Geoffrey Gaul suggested, about eight months. The Crown expected to add the additional seven charges to their indictment against Pickton, for a total of twenty-two counts, Gaul said.

At this point, we discovered that the defence team now had ten lawyers on board. And when Peter Ritchie told reporters that his client was keen to get started, he acknowledged that his relationship with Pickton was distant. "I don't speak to him much," Ritchie said.

—

The court hearing began on May 25, 2005, as expected. Pickton was not present to face the new first-degree murder charges before Judge Geoffrey Barrow; instead, he appeared by video link from the North Fraser Pretrial Centre. What was unexpected was the number of new charges—instead of the seven mentioned earlier by the Crown prosecutors, there were twelve.

The seven charges we had known about were the ones mentioned by Judge David Stone at the end of the preliminary hearing in July 2003. At that time, he sent Pickton to trial on the fifteen original charges; because the extra seven cases came to light a few days after the hearing began, he preferred that the Crown prosecutors lay the new charges as direct indictments, a step that was possible because the evidence had been heard in court. These seven charges included the murders of

An artist's rendition of Pickton, then fifty-five, appearing via video link from jail on April 9, 2002. (*Drawing by Jane Wolsak*)

Marnie Frey, Tiffany Drew, Sarah de Vries, Cynthia Feliks, Angela Jardine, Diana Melnick and an unidentified woman known as Jane Doe. The five new ones, filed by Mike Petrie, were for Cara Ellis, Andrea Borhaven, Kerry Koski, Wendy Crawford and Debra Lynne Jones. And the fifteen that had already been filed were for the murders of Sereena Abotsway, Mona Wilson, Jacqueline McDonell, Diane Rock, Heather Bottomley, Andrea Joesbury, Brenda Ann Wolfe, Jennifer Lynn Furminger, Helen Mae Hallmark, Patricia Rose Johnson, Georgina Faith Papin, Heather Chinnock, Tanya Holyk, Sherry Irving and Inga Hall. Willie Pickton had achieved a Canadian record: twenty-seven charges of first-degree murder.

But the Crown prosecutors weren't the only ones with a big news story to spring that day. Peter Ritchie had one too. He told Judge Barrow that his client needed a much stronger publication ban than the protection offered by the Criminal Code during this new phase of pretrial hearings. Although the Canadian press had respected the ban since January 2003, and there had been only one breach by American reporters, Ritchie insisted that Pickton needed to be protected from leaks in foreign publications and on the Internet while the voir dire ran. He asked Judge Barrow to either close the court entirely, preventing the public and the media from entering, or order reporters not to tell anyone, not even their editors and producers, anything of what they heard. The ban would even mean that family members couldn't tell other family members what they had heard in court.

Though conceding that he knew "of no case where there has been a breach or an alleged breach . . . which is significant," Ritchie justified his request by saying that the first motion he planned to put before the judge would "involve allegations that arise from the police investigation concerning potential involvement of others in the murders. We are pursuing potential avenues of defences for our client and if others are affected by that, it's my submission [that] that should be a concern for the Crown."

Reaction to Ritchie's request was quick and severe. Many people said it was an attack on free speech. "It's unworkable, it's unenforceable, it's nuts, with respect, and it's of no efficiency," Robert Anderson, the media lawyer for the *Vancouver Sun* and the *Vancouver Province,* told Judge Barrow. While a *Sun* editorial acknowledged that the Internet had "limited the effectiveness of traditional publication bans," the solution Ritchie sought, the editorial said, "would have us seal up the courtroom, if not physically then by gagging everyone on their way out the door. His solution would do more harm than good. . . . Except in extraordinary circumstances, courtrooms must operate under the public eye, otherwise there can be no justice as we know it."

Michael Skene, the lawyer acting for CTV and the *Globe and Mail,* concurred. If the judge ordered people not to talk about what they heard in court, it would represent an unprecedented restriction on freedom of speech. "If Mr. Pickton is granted the order he is seeking, it sets a very bad precedent," Skene said outside the courthouse. "It says that people who attend the court, when they leave it, aren't free to talk to other people about what they've seen or heard."

Three days later, on May 28, 2005, Judge Barrow was expected to rule on Peter Ritchie's request. But when the sheriffs went into the courtroom, Barrow wasn't there. They were shocked to find out that, instead, Patrick Dohm would be in the judge's chair.

"Dohm!" exclaimed one of sheriffs. "What's he doing here?"

The explanation was surprisingly brief and completely

baffling: Judge Barrow had discovered, Judge Dohm said, after only two days of presiding over the Pickton case, that he faced scheduling conflicts that would not permit him to take on this trial. The new judge would be Justice James Williams, who was already based in New Westminster's Supreme Court. The whole thing seemed odd to many of us who were following this case closely, even one following it from Jerusalem, but no better explanation was forthcoming.

Williams, a slender man with short, thick, grey hair and a full moustache, was born in Brooks, Alberta, but grew up in Yellowknife and Calgary. In 1970, he graduated from the University of Alberta with a Bachelor of Arts degree. He joined the RCMP, spending most of his time there working in commercial crime. In 1981, after several years on the force, he returned to university to study law. This time, he attended the University of British Columbia. He had to work part-time as a Greyhound bus driver to support his wife and three children. Williams graduated from law school in 1983, articled under Len Doust (often called the finest criminal defence lawyer in the province) and was called to the bar in 1985. He soon joined the downtown Vancouver law firm of Doust Smith, which had been set up in 1988 and was managed by Bill Smart, one of the province's most skilful criminal defence lawyers and another of Len Doust's former articling students. By 1990, Williams was a partner, working in criminal defence litigation and prosecution, where he was valuable in the firm's other speciality, defending police officers in trouble. In 1991, the firm's name changed to Smart & Williams, and Williams began to be better known in the province's legal community. He volunteered for various legal programs and served as an instructor or panellist for a number of courses for the Continuing Legal Education Society of British

Columbia, the Justice Institute of British Columbia and the Trial Lawyers Association of British Columbia. Although lawyers knew who he was, his name wasn't familiar to the general public until he became involved in several high-profile cases. He acted for RCMP officer Hugh Stewart, who had pepper-sprayed student protesters during the 1997 Asia-Pacific Economic Forum in Vancouver, and he defended hockey star Marty McSorley after he bashed another player, Donald Brashear, with his hockey stick in February 2000.

In April 2002, two months after Willie Pickton was apprehended, Williams had been appointed to the Supreme Court of British Columbia and assigned to the New Westminster court. Williams had a reputation for a sharp wit, and he was known to be bright. But did he have enough experience to manage what appeared to be the biggest criminal trial in Canadian history? Over the three years he had been a judge, he had handled only thirty cases.

When local lawyers heard the news that Williams would be presiding over the Pickton trial, the reaction was positive. "I think we're lucky to have him running it," lawyer George Macintosh told the *Globe and Mail*'s Robert Matas. "He is even-handed to an unusual degree." Richard Peck, one of the defence lawyers on the Air India trial, also spoke highly of Jim Williams. "He's got tremendous common sense and doesn't bring a bias with him," he told Greg Joyce of Canadian Press. Williams's strength, Peck said, was his "even-handedness, his equanimity."

When he appeared for the first time, on June 8, 2005, Williams appeared calm and confident. It took him only a few minutes to put his mark on the case. He denied Peter Ritchie's request for draconian publication bans, saying standard rules would suffice—but he also took the precaution of prohibiting any publication or broadcast that could help people find banned information "by any means, including the Internet . . . information that would tend to identify websites or other sources from which prohibited information about these proceedings can be assessed, including, but not limited to, the names and addresses of any such websites and sources."

—

By early July 2005, David and I were back in Canada, and the Pickton story dropped to the bottom of my priorities. Our younger daughter, Amy, had become engaged in May to a young man called John Rowley, and they had scheduled their wedding for our own fortieth wedding anniversary weekend, on September 12, 2005. (David and I had been married on September 11, 1965.) The summer was a frenzied and very happy writeoff of meetings with our minister, organist, soloist, caterer, dressmaker, florist and all the other people whose presence became suddenly urgent and completely absorbing. It was, thank God, a lovely wedding with no glitches, and it went by for me without a thought of Willie Pickton. But a few days afterwards, I had to figure out when to go back to Vancouver and, once again, where to live and how to get around.

The voir dire was now scheduled to begin on October 3, 2005—not in September as first announced—in New Westminster. This time, I used a website to help me find a place to live and found a large, comfortable apartment with a wood-burning fireplace on the second floor of a big house close to Point Grey Road. Once again, I shipped out our latest car and all my research, and hoped for the best.

I arrived in Vancouver on Sunday, October 2, 2005, rented a car until mine arrived and moved into the apartment, where I found something I had been longing for: a window with a view over the ocean to the mountains. I fell into bed with the windows open, and that familiar smell of damp cedar and pine drifted into the room.

The next morning, I drove out to the New Westminster courthouse, at Begbie Square on Carnarvon Street. I was late. By the time I got there, whatever had gone on in court that morning was over, and the sheriffs were locking down the courtroom. I found the Crown prosecutors, still gowned in their black robes and white starched shirts, lining up at the little coffee shop across the street, right beside their offices. Mike Petrie and Derrill Prevett introduced me to two new members of the team, Satinder Sidhu and Jennifer Lopes, both experienced prosecutors who had been working in Surrey before moving to this case. The group had bad news for me. The voir dire I had moved out to attend had just been postponed until January 2006. I could have stayed home and spent many pleasant hours looking through honeymoon pictures and helping Amy and John admire their wedding presents.

Before I left that day, I walked back to the courthouse and past the old red brick office building that formed the side of the courthouse square. The next lot was full of trucks and backhoes clearing a large site for the construction of a new condominium. Trude Huebner had told me the company doing the demolition and clearing work was Dave Pickton's. I watched the activity for a while, wondering if Dave ever came by to help and if he would venture into the courthouse itself, once the voir dire started, to sit in one of the two chairs set aside for Willie's family. I doubted it. Dave had already told reporters he didn't want to have to deal with the media, who would have hounded him for comments. I doubt anyone would blame him for staying away.

I had to tell my nice landlords I wouldn't be staying for several months, after all. But I did stay the month, spending much of it in the Downtown Eastside. As far as I could see, nothing had been done to improve the lives of the community's inhabitants—certainly not for the prostitutes and drug addicts. Three years after I first got to know this community, there were no more detox beds and housing was no better, despite all the interest in the case of the missing women. The women were as much at risk from sexual predators and psychopaths as they had ever been.

One change for the better was the Four Pillars policy. Championed by Larry Campbell when he became mayor, it was a plan to establish North America's first safe, legal injection site for addicts, so that fewer would die from overdoses or from diseases and infections caused by dirty needles and contaminated water. And despite an uproar from many quarters, including a fair segment of the Vancouver police, it was put in place. But in August 2005, when he was close to the end of his three-year term, Campbell had accepted an offer from Prime Minister Paul Martin to become a Liberal member of the Senate in Ottawa. I'd heard that Campbell had not particularly enjoyed his time as mayor and disliked the bureaucratic side of the job, but I was surprised to see him go to the Senate, which meant spending time in Ottawa, a far more bureaucratic place than City Hall. I thought it was a shame. It seemed he had not been able to help the Downtown Eastside as much as he had hoped to.

It was not for lack of will or good ideas. The Downtown Eastside is crammed with a wide variety of social agencies, drop-ins, food banks, shelters of one sort or another, and people who want to help. Many of these overlap with one another and, for the most part, they get along. Several important and carefully planned programs have been instituted to try to "fix" the neighbourhood, all designed to include the different groups who live there, whether they are long-time residents of Chinatown, the local Aboriginal societies, the yuppies of the nearby gentrified Strathcona area or the poverty-stricken, addicted residents of the local single-room occupancy (SRO) hotels. But with such a mix, there are territorial issues and conflicting demands and needs. The city faces pressure from condo developers who would like to take over the area, now one of the last undeveloped parts of central Vancouver. But if the developers succeed, where will these people go?

Simple statistics underline the area's problems, problems that it would take the combined political will of every layer of government to fix. The Downtown Eastside has thousands of addicted residents but, as we have seen, pitifully few detox and rehab services for people who want to kick their drug habits. Ninety percent of the residents rent a place to live, and for most it is a room in an SRO hotel. The area has twice as many seniors as the rest of the city, and far fewer children and youth. A high percentage of the people here do not live in families; of that group, fifty percent of what the city calls "non-family persons" live alone, compared to twenty percent in the rest of the city. Unemployment here is running at twenty-two percent, compared to eight percent in the rest of the city. As one City of Vancouver report points out, in 2001, "the median household income in the DTES was $12,084, less than thirty percent of the city's median household income figure ($42,026). In 2001, while Vancouver has seen an increase in both the median and average household income, the median household income has dropped slightly in the DTES."

Another running sore for the neighbourhood was the continuing failure of the Vancouver Police Department's Missing Persons Unit to do its job properly. Ever since I'd first come to Vancouver, I had heard about this unit's refusal to accept missing persons reports from the family members and friends of the missing women—or, when it did take reports, its sloppiness or outright neglect in investigating them. I knew that Doug LePard, a deputy chief constable of the Vancouver Police Department, had been working for two years on a report about the way the VPD had handled the missing women case. One of the subjects of his report would be the Missing Persons Unit.

A well-respected cop with a degree in criminology from Simon Fraser University, where he had become a friend of Kim Rossmo's, LePard had become an internationally recognized expert on stalking offences but also had wide experience in the force and several bravery commendations. He was now one of the most powerful officers in the city. I'd been told his report would be highly critical of his force, but that it wouldn't be released until the Pickton trial was over.

However, an important part of LePard's report did come out early, under a freedom of information request filed by the *Vancouver Sun*. In late September 2005, *Sun* reporter Chad Skelton published a shocking story about the VPD's Missing Persons Unit that finally answered many of the questions people had been asking for years. A fifty-four-page internal audit completed in October 2004 and written by retired VPD inspector John Schouten blamed "overworked officers, inadequate supervision and shoddy record-keeping" at the Missing Persons Unit "for compromising its ability to solve cases including possible serial crimes," Skelton reported. The audit found that the unit, which had had 3,847 missing persons complaints in the previous year—315 of which remained unsolved—had only one police officer working full-time with the help of a part-time civilian worker, both supervised by John Dragani, a sergeant with other duties. Dragani spent so much of his time working with the police union and the police pipe band that he had little time for the unit, but far more disturbing was the fact that he was under investigation for possession of child pornography on his home computer. He had been suspended since April 2005. The part-time clerical worker was sent to crime scenes, Chad Skelton reported, "and cases were assigned to empty desks. A missing person call may not be assessed for 84 hours, or longer, on holiday weekends."

Skelton also wrote that, according to Schouten's audit, there was "little active investigation of files" after the first forty-eight hours, and that the lack of follow-up had "the potential to embarrass the Vancouver Police Department and could possibly result in civil liability." No one reviewed old unsolved missing persons cases, and missing data in computer files meant information was not "accessible for follow-up investigators, or to identify trends or possible serial crimes." There were no clear guidelines on when a disappearance should be considered a homicide, Schouten said. "In those cases where suspicious circumstances are involved it is imperative that the police conduct a thorough investigation, at the earliest opportunity, so that no evidence is lost."

One of the most shocking findings of the audit was the fact that cases were still assigned to officers who had left the unit, leading, Schouten wrote, "to a concern that investigative

leads that could have been pursued were abandoned and con-
tinuity of the investigation is lost."

And then there was the finding that the unit had not been
helpful to the joint RCMP–Vancouver Police Department
Missing Women Task Force.

Schouten concluded his audit with fifty recommendations
to fix the problems, including adding more staff and giving
them better training, but when Skelton tried to find out if any
of these had been implemented, the VPD's media relations
section said it was too busy to answer his questions.

All of the issues raised in Skelton's stories about the
Schouten audit confirmed what the families of the missing
women had long suspected.

—

When I look back at my years of commuting to Vancouver,
I see the time punctuated with car disasters. Having my Jeep
stolen was unpleasant, but later, I had two serious accidents
in rented cars. The first time, I was sideswiped on Broadway
by a student who pulled out in front of a bus while I was
driving past it; the bus driver filed a report stating I was not
to blame. The car, I am willing to bet, was a writeoff to the
rental company because the side was caved in. I wasn't hurt,
and neither was Elaine Allan, who was with me. The second
accident occurred in October, a few days after the voir dire
was postponed. I was driving along a quiet side street in my
Point Grey neighbourhood, and a woman shot through a
stop sign to whack my driver's side, shoving my vehicle to the
corner of the intersection. She had two small children in her
car, both of whom spoke better English than she did, and
they tried to comfort her as she wept. No one was hurt, but

once again, my rental car was wrecked. And once again, thank God, a witness happened to be nearby when it happened and she, too, filed a report. The rental people were very nice.

"You got T-boned, eh?" one man inquired as he surveyed the mess. "Wow. You were lucky, lady." I certainly was. My own car, an elderly BMW, arrived soon afterwards, and I prayed no one would hit this one; it was David's pride and joy—and back home, he was getting around on a bicycle.

A few weeks later, it was time to pack up all my stuff again. David took pity on me and came out to help. His presence turned a miserable time into fun. We visited family members, took wonderful drives and enjoyed the city like tourists. We sat on benches in the Granville Market, watching the boats go by and sipping cappuccinos; I dragged him around to my favourite bead stores; we ate crab club sandwiches at Troy's in Horseshoe Bay. He even went with me when I was looking for Maggy Gisle, who had suffered a relapse, lost her daughter, Lisa-Marie, to foster care and disappeared into the Downtown Eastside. This time, trawling through the bars on East Hastings and going through the floors of a couple of the seedy hotels was an experience I saw through David's eyes; he was as shocked as I had been on my first visit. I did not find Maggy there, but she turned up a few days later, and our last days in Vancouver were spent trying to get her out of the Downtown Eastside and into an apartment in a safe neighbourhood so she could get her daughter back.

When it was time to go home, we stored almost everything in a friend's basement. She even agreed to let me leave the car in her garage. Then we went back to Toronto to wait for the voir dire to start.

FOURTEEN **NEW WESTMINSTER**

At the end of January 2006, I flew back to British Columbia, rescued my car from my friend's garage and moved into my tenth Vancouver place since starting research for this book in the spring of 2002. This was the best so far: a small two-bedroom house in Southlands, the south side of West Point Grey and the horsy part of Vancouver, an area where I could probably never afford to buy a house. It belongs to a young woman who is both my friend and my daughter Amy's; because she would be in graduate school in the United States and tenants were moving out, I could have her house for several months. It was a bright, sunny place with big windows, including doors opening onto a lovely private garden, full of old roses, shrubs and herbs. There was an office for me and one for David when he came out later in the year. And to make it perfect, it was close to South West Marine Drive, which led me straight east to New Westminster in about thirty minutes.

About a mile south of the house is the Fraser River; beyond that, in the distance, is the Vancouver Airport. In the Southlands area, I felt as if I were in Brigadoon, a lost community of people living in another era. There are farms, riding stables and barns, horse trails, old shacky houses mixed into a community of expensive new ones, all more or less Craftsman style, with shingled roofs and old-fashioned gardens. Sometimes I'd walk down to the river and along the path there, ducking the blackberry vines and getting out of the way of riders and horses when they came by. On each side of the Southlands community are golf courses, some on Indian land, so the whole area is a long stretch of protected, well-cared-for recreational and residential property. *I could get used to living like this, but I'd better not.* To bring me back to earth, one friend pointed out that my next-door neighbour appeared to be running a grow op in his basement. *So that's why the lights are on there all the time,* I thought.

I had to get up early on Monday, January 30, 2006, the date the voir dire phase of the trial was to begin. A strict publication ban still applied. This phase, predicted to last four months, would hear the applications—the voir dires—from the defence team about the admissibility of evidence; in other words, the defence team would argue about why prosecution evidence should be dropped, and the prosecutors would argue about why it should be kept. Once the judge had finished ruling on these applications, he would call a jury and the trial proper could begin.

Like the courthouse in Port Coquitlam, the Supreme Court building in New Westminster is a relatively new structure, and an attractive one, set in a space called Begbie Square, halfway up a very steep hill. The glass wall of the courthouse entrance is at the side of Begbie Square, up a broad and shallow set of steps from the sidewalk. A spacious courtyard in front, edged with deep perennial beds, offers plenty of places to sit, and a waterfall courses down the side, from the top of the hill. At the top of the staircase are a number of new condominiums, and at the side facing the courthouse there are more.

Without a reserved media seat, I needed to line up in time to get one of the public seats in the courtroom, so I was there at 7:30 a.m., the first person to arrive. From all the hype, I had expected a mob scene of press and public, but there was no more a mob in New Westminster than there had been in Port Coquitlam on the first day of the preliminary hearing three years earlier.

And there *had* been a lot of hype, most of it generated by the Attorney General's office. The people there assumed that the world was watching this case and the world would be present, if only through the media. So, months earlier, they had rented a large, empty office space a block away from the courthouse, on Victoria Street. It was the back half of an office that fronted, like the courthouse itself, on Carnarvon Street, and felt like a small warehouse. Here, they had installed a media centre with video monitors. Long tables stretched down one wall and in rows across the width of the room, with enough chairs for thirty-five reporters. Each space had plugs for power, a telephone and a high-speed Internet line. There was a desk for a sheriff, who would be present at all times, a podium with a blue wall behind it for press conferences, a tiny kitchen area for coffee, and washrooms in nearby corridors. Although there is a press room in the courthouse, it has space for only one or two people. The new room, they told us, was considered an extension of the courtroom itself, so most courtroom rules would apply; although we could take food in there and talk to each other, we had to behave with decorum and leave during the lunch breaks, when it would be locked down.

The hitch for me was the cost. The AG's office said we had to sign two-year contracts for our spaces, at a cost of $500 a month. Internet and phone would be extra. I decided to pass. I didn't need to file daily stories, and while it was always fun to hang around other reporters, gossiping and analyzing the daily events, it wasn't really necessary that I do so. I would be covering my own costs (the generous advance from my publisher had run out, oh, years ago); everyone else had newspapers or networks paying for them. What was interesting was that very few media outlets bought into this media room. Only half a dozen of the spaces were booked. If the AG's media people were chagrined by the lack of interest in renting space, they should have realized that most newspapers, broadcasters and magazines are not going to send reporters to cover cases that are still under a publication ban. If they can't report on the news that night, forget it. That's why there were almost no reporters present for most of the preliminary hearing. And so it would prove to be for most of the voir dire.

But the hype extended to New Westminster itself, a city of about sixty thousand people that had once been the provincial capital. In late January 2006, the Attorney General's office, along with city officials, had held a meeting to brief local merchants and business people about the boom the trial would bring to the city. Local, national and international media would be descending, they advised everyone, and they'd be pouring into the coffee shops and restaurants, using services, buying goods. Parking would become impossible. The city had decided to charge television trucks $60 a day to park on streets with meters, and had designated another street for more trucks. One woman who owns a consignment shop on Columbia Street (the main shopping street, two blocks south of the courthouse) told a reporter she thought the whole circus would be bad for her business.

Having read the stories about the business boom that would hit the downtown, I walked along Columbia Street to see what the big attractions would be. I counted seven bridal stores, a couple just for grooms and their ushers and best men, and the rest for women. There was an antiques mini-mall, where the most interesting items were Nazi mementoes from the Second World War—weapons, inkwells, cigarette cases and badges. On another block, there were a couple of small antiques shops and three or four modest restaurants and coffee shops, including a Starbucks. I think I saw a dollar store and a small department store. The four-storey yellow brick Burr Block—the city's best-known business block, named after Raymond Burr, the New Westminster actor who played Perry Mason in the long-running television series—seemed rundown and pretty well abandoned; painted on the side of it in large letters was the word ROOMS. The street also boasted some payday loan outfits.

I've seen promotional literature for New Westminster that compares it to San Francisco because the city drops so steeply to the edge of the Fraser River. But that's where the comparison should end. To get down to Columbia Street from the courthouse, you have to walk down a steep stair-case past the Crown prosecutors' red brick Victorian offices, easily identified by the sight of Mike Petrie standing outside smoking. Just below his offices, you cross through a centre for the homeless, easily identified by the men lounging in front of it, also smoking. Below Columbia Street, running parallel to it and down another steep hill, is Front Street, which has some second-hand shops and a military surplus store. They face a dark and shabby area of rail yards and, eventually, the Fraser River. It's an industrial site here. But near each end of Columbia Street is an entrance to a road that can take you to Westminster Quay and a public market, a pleasant development of shops, hotels and condominiums.

It is not easy walking distance from the courthouse; it is, in fact, a drive. You would not go there for coffee or lunch if you had an hour's break from the court. At the east, on the way to Port Coquitlam, Columbia Street ends at what was once the British Columbia Penitentiary. Most of it has been demolished, but what is left has been transformed into pleasant townhouses and condominiums.

New Westminster has charming neighbourhoods, with historic buildings and lovely parks, but the old downtown, near the courthouse, is not one of them. A lively, prosperous business section has developed a few miles away on Sixth Avenue; that's where you'll find good shopping, restaurants and plenty of banks and services. Most out-of-town reporters planned on staying in Vancouver and commuting. Businesses near the courthouse that expected to be transformed by the Pickton voir dire were, I think, sorely disappointed. As far as I know, the only ones that got extra customers were the coffee shop across the street from the courthouse, an excellent Japanese restaurant around the corner, and Mugs and Jugs, a tavern with strippers, just down the street on Carnarvon and said by knowledgeable barristers to be a favourite lunch spot.

—

Monday, January 30, 2006. Three years and two weeks after Willie Pickton's preliminary hearing began in Port Coquitlam, a small crowd was gathered in front of the New Westminster courthouse, and a few television vans were parked on the street. There was a long lineup to get in—not just reporters on the Pickton story, but people attending other trials—and it was slow because of the heavy security at the entrance. Once again, the sheriffs' careful search of every bag, wallet and pocket meant delays as they confiscated cameras and camera phones, recording devices (except those belonging to the media) and occasionally even needles, spliffs of marijuana and small packets of cocaine or heroin. Visitors didn't get any of this back when they left; in fact, I saw people arrested as they tried to enter carrying drugs. Everyone had to pass through a security gate, after which another team of sheriffs carefully patted each person down with a metal detecting wand, working up and down each arm and leg and across the back and front. The only people spared the searches were lawyers, judges, police and security people.

Near Courtroom 102, Judge Williams's courtroom, at the far end of the main floor, was yet another team of sheriffs performing the same searches again, including a second pat-down with a wand. Just behind their search station there was a large room with chairs, washrooms and a water fountain; this was a kind of lounge, a place to go during the morning and afternoon breaks or to escape to for a private talk. On one side of this room was Judge Williams's courtroom, 102; on the other side was a much larger courtroom that had been set aside as an overflow room for the Pickton trial. The court staff had installed three large monitors in here so anyone who couldn't get into the judge's courtroom could watch proceedings in here. Even though the interesting part of the trial was not starting yet, and despite the publication ban, people were here because . . . well, you just never know. Maybe Pickton would plead guilty and spare everyone a long trial. That's what Gary Leon Ridgway, the Green River Killer, had done. No such luck this time. Pickton was clean-shaven and wearing a short-sleeved grey shirt and black jeans. He also had on new white running shoes with Velcro fasteners; I wondered about these until I suddenly remembered that prisoners are not allowed shoelaces. The last time I had seen him in court, on the final day of the preliminary hearing, his hair had been short; now, it was long and greasy. A mauve bracelet he wore on his left wrist must have been a prison identification band. As usual, he had a notepad with him, and he scratched away on it throughout the day.

When the indictments were read out to him, Pickton, in a strong, clear voice, pleaded not guilty to twenty-six counts of first-degree murder. There were twenty-seven counts against him, but his lawyers were disputing one of them, a murder charge in the case of one Jane Doe, and they refused to allow him to enter a plea one way or the other on that charge. Judge Williams later entered a plea of not guilty for him.

The people in Pickton's corner that day were Peter Ritchie—who later told reporters that he was dealing with 750,000 pages of material from the prosecutors—as well as Patrick McGowan, Adrian Brooks and David Layton. The Crown prosecutors included Mike Petrie, Derrill Prevett, John Ahern, Geoff Baragar, Satinder Sidhu and Jennifer Lopes; the only member of the prosecution team missing was the latest addition to the team, Jay Vogel. People looked pretty much the same as they had in 2003, except for McGowan, who looked less like a student and more like a veteran lawyer, and Prevett, who had lost a lot of weight, as well as his moustache, and looked younger.

I knew most of the sheriffs who were present; they'd been at the preliminary hearing in Port Coquitlam. Freda Ens was back in her role as a Victim Services worker. One newcomer was a tall, casually dressed, pleasant-looking man of about fifty-five or sixty who entered the courtroom with the lawyers; he was clearly not a reporter or a member of the public, although he sat with us. During a break, he told me he was Bob Stone, a retired member of the RCMP. He would be attending the trial every day to take notes for the Missing Women Task Force, which he was working for on a temporary basis. He was also responsible for managing the task force budget. It turned out that Bob Stone was a former Chief Superintendent of the RCMP for the Surrey region. He was a nice guy, but we reporters viewed him with caution, wondering if part of his job was to take notes on what the media were saying.

Our veteran court watcher, Art Lee, was back as well. I missed Russ MacKay, who—though I didn't know this at the time—had been suffering from lung cancer during the preliminary hearing. I had certainly noticed that he was getting thinner and thinner, but I'd thought he was cutting back on beer; at least, that's how he had explained it. But Russ had died before the voir dire started, and I would miss his good company. Russ had never had a problem with the Picktons on his welding jobs at their farm, so his even-handed reaction to testimony was always a good reality check. He had an ironic sense of humour, he was smart, and he listened carefully, so he frequently picked up allusions or facts I missed, and we would talk them over on the breaks. His knowledge of Port Coquitlam and many of the players in this story was invaluable. I hoped his family was keeping his dahlias in good shape. I was sure they would.

Judge Williams introduced the lawyer who entered the court with him as "Christine Judd, counsel to the court." In other words, his counsel. None of us was sure what that meant, but we assumed she would assist him with preparing rulings. Although she was gowned in formal robes like the other lawyers, she did not sit with them. The well of the court was so small that there was no appropriate place for her to sit, so she took a seat in the jury box.

Even after all the fuss, the public gallery of the little courtroom wasn't full. Because cameras weren't allowed inside, the TV reporters came in for brief periods, took notes and rushed out to the courtyard to do pieces on-camera, with the courthouse behind them as a backdrop. A group of women, some of whom knew or were related to one or more of the missing women, had gathered in the courtyard with a large quilt and banners, and some of them were drumming and chanting. We could hear them inside the courtroom, and they became part of the story on television that night.

I wasn't surprised when the TV reporters were absent the following day. They didn't return for months, and who could blame them—all they could report was that the trial had started. And if reporters turned up from the United States or any other country, we didn't see them. But we heard they had decided to honour the publication ban.

I didn't have to arrive at 7:30 a.m. any more; after the first day, there was plenty of room when I got to the courthouse around 9:00. Within a few days, the Attorney General's media people relented and gave me a pass to sit in the front row, but even there, after a few weeks, just a few of us were left.

Lori Culbert, one of the strongest reporters on this story from the beginning, came every day. It was a long commute from her home in North Vancouver. Every morning, she biked from her house to the bus station, took the bus to downtown Vancouver and then caught the SkyTrain to New Westminster.

Bob Matas was there every day as well. Bob was an old friend; we had shared a pod at the *Globe and Mail* for a couple of years, and I remember how reluctant he was when he heard that the paper wanted him to transfer to the Vancouver bureau. "Bob, it's a gift from God," I told him then. "Go!" Now, he told me, he would never leave. By coincidence, he lived just a block from my little rented house, and he was hugging himself that he'd bought in the area before the big jump in Vancouver house prices. Bob hadn't covered the prelim; that had been Jane Armstrong's job. I liked to think of him as a newcomer to the story, because I was jealous that he got to write about it every day. *He and Lori will get all the scoops,* I thought, and it made me crazy.

And if they didn't, Greg Joyce would. Greg, who had also covered the prelim, was one of my favourites. A tall, laconic guy, he had been with Canadian Press for years, and he was smart. I counted on him as my common sense detector. He also had a wonderful sense of humour and never missed the slightest hint of cant in any lawyer's speech.

The *Province*'s Ethan Baron was another regular now. Ethan, a sunny-natured American, was a delight, and always knew the best places to eat lunch. French CBC's Pierre Claveau, another prelim alumnus, whose accent was as strong as it must have been when he left Quebec nearly thirty years earlier, rode to New Westminster on his Harley-Davidson, much admired by the sheriffs. Susanna de Sousa, a bright young intern for the CBC who won friends and admirers throughout the court with her cheerfulness and work ethic, was there every day, usually in the media workroom, monitoring every development and sending her notes back to the newsroom.

And that was it. Our modest tribe wasn't going to make much of a difference to the New Westminster restaurant scene, especially since Lori and Bob always packed a lunch.

But I was lucky to have such agreeable colleagues. That has always been the best part of being in my business.

The biggest challenge we had, which was described well by media lawyer Dan Burnett in an article for the UBC journalism school, was the publication ban applied to the voir dire. Burnett and Michael Skene, the lawyer who had organized the transcripts subscription for some of us, often appeared in Williams's court, representing various media organizations. Both had worked on the successful arguments against Peter Ritchie's unusual demand for a complete shutdown on information during this phase of the trial.

In his article, published on January 29, 2006, Burnett wrote:

> By the time the trial is in its fifth or sixth month, there will have been countless voir dires, some lengthy, some for just a few minutes, at various times through the trial. Reporters' notes will be littered with references to testimony, exhibits, and arguments. Few will be able to attend every day. Somehow they will need to keep track of what information came out during voir dire and remember to obey the ban.
>
> The temptation to simply 'put down the pencils' when the jury is absent would be a mistake because the ban is only temporary until the jury retires to consider its verdict . . . therefore, if the case comes to an abrupt end due to a plea or another development, the information from the voir dire will become the sole record of much of the evidence. Also, when the trial is over, the information from the voir dire that the jury did not hear will be a fascinating series of news stories.

Although the voir dire situation is difficult for outsiders to grasp, Burnett's comments seemed right on the money to me. These were the reasons I'd come to Vancouver and was staying so long. To me, the voir dire was as important as the preliminary hearing. And I couldn't take the chance that there would be an "abrupt end" and I wouldn't know exactly how it had happened.

As far as the general public went, few ever came. About once a week, a high school group would troop in, sit in a row for an hour or so—bored stiff, for the most part—and leave. No one ever came for Willie Pickton.

The only other person there day in and day out was a man called Lance Henry. Shy, uncertain, uncomprehending Lance. A sweet man with a good sense of humour who always wears a baseball cap, Lance is the brother of Janet Henry, one of the Downtown Eastside's missing women. She disappeared in June 1997 but has never been identified as being on the Pickton farm, and Willie Pickton has never been charged with her murder. Janet was also Sandra Gagnon's sister. These three had been among thirteen siblings in a Native family from Alert Bay. Most of their brothers and sisters were now dead, and most had died violently. Lance, who was unemployed, was there to pay homage to his sister and the other missing women on behalf of his family; it was all he could think of doing to support them.

Because this voir dire phase was all about testing evidence—with the defence working to exclude it and the prosecutors trying to retain it—and because so much case law was cited, hour after hour, it was often difficult for Lance to understand the arcane arguments the lawyers were batting around, and he was baffled by the precedents they cited. But he was anxious to learn. We all briefed him on what was going on, and no one was kinder to him than Bob Stone. One day, Lance broke down, and Bob led him out gently and sat with him until Freda was able to come and take over.

Sandra Gagnon came to court from time to time, and at first she and Lance sat apart: "We don't really get along," she confided in me one day. But she didn't tell me what went wrong between them. All she would say was that something had happened and they weren't close any more.

FIFTEEN THE VOIR DIRE

January 30, 2006: Pickton at first day of the voir dire
(Drawing by Jane Wolsak)

T he voir dire phase of the trial was supposed to last four months. It took well over a year. But Dan Burnett was right: it was worth attending, and it was often fascinating. Had Willie Pickton decided to stop the proceedings with a guilty plea, we would have had some great stories from it. Stories we had heard in the preliminary hearing came back in the voir dire—but this time with more detail.

But I have to admit that much of the time it was just . . . tedious. The job of the defence in this phase of the trial was to challenge the Crown's evidence and argue for the removal of as much of it as possible, while the Crown prosecutors fought to keep it. This process often involved listening to witnesses. We had seen some of these witnesses in the preliminary hearing; others were new. The main weapons used by both sides were lengthy citations of case law, in which one learned judge after another would be quoted at stultifying length. Nice as he is, Adrian Brooks, without a doubt, won the prize for wearing down the rest of the room with talk. Even the hyper-alert Bob Stone was sometimes heard snoring gently in his back row seat.

Day after day, the legal teams plowed though the evidence and argued over what could stay and what could not. Pickton followed everything with interest and made notes, sometimes on lined paper in a three-ring binder, sometimes on a pad of lined legal-sized paper; once in a while—say every few days—he would tear off a sheet and pass it to one of his lawyers. Because we journalists sat right behind him, no more than a yard away, we couldn't help but see the writing on the paper, but reading it, we discovered, was impossible. Whenever a sheriff or any of the defence team spotted us looking over Pickton's shoulder, we got a reprimand from the judge, who would stop the proceedings briefly to tell us to cease and desist. After three such warnings, we got together and wrote a letter to Judge Williams, saying our job was to observe what was happening in the courtroom and if Pickton was writing stuff down we were going to report that. The judge did not respond, but the reprimands ceased and we tried to be more careful.

The first big news that came out of this process was Judge Williams's decision, announced on March 7, 2006, that he had quashed one count in this case: Pickton would now go to trial on twenty-six counts, not twenty-seven. The one Williams threw out—saying the charge could not proceed because it failed to meet the minimum requirements set out in the Criminal Code—concerned a Jane Doe, the only victim among the twenty-seven whose identity is still unknown.

As the voir dire continued in Courtroom 102, news occasionally surfaced from the outside world. Business was business in the Pickton family, and the siblings were headed, if only through their lawyers, to a different Supreme Court to contest the tax assessment on their Dominion Avenue farm. On March 14, 2006, *Vancouver Province* reporter Keith Fraser wrote that the family was upset that the Property Assessment Appeal Board of B.C. had rejected their appeal regarding a $5.9-million assessment on the land. Fraser's story said the Picktons had complained that they had been kept off the land from February 5, 2002 (when Willie was first arrested), until December 1, 2003—although the police had, in fact, left the property on November 18, 2003—and that because of the investigation any residential development would be delayed for years. They now planned to use the land for farming, they asserted, and therefore their taxes should be reduced. The board rejected their argument, pointing out there was no plan for the land, as Fraser reported, "that would have produced the required volume of agricultural production within the next 12 months."

Back inside the tiny world of Courtroom 102, we began to see the strength of the defence team. Not just in ability, but in numbers. In the late fall of 2004, Peter Ritchie had had four full-time and four part-time lawyers working on the case, as well as support staff, researchers and experts, and once again, as he had done in Port Coquitlam during the preliminary hearing, Ritchie had opened a second office near the courthouse. But by late March of 2006, the names of fourteen defence lawyers had sifted their way through the system on various documents.

Ritchie turned up far more often in the New Westminster courtroom than he had at the preliminary hearing, but Adrian Brooks continued to take the lead on most of the applications and arguments delivered before Judge Williams. The other mainstays of the defence team for the first few years had been Marilyn Sandford and Patrick McGowan; we now grew familiar with seven others: Glen Orris, David Layton, Peter Schmidt, Richard Brooks, Frida Tromans, Chris Karlsson and Joseph Saulnier.

Glen Orris may be even better known than Peter Ritchie. A stocky bald man with a pugnacious lower lip and, I'm told, a lovely sense of humour, he has a way of pacing the courtroom with his head thrust down so low and pushed forward so far that all you can see from the back is his neck. So the opening line of his minimalist website surprised me: "Let us be grateful to the people who make us happy; they are the charming gardeners who make our souls blossom"— Marcel Proust.

One of Vancouver's famed defence lawyers, Orris is a sole practitioner, and he is well-liked by other lawyers. Educated at Simon Fraser University and the University of Manitoba, where he took his law degree, he has been a practising criminal defence lawyer since 1973. He is a past president of the Vancouver Bar Association and is very involved in legal education. He has acted for several infamous murderers, including Terry Driver, known as the Abbotsford Killer, who was convicted of murder after he killed a teenage girl with a baseball bat, injured another, then taunted police with phone calls. Orris also defended John Oughton, the Paper Bag Rapist. But Orris made only a cameo appearance in New Westminster, to lead arguments on one of the voir dires.

David Layton and Peter Schmidt had come in to help from another criminal defence firm, Gibbons Fowler Nathanson. Founded in 1997 by the late David Gibbons, another of B.C.'s celebrity criminal lawyers, with his partner Richard Fowler, the small firm now had six lawyers. They all appeared impossibly young, but they all had strong credentials. Layton, a tall, lanky man with untidy hair, a tendency to stoop and glasses that always looked as if they needed cleaning, has an impressive resumé. After graduating as the gold medallist from Dalhousie Law School in 1987, he took a post-graduate law degree at Oxford University and returned to Canada in 1990 to clerk for Brian Dickson, the late chief justice of the Supreme Court of Canada. After ten years of practising criminal law in Toronto, he moved to Vancouver to work for Gibbons Fowler Nathanson. Layton is a talented writer who contributes to many journals and books; in fact, he and co-author Michel Proulx, a former judge of the Quebec Court of Appeal, won a prize for their 2003 textbook *Ethics and Canadian Criminal Law*. His strength, the firm says, lies not just in all aspects of criminal law, but especially in "providing research, writing and oral argument on trial and pre-trial matters."

I suspected that it was Layton's fine Italian hand behind the lively and informative blog on the firm's website, especially a four-part series on lengthy trials. And I was interested to note that he took part in a September 26, 2006, trial lawyers' conference in Vancouver with his partners Richard Fowler and Matthew Nathanson; their panel was called "When Your Client Sings Like a Canary: Statement Exclusion Strategies."

Layton's colleague Peter Schmidt has a criminology degree from Simon Fraser University. He took his law degree at

Dalhousie and articled for both Gibbons Fowler and the B.C. Supreme Court before being called to the bar in 2004. He had to be one of the youngest lawyers at Pickton's defence table, but I guessed he was one of his firm's lively bloggers.

Richard Brooks, whom we'd met during the preliminary hearing, came back occasionally to argue a special file. As we had seen before, he was tough as nails.

Frida Tromans seemed to be the only New Westminster lawyer working on the Ritchie team. Before she went to UBC Law School, Tromans had worked for community agencies that provided employment services for adults with developmental disabilities, as well as for Douglas College's occupational education program. After being called to the bar, Tromans practised criminal law and civil litigation for a few years for the Vancouver firm Singleton Urquhart, then returned to New Westminster to work for the Insurance Corporation of British Columbia. Like her new boss at the Pickton trial, Tromans is a gifted musician; she sometimes plays guitar in a small band with other lawyers.

The last members of the team thus far were Chris Karlsson, a volunteer for the Community Legal Assistance Society, who had been practising for only a short time, and a newcomer, Joseph Saulnier.

Few of these newcomers were on the Pickton case full-time; most were juggling a number of other clients. Peter Ritchie himself was still taking on new cases; he was acting, for example, for the teenage daughters of Gerald Foisy, a passenger on the *Queen of the North*, a B.C. ferry that hit a rock and sank just south of Prince Rupert on March 22, 2006, with 101 people on board. Ninety-nine people survived, but Foisy and his girlfriend, whose bodies have never been found, were presumed drowned. In the week of May 13, 2006, Ritchie launched a suit against British Columbia Ferry Services Inc. on behalf of Foisy's daughters, claiming they had lost "support, guidance, care and companionship, inheritance, dependency and services as a result of the negligence of the company."

Ritchie defended the size of his publicly financed team by pointing out that they had received 750,000 pages of documents from the prosecutors. "If Mr. Pickton only had one lawyer, that lawyer would be reading this [investigation's] disclosure material for years and the matter would never get to court," he said to Canadian Press reporter Greg Joyce. "So there are efficiencies that have to be engaged here."

—

Good news doesn't seep into the Pickton story often, but one day there was an extraordinary turn of events: one of the women who had been on the official missing women's list since 2002 turned up alive and well and completely unaware that she had been on it.

On Monday, June 5, 2006, Linda Grant was surfing the Internet for news about the Pickton case, as she told The *Sun*'s Lori Culbert the next day. Although she now lived in the United States, Grant came from Port Moody and had heard about the Pickton story from a friend. To her shock, she discovered her own face among the pictures of the missing women, with a note saying she had last been seen in 1984. She emailed Wayne Leng, whom she found through his website, and he put her in touch with the Vancouver police. Almost immediately, she was reconnected with her family in British Columbia.

When Lori Culbert interviewed her, Grant explained that she had left Canada in 1983, when she was twenty-five years old, because of a bad family situation during which she had lost custody of her two little girls, Brandy and Dawn. She went to the southern United States—"the furthest place I could go." After giving birth to a third daughter, she gave the baby up for adoption. Eventually, Grant made a new life for herself and had a new family. But the timing of her reunion with her old family was extraordinary. On April 10, 2006, just two months before Grant checked Leng's website, her third daughter, Briana, who was living in New Westminster, posted the following note to the MissingPeople.net message board:

> Linda Louise Grant is my birth mother. I never knew her as I was adopted as a baby. I found my birth family 6 years ago, and found out about the missing women. So far they have not found anything on my mother. I still have hopes of finding her, though I know that will probably not happen. My heart goes out to all the family's [sic] of the women who have been found on the farm. As well as to those who still don't know where their loved ones are. Keep hope in your hearts. If anyone has any information about my birth mother, or even knew her at some point, please email me as I would love to know her through others . . . not just the family. I will keep praying for all the women who are missing.

A few weeks later, on May 25, 2006, the same message board had a posting from Dawn Grant:

> My mom is Linda Louise Grant. She went missing 23 years ago and was last seen a block from the

Pickton pig farm. I miss her very much and hope she is still out there some where. When I was a kid I always thought that she just abandoned me and when I heard about the pig farm I was hoping more than ever that she abandoned me. . . . I used to be mad at her for missing me grow up and for not being there when her first grand-child was born. But now I just hope she is still alive and safe and happy. I feel robbed as I imagine that all the families of the missing women do. . . . All I know is that I want my mother back and if she is still out there and you have any information about her please e-mail me . . . even if you don't think it's important. I just want to know anything about her.

By June 7, 2006, Linda Grant and her daughters had talked to each other and were planning to meet.

—

By the middle of June, it was time for me to go home. David, who had been on sabbatical from the University of Toronto since January, had come out for the last three months, and we'd spent our spare time visiting family and taking a few weekend trips. We decided to drive back east, and we took the slow road the entire way. I'd never driven down Highway 97, which runs south along the length of Lake Okanagan; I'd never been to Osoyoos or into the Kootenays. I wanted to see it all—the orchards and market gardens, the vineyards, deserts and farms. We drove through the Badlands of Alberta, which looked to me like parts of the Negev Desert, and visited the Cypress Hills in Saskatchewan, where we counted twenty-four white pelicans on Cypress Lake. We stopped in the eastern Saskatchewan park area to explore the RCMP's first headquarters at Fort Walsh. We trundled along Saskatchewan's empty southern highway, passing through dozens of little ghost towns and a few bustling centres, including Weyburn, where we expected to find many memorials to their most famous resident, former Saskatchewan premier Tommy Douglas. As Douglas was the first leader of the New Democratic Party and the winner of a national contest for the "Greatest Canadian," we were sure Weyburn would be trumpeting their local boy. Not at all. The local museum knew of only one place where we might see some Douglas mementoes: the old clapboard church where he had served as a Baptist preacher for many years. When we found it (no one was sure of how to get there), it was closed—but on the side of the building there was, at least, a large poster of a newspaper article announcing the birth of medicare in Saskatchewan, Douglas's greatest political triumph.

We also visited David's grandparents' homestead in Treherne, Manitoba, clambered around the lift locks in Sault Ste. Marie and explored Manitoulin Island. All places a little off the Trans-Canada Highway, all taking extra days. So what? we said to each other.

It was exactly the distance I needed from the ugliness of the Pickton story. But it still managed to reach me. While on the road, I received two pieces of shocking news. The first was a call from Freda Ens with the sad news that Lance Henry had died. As soon as possible, I talked to his sister, Sandra Gagnon, about what had happened.

Sandra and Lance had started to talk again. They went for lunch and finally hashed through the issues that had divided them for so many years. After that, their friendship began to strengthen—sometimes they even sat in court side by side. One day, people were surprised when Lance didn't show up in court. It wasn't like him. He wasn't there the next day either. Lance's son Cody, worried that he hadn't heard from his dad since they'd spoken on the phone the night before, had gone to Lance's apartment and found him dead at his computer, still sitting at his desk, still holding the phone. Lance, who was only forty-six, had suffered a heart attack before he could hang up after talking to his son.

Around the same time I heard that John Dragani, the now-retired Vancouver police officer who had been in charge of the Missing Persons Unit, had been arrested on June 19, 2006, and charged with the possession of child pornography on his home computer. Dragani, the man who was too busy with his responsibilities for the VPD's pipe band to pay attention to the missing persons' cases, had been suspended without pay in April 2005. "There is no question that allegations concerning this officer's conduct were embarrassing for the VPD," Tim Fanning, a VPD spokesman, told the media, "but it was also an opportunity to clearly demonstrate that on those rare occasions where criminal conduct is alleged against a police officer, the department takes it very seriously."

But in addition to the disturbing news, I also heard some good news: another of the women believed to be missing had turned up alive and well. Mary Florence Lands had disappeared in 1989 and was reported missing in 2004. In fact, as Lana Haight, a reporter for Saskatoon's *StarPhoenix* reported, she was living in Cochin, a small community in northern Saskatchewan, and she too discovered, in the week of June 24, 2006, that she was listed on the Missing Women

Task Force poster. Like Linda Grant, she had gone through a rough time. Although she told Haight she had never been a prostitute, she did admit she had been a chronic alcoholic and lived near the Downtown Eastside. Ill with diabetes, Lands said she had suffered a stroke in 1987 and had to give up her three children to a cousin, who promised to adopt them and take care of them. Lands moved to Winnipeg and never knew that the cousin decided she couldn't manage and that the children had gone to separate foster homes.

"I never tried to hide from anybody," Lands told Haight, adding that she had tried to find out where her children were "by sending messages to community centres in Vancouver's Downtown Eastside to post on their bulletin boards, asking that her children contact her 'if they wanted.'" After six years of her attempts, a relative saw one of the notices and the family was reunited.

"I was telling [police] from day one that she shouldn't have been on that list," her son Michael Lands told Haight at the airport when he arrived to visit his mother. "No one was believing us at the time. The truth finally gets to come out now. We have her and we've got her side of the story and it's great."

Mary Florence Lands and Linda Grant were both alive and doing well—two of the very rare happy stories in this massive tragedy of neglect. The official list of missing women shrank from sixty-nine names to sixty-seven.

—

As soon as we got home, we packed again and went to Israel, where David was attending a meeting at the Hebrew University, for ten days. We spent the rest of the summer at our cottage in Quebec, where my boxes of binders and chapter drafts were waiting for me.

In August came news I did not expect. Judge Williams had ruled in favour of Peter Ritchie's application to separate the twenty-six remaining counts of first-degree murder against Pickton so that there would be two trials instead of one. Ritchie had argued that a single trial could last for up to two years, which would put too much strain on a jury. Mike Petrie argued against this notion; he was in favour of one trial. But the judge agreed with Ritchie and decided to split the process into two trials, one on six counts and one on twenty. The trial on six counts would include charges related to the murders of Sereena Abotsway, Mona Wilson, Andrea Joesbury, Brenda Wolfe, Marnie Frey and Georgina Papin.

"The evidence in support of those counts is materially different than that with respect to the others such that it justifies this outcome," said Judge Williams, explaining the reasoning behind grouping these counts together. "I am satisfied that the interests of justice require severance from the present indictment," he added. "Proceeding to trial on the indictment as it is presently constituted will impose an unreasonable burden upon the members of the jury in terms of the anticipated duration of the trial, the volume and nature of the evidence, and the complexity of the legal tasks that this case will require of them.

"Some inconveniences will result from this order," Judge Williams conceded. "However, the proper exercise of my discretion to maximize the likelihood that this trial will proceed properly to verdict without mistrial makes necessary an order for severance."

Judge Williams reassured everyone that the remaining counts would still go ahead—just at a later date. "Each count will be permitted to proceed," he said. "The effect of this order is simply to require that the matter be dealt with in separate trials rather than one large trial."

I felt frustrated to be in the east. I needed to be in New Westminster, where I might have had a chance to grab some officials outside the court to see exactly what this meant. Instead, all I could do was read the formal statements in the transcripts.

"What is vitally important to understand is that the court has not ruled that any of the twenty-six counts should not proceed," said Geoff Gaul, the spokesperson for the province's provincial justice branch. "All twenty-six counts remain very active."

I wasn't so sure. And most of the colleagues I contacted by phone or email over the next few days were just as cynical as I was. We figured that if the Crown won a conviction on the six counts, they would simply slap Pickton in prison and stay the remaining counts against him. That would be the sensible thing to do, and it would save taxpayers millions of dollars in legal fees and court costs.

It would also mean that the publication ban we'd obeyed all these years would finally be lifted. We could go right back to the earliest days of the preliminary hearing and write all about it and get it published. We could write anything we liked from the voir dire phase. We might even be able to find out what taxpayers had spent on paying for Pickton's defence. So, to be honest, part of me saw a silver lining if that's how it played out.

But I didn't want it to happen that way. I empathized with the families of the other twenty women. I also knew how painful it was for the families of women whose DNA had been identified on the farm but whose murders Pickton had not yet been charged with. And then—then there were the families of women who were still missing, families who were sure that their loved ones had died on the Pickton farm but were waiting for some proof, however fragile.

I could see an unfortunate hierarchy developing among the victims' families. If Pickton had been charged with your child's murder, or your mother's or sister's or aunt's, that put you in the top rank. You knew for sure that she was dead. You knew for sure that someone had been charged. There was a lot of use of that dreadful word "closure." If your relative was in the six, well, you were kind of at the top of this group. If your girl was in the twenty, on the other hand, it was easy now to feel that her death seemed less significant to authorities, even though the authorities did everything they could to persuade families that that wasn't true. And if there were no charges related to your family member, it seemed, to many, as if no one cared at all.

If there was ever to be a second trial on twenty counts, those counts would include the first-degree murders of Jacqueline McDonell, Diane Rock, Heather Bottomley, Jennifer Furminger, Helen Hallmark, Patricia Johnson, Heather Chinnock, Tanya Holyk, Sherry Irving, Inga Hall, Tiffany Drew, Sarah de Vries, Cynthia Feliks, Angela Jardine, Diana Melnick, Debra Jones, Wendy Crawford, Kerry Koski, Andrea Borhaven and Cara Ellis.

—

For the first two weeks of August 2006, I worked on my book. I was writing steadily now—as far as I was concerned, the research phase was over. It had to be. I had spent enough time on this. As the trial rolled along, my plan was simply to go back to the manuscript and stuff any relevant new facts into old chapters, then wind it all up with a brisk summary of events. I tried to ignore the fact that there would probably be two trials and it could be many years before this story would be finished. My deadline had passed about two years before, and I couldn't bear to think about it. How could I finish a book when there hadn't been one trial yet, let alone two?

"And knowing the prosecution evidence isn't enough," a retired judge told me. "What about the defence evidence? What about that? They won't be revealing that for months, maybe years." The warning was a good wake-up call.

Still, I tried, studying the voir dire transcripts as they rolled into my email inbox.

When I tired of worrying about my book, I worried about the most boring subject in our family conversations: my right knee. It had been severely arthritic for close to ten years. It hurt all the time and gave way regularly, dumping me in a heap any old place—on the street or down a set of stairs. The last few months of coping with New Westminster's steep hills had been a nightmare. Dear, gallant Pierre Claveau would always offer his arm, which I took gratefully.

On August 15, 2006, I drove to Toronto from our cottage for a consultation with Dr. John Murnaghan, a surgeon at the Orthopaedic and Arthritic Hospital on Wellesley Street, quite close to my home. After nearly four hours of tests and X-rays, Dr. Murnaghan told me I needed a total knee replacement. I was not surprised. Cortisone and hyaluronic acid shots had kept me going for the last few years, and had even allowed me to dance at Amy's wedding a year earlier, but they were no longer working. Not at all. I was in constant pain, and I couldn't walk more than half a block.

But I was shocked to learn that they could perform the operation in two weeks. I couldn't return to the cottage, and I couldn't go back to B.C. in the fall. Instead, on September 1, the doctors replaced my right knee with a two-pound mix of plastic, stainless steel and titanium. I was in hospital for nine days and spent the next six weeks setting my BlackBerry to go off every three and a half hours around the clock—as the nurses had taught me—to remind me to take my pain medication. If I waited four hours, the effect of the pills would have worn off and it would take me another hour to start feeling human again. I couldn't drive for six weeks. But for three weirdly happy months, I would stagger off to physiotherapy sessions at the hospital, where everyone else was as wrecked as I was. When my physiotherapist, the tough and completely adorable Ana Szafirowicz, finally discharged me, I felt as if I'd lost my best friend. I joined a sports club, started an aquafit program and worked out in the gym. I wanted to be able to go back to New Westminster and walk again without help.

Because I was stuck in Toronto, I consoled myself with an enchanting new puppy, a cairn terrier with the most agreeable temper of any cairn we'd ever had—and there had been many of them over the years. I would usually ask for the one in the litter that seemed the liveliest, the "go-getter," as the breeders would call them. This time, when the breeder told me about the little girl who was "snuggly," I knew right away that she was the one for me. We called her Frances. She became my constant companion as I learned to walk again, and she snoozed under my desk as I wrote.

And the transcripts flowed in, day after day. The voir dire phase was far from over.

SIXTEEN **SEVERING THE COUNTS**

I n all these years, as we inched towards a trial, we had never heard from Willie Pickton himself. I certainly felt I knew him well; I had interviewed many people who had been close to him, and I had a good sense of his interests, his sense of humour, his intelligence and how he spent his time. But I had not spoken to him. Peter Ritchie had scared off reporters, denying all access to his client, and like sheep, most of us— including me—had accepted his prohibitions. It took me a while to understand that the person who decided who Pickton could see was Pickton himself; his lawyer had no power to stop him from having visitors in jail. I wrote him directly to ask for an appointment, but got no response. I knew he was seeing a few people; I even heard that he had given interviews to a reporter with CBC Television. So I knew I had to persist.

In the meantime, however, Pickton was reaching out to other people. On September 3, 2006, through a scoop by the *Vancouver Sun's* Lori Culbert and Neal Hall, the public was able to read his thoughts in letters he wrote to a stranger, a man called Thomas Loudamy. A warehouse worker from Fremont, California, who had told Pickton he was a woman called Mya Barnett, Loudamy's hobby was writing convicts in prison, especially famous serial killers. One of these was Clifford

Olson. Sometimes, he told Lori Culbert, he would tailor his image to suit the person he was trying to reach; in Olson's case he used his real name. But when he wrote Pickton, he decided to pretend he was a woman going through hard times, reasoning that Pickton might be more apt to reply to a letter from a woman. Pickton fell for Loudamy's pitch, sending back three letters—the first in late 2005, which Loudamy wasn't able to find for the reporters, and two others, which Loudamy received in March 2006 and on August 29, 2006. He gave copies of these last two letters to the paper, which ran excerpts and pictures of them after making sure they were authentic.

The letters, neatly printed in capital letters, full of spelling mistakes and crammed with biblical references, showed that Pickton was following his court process closely and even knew how much it was all costing. And they showed that he was wary of strangers.

"I have received letters from all over the world," Pickton said in a letter dated February 26, 2006, "and there are many I do not write back in reguards some does not make sence, others testing me over and over again while time goes on to this day."

In the same letter, he wrote, "I like what the judge has said in coart that I want to give this con-demn-man a half decent-trial and I smiled and said to myself my father also was a con-demned man of no wrongdoing, and for that I am very proud to be in this situation for they are the biggest fools that ever walked the earth, but I am not worried for every thing on earth will be judged including Angles."

The August letter shows he was pleased with Judge Williams's decision to sever the twenty-six counts to six and notes the number of days he had been in jail so far: "By the time date of August 29th 2006 I will have been in hear at N.F.P.T.C. [North Fraser Pretrial Centre] for a total

AUGEST 22ND 2006

PAGE
1

TO MYA;

IT'S HAS BEIEN QUITIE SOME TIME SINCE I HAVE REALLY HEARD FROM YOU, OF WHICH I WROTE YOU BACK IN MARCH OF THIS YEAR (2006). I AM VERY - VERY PLEASED TO HEAR OF YOU ARE DOING QUITE FINE, AND ALSO TO HEAR THAT YOU ARE STILL CONTINUE-ING WITH THE SAME JOB THAT YOU GOT AT THE TRAVEL AGENCY AT THE BEGINNING OF THIS YEAR OF 2006.

I SEE THAT YOU HAVE HEARD IN THE NEWS OF - WHICH THE COART OF LAW HAS DROPPED A LOT OF CHARGES. THEY HAD TO, THEY HAVE NO CHOICIE BUT TO, IF NOT THERE WILL BE A WHOLE LOT OF COART TIME WAISTED ALL FOR NOTHING IN WHICH THERE WILL BE IN NEED A WHOLE LOT OF ANSWERS TO MANY QUESTIONS BY THE POLICE AND THE R.C.M.P. WHEN THIS COART CASE IS OVER BY THE WAY OF THE PUBLIC OF WHEN THEY FIND OUT THAT I AM NOT IN-VOLVED AT ALL.

IF THE COART DID NOT DROP ALL THESE CHARGES I COULD BE IN COART FOR AT LEAST TWO OR MORE YEARS AND IT REALLY WILL BE HARD TO **KEEP A JURY TO-GETHER** FOR SO LONG, OF WHICH FAMILYS COULD BE BROKEN UP FROM THE — PRESSURE OF THE STRESS, AND FOR THAT IT COULD END IN A MIS-TRIAL HALF WAY THROUGH COART. THERE WILL ALWAYS BE TIMES YOU HAVE TO TRAVEL DOWN A LONG ROAD AND - FOR ONLY TO GO A SHORT WAY WHICH HAS NO SENCE AT ALL FOR ALL ROADS WILL CROSS AT THE END WHILE TRUTH COMES OUT TO THE SUR-FACE.
"THE LONG ROAD OR THE SHORT ROAD," THE TRIAL JUDGE WENT FOR THE SHORT ROAD. → "(HE'S SMART)"

of—1,650 days to date, of which is just over 4 1/2 years in a-waiting for trial."

He also told "Mya" about the sheriffs escorting him to court each day and about how much this investigation was costing. "I have heard my case is over $100,000,000.00 one hundred million dollar case and for the police are no ferther a-head now than when they had first started way back in

February of 2002," the August letter says. "The short way is to put surveillance-cameras and to see who is doing all this. For then they well know the truth and to have the right people behind bars . . . they would save many other lives while the criminals that are in-volved still at large but no-body-cares for they got me as a fall-guy-any-ways."

Telling people he was the fall guy was a strategy for Pickton. Although he was kept away from other prisoners for his own safety, there were a few times when he was able to talk to another inmate across an exercise yard. When the man asked how he was doing, Pickton said he had been set up to take the fall for the real killer, a truck driver who worked for his brother, Dave.

—

While Willie sat out those last weeks in jail before the trial started, Dave Pickton had problems of his own. He had started another siege against the tax assessors. His plan was to return the seventeen acres of land on Dominion Avenue to farming, he told a reporter in early October 2006 outside the B.C. Supreme Court, where he was preparing to ask the court to grant the property farm status instead of its present residential status. The family had been successful in pulling the property out of the province's Agricultural Land Reserve in 1986; now, they wanted it back in. Because the police had been on the farm since early 2002, his argument went, the family shouldn't have to pay residential taxes for the years 2003, 2004 and 2005.

Dave Pickton had tried twice before to win tax relief on the property, and had failed; the tax assessors maintained it was in an area of residential development and should remain assessed as residential land. Right now, the land was assessed at $7.1 million. It wasn't going to be an easy case to win, given that the Picktons had already sold off most of their land for subdivisions and a school, but Dave Pickton assured everyone that he was planning to seed the land for hay and put some horses on it right away. Were he to win, it would be assessed for about $1 million, something that, no doubt, would distress interests that counted on it maintaining its value. These included the Attorney General's office, which had put a lien on the third of the property owned by Willie Pickton, and also included Karin Joesbury, Andrea Joesbury's mother, who had launched a civil lawsuit against Pickton in 2002 and registered a claim on the land as well.

Dave Pickton did arrange to have a portion of the farm levelled with layers of new topsoil, and he did arrange to have it seeded. But only a portion. The rest? The rusted machinery and old trucks are still there, shoved to the edges of the property. Piles of junk remain, hidden by vast domes of dirt and grass, all around the back corners of the land. Thick concrete blocks mark entrances and keep vehicles out. A chain-link fence, gates and a jumble of small sheds clog the Dominion Avenue entrance, and deep pools of stagnant water seep into the sandpits along the eastern edge of the property. This does not look like a farm in waiting, not with road construction continuing along Dominion, not with the new sidewalks, gutters and street lighting that will soon stretch all the way down to Burns Road, not with the continued growth of the shopping centre across the street, not with the aggressive development of the new subdivisions surrounding the Pickton land.

Just as Dave Pickton was preparing for his tax battle in court, there was a bizarre story in the news: On Tuesday, October 3, 2006, one of his former employees, Brian Arthur Betker, a fifty-four-year-old truck driver from Maple Ridge, was charged with attempted murder for allegedly pulling up to another truck on the Lougheed Highway in Pitt Meadows the day before, bracing a sawed-off .22 calibre rifle out his window and firing at the man driving the truck. In addition, Betker was charged with illegal possession of a loaded prohibited firearm, transportation of a prohibited firearm and possession of brass knuckles, which are also considered a prohibited weapon.

Crown prosecutors and Dave Pickton refused to talk about the case; the only person who would comment was Bill Harris, who works for Dave Pickton's company, D & S Bulldozing Ltd. "We do not know anything about it," Harris told Robert Matas, who called him for the *Globe and Mail*. "It has nothing to do with the company. We do not know what is happening. . . . We are totally miffed." He also told Matas that Betker didn't work for D & S—if he had, he added, "it was quite a while ago."

During this period, Courtroom 102 in New Westminster's Supreme Court continued to see long arguments between the prosecutors and the defence counsel on defence applications to exclude evidence from the trial. I began to wonder if the trial would be postponed. I couldn't see how they could wrap everything up and choose a jury before the start date of January 9, 2007. In Toronto, I read the court transcripts that arrived in my email inbox every couple of days with anxiety; once again, I would be heading to Vancouver, trying to find a place to stay and booking my flights—and I couldn't be sure we'd start on time.

Suddenly, while I was musing over flights and the possible implications of the charges against one of Dave Pickton's truck drivers, there was an announcement about another missing woman. An officer from the Victoria police told reporters that the Missing Women Task Force had obtained evidence that connected a local missing woman to the Pickton farm. Nancy

Clark, a twenty-five-year-old Victoria sex trade worker, had disappeared on August 22, 1991, but no one had ever guessed that she might be connected to the Pickton investigation. No woman working in the sex trade outside the Vancouver area was on the formal list of missing women.

Victoria police inspector Les Sylven wouldn't tell reporters whether Clark's DNA had been found on the farm, nor would he say whether another charge would be laid against Pickton. "All I can say," he emphasized, "is that they collected some evidence that connects with our Nancy Clark missing persons file in relation to their investigation in the Lower Mainland."

While the defence and the Crown wrangled about evidence throughout November, the process of choosing a jury was under way. At first, there was a lot of talk about how difficult it would be to find people willing to take on a trial that could last a year, but by mid-November it was clear that many people would agree to do the job. By December 9, 2006, an initial list of 3,500 possible candidates was winnowed down to a potential jury pool of nine hundred people. Two days later, the selection began.

It was going to be a long and difficult trial. The money, paid on a scale set out in the *Jury Act*, wasn't great—$20 a day for each of the first ten days of the trial, $60 a day for the eleventh to forty-ninth days and $100 a day for the fiftieth and each subsequent day of the trial. The court would likely sit for only four days a week; if it sat for a year, with a couple of weeks off for holidays, each juror would make about $17,000. Under B.C. law, those jurors with work contracts would be paid by their employers the money it took to bring them up to their regular salaries.

As it happened, it didn't take long for Judge Williams to find fourteen people willing to serve, people who were acceptable to both the Crown and the defence. Two of the fourteen were alternate jurors, there in case two of the chosen jurors should have reason to step down before the trial started. On the first day of the trial, the judge told them, the two alternates would be dismissed and the trial would start with a regular jury of twelve.

As I expected, Judge Williams did delay the start date. January 9 would not be possible, he conceded; there was simply too much to do. He told everyone the trial would begin on January 22, 2007.

—

January 22, 2007
Back where I started.

That's what I think when my alarm goes off at three a.m. on Monday morning. I'm staying at a small hotel run by the Vancouver School of Theology at UBC, but I am not back on the hard futon provided by my own Presbyterians. The theological precinct here has been in a state of major upheaval since I first arrived in the summer of 2002; developers have bulldozed and excavated every inch of available green space around the colleges—even tearing down many of the college buildings—to build expensive condominiums and town-houses, places few students, professors or theologians would ever be able to afford. The prices for the individual units soar into the millions of dollars.

The old stone building where I'm staying, called Iona, is owned by the United Church and is the centre of this old complex. It has been gutted and rebuilt. One of the additions is a small hotel with pleasant rooms and views out over the ocean and the North Shore Mountains. It's perfect for me. The best surprise is the Starbucks on the main floor, right next to the H.R. Macmillan Theological Library.

Right now, I am anxious about getting a seat in the judge's courtroom. From everything I have been reading in the newspapers, I am competing with 350 accredited members of the media from around the world. There is to be a raffle, for goodness sake, for the thirty-five media seats in Courtroom 101, now known as the overflow courtroom, which holds one hundred people. Thirty-five seats have been set aside for victims' family members; the rest are for the general public and court officials. If I am really lucky, I will get a seat there.

But that's not where I need to be. I need to be in the judge's courtroom, 102. I want to see the jury; I want to watch Pickton; I want to see who is sitting in the public gallery. But there are only forty-five seats in that courtroom, and as they have done twice before—at the preliminary hearing in Port Coquitlam in 2003 and at the beginning of the voir dire phase of the trial in January 2006—local media outlets have formed a committee and parcelled out the fifteen media seats to themselves, the group they call "the stakeholders." No one considers me a stakeholder, so I have to try to get there early and line up for one of the fourteen public seats.

This morning, there is a complication. Weeks ago, *The Early Edition,* the CBC's local early morning radio show, invited me to co-host the program with regular host Rick Cluff from six to eight-thirty in the morning. Their plan is to broadcast the show on location at the courthouse itself, from a borrowed condominium overlooking Begbie Square. No, I told them, I can't. I have to line up for a seat in the judge's courtroom. They countered with an offer to have someone line up for me. *Oh great,* I thought, *that will cause a major fight with others waiting in line—maybe we'll even be caught on live television.* Eventually, we compromised: I will get there at five a.m. to line up, someone from the CBC will take my place at six, we will explain our situation to the others in line and pray for their mercy, and I will come back at eight a.m.

I am so wired that I'm already awake when the alarm goes off, and I am on the road to New Westminster by four a.m. I have to do some television interviews later today, so I have put on what I call TV clothes (tailored jacket, well-ironed bright pink shirt—nobody notices your pants and shoes) and made sure I have TV hair (neat and styled, sort of) and TV makeup (foundation, powder, lipstick, mascara). As I drive into New West, it's black night outside, with no hint of morning sun, and rain is coming down steadily.

The CBC people had decided they wanted to be right on the courthouse square as the trial started, and the only option was a condominium. They knocked on doors until they found an agreeable woman with a spare room who thought this would be fun. Now, the condo owner guides me into her parking space and we climb three flights of stairs to the top room of her home, which boasts a sweeping view of the square, the front doors of the courthouse and all the people milling below. The television networks have set up a line of white tents across the front of the square, and cameramen are already figuring out the best places for shots, while sheriffs are arriving for work, paper coffee cups in one hand, uniforms on hangers slung over their shoulders. I can see that some people are lining up already.

Anu Dawit-Kanna, the young CBC broadcaster who will line up for me, is sipping coffee and looks far too relaxed. I am in full panic mode, and she gets the message and heads downstairs. The producers decide to let her "test the line"—asking people if it's okay to stand in for me—and she reports back that it's friendly. She will be filing quick hits by cellphone to the CBC about the lineup and what people are saying.

The producers prefer that I stay put and read the scripts. They find me some coffee and try to get me settled, but I can think only about whether I am going to get into the courtroom.

Laura Palmer, the executive producer, has an interesting lineup of guests. Aside from Lynn Frey, Marnie Frey's step-mother, they are all new to me and one, Alex Abdul-Malik, an expert on psychological trauma, has a fascinating assignment here today—he tells listeners what could happen to people just by listening to the news on this case, or reading the papers. Abdul-Malik ran a workshop called "Vicarious Traumatization" for reporters covering the Pickton trial; one of these was the CBC's Shana Hugh, who works on this morning radio show, and she found it very helpful. Traditionally, Shana tells me before his interview, "trauma is from direct impact . . . but hearing or retelling of an event can have that same effect. And you know the event is getting to you when . . . you may start to notice an acute reaction, such as feeling overwhelmed, you are being bombarded with intrusive thoughts, or you suffer from nausea or sensitivity of anything related to that issue, for example. You may even suffer from the cumulative impact over time, as you are exposed over and over to news or information about the event. And the impact it can have on you is that it can change the fundamentals of how we see ourselves or understand what people are capable of. Sometimes the event challenges ideas we have about the world we live in.

"The effects may be worse for some people, particularly those who have been exposed to something traumatic in their own life . . . this helps it resurface. It's not common, but it can happen."

Tom Collins, a former sheriff, is now head of the media liaison for the Attorney-General's department and he is, he admits, totally excited about today; organizing space, accreditation and all the other minutiae of making it possible for hundreds of journalists to work here, has been exciting and he is beaming this morning; so far, there have been no glitches. One of the journalists is the CBC's Natalie Clancy, who has been covering the case for the national news ever since Pickton was arrested in 2002; she is on the show today to talk about her experiences. Then there is Donna Turko, an experienced defence lawyer, who explains what the defence team's strategy might be. A former journalist herself, Turko has worked with most of the senior people on Peter Ritchie's team and has appeared before Judge Williams herself, so she is a good person to steer us through the legal issues we'll see today. Susan Burgess, a doctor who is an HIV specialist, works on the Downtown Eastside and is the person who reported Andrea Joesbury missing in June 2001, is also here; she knew at least six of the missing women well and is powerful here this morning because of her passion about the way people are treated in the Downtown Eastside and about the lack of detox and recovery beds.

The program is being run out of a spare bedroom that has been cleared of furniture, and despite one tiny glitch after another, Laura, Rick and the rest of the CBC team remain calm. The lineup below us is snaking around the corner of the courthouse; I force myself to stop looking out the window. I try to ignore the television lights flaring in the dark. Still, out of the corner of my eye, I can see the lawyers pulling legal bags on rollers through the doors of the courtroom. It is now 7:15, and it's still raining. I know Peter Ritchie's team is in because I can see Ritchie's beret and Patrick McGowan's red hair.

The CBC folks turn me loose at eight, and I hobble down the flights of cement steps to the square below. Everyone in the queue is now inside the courthouse, half an hour before the usual time. Where is Anu? I line up at one of the four sheriff's stations to be searched. I still can't see her. Fast as I can, I make my way down the long hall to Courtroom 102. I hear voices urging me on. If Anu gets to the second bank of sheriffs, they will give her a pass, and it will not be transferable. There she is. Just ahead of her is Elaine Allan, and I know everyone else there. No one complains when Anu slips out, giving me her place. I get through the sheriffs, and there is a pass for me into the judge's courtroom. I begin to breathe.

Inside, the stakeholders are filling the front row and the half of the second row reserved for the press, all marked with purple tape. Greg Joyce, who has been covering this case for years, is here for Canadian Press. Jeremy Hainsworth is reporting for Associated Press; Allan Dowd for Reuters; Bob Matas for the *Globe and Mail*; Lori Culbert for the *Vancouver Sun*; Ken MacQueen for *Maclean's*; Stephen Smart for CKNW Radio; Kelly Ryan for CBC Radio; Natalie Clancy for CBC Television; Ron Bencze and Darlene Heidemann for Global Television; and Lisa Rossington, Janet Dirks and Todd Battis for CTV. A

A cameraman arrives at Begbie Square at dawn to shoot live interviews for morning news shows. Media tents are set up in front of the courthouse (right).

few other reporters, like me, sit in public seats; many more, we know, are in the overflow courtroom next door, watching the proceedings on monitors; more still are watching on monitors in the media workroom a block away.

Family members of the victims are settling into the next batch of seats, marked with pink. Lynn Frey is here with Marnie's daughter, Brittney, and Lynn's foster sister, Joyce Lachance. Ernie Crey, the brother of Dawn Crey—a missing woman who has not yet been identified as a Pickton victim but whose family was told in early January, 2004 that her DNA had been found on the Pickton farm—is here, along with his sister, Lorraine Crey.

The thirteen of us lucky enough to obtain public seats, set aside with orange tape, fall into them. Behind us sit court and police officials and Victim Services workers. Their seats have acid green tape on the arms. Freda Ens is here, and she always makes me feel better. Bob Stone, the note-taker for the RCMP, takes his usual seat in the back row. Also present is Fiona Flanagan, who works for the Missing Women Task Force as a witness wrangler, my own term for the person who makes sure witnesses arrive on time for their court appearance and finds them a private place, away from the media, to wait until they are called to testify. Beside us, against the side wall, one in front of the other, are two chairs marked with pale green tape. These are for the Pickton family and friends; they are, as they always have been, empty.

The lawyers come in, adjusting their vests and gowns, flipping their long black ties in place under their starched white wing collars. They start unpacking their big cases and putting folders and binders on their desks. Derrill Prevett is at the far left of the front table set up for the prosecutors; beside him on his right, in order, are Mike Petrie, Geoff Baragar and

Satinder Sidhu. Behind them, at the second table, are Willie Pickton's lawyers: Richard Brooks, Patrick McGowan, Marilyn Sandford, Adrian Brooks and Peter Ritchie. Several members of the teams are missing; there is no room for more in this courtroom.

The court clerk arrives and settles in beside the court reporter. Sheriffs array themselves around the well of the court, where the judge, clerk, reporter, lawyers, jury and the accused sit, and two more sheriffs flank the public gallery, behind the bulletproof Plexiglas, where the rest of are waiting. The judge comes in, followed by his assistant, Christine Judd. The courtroom is so small and so crowded that there is no place for her; she perches in a chair beyond the jury box, out of sight.

Finally, a sheriff escorts Willie Pickton into the room, and he takes his place in the Plexiglas box, facing the judge. It's the first time we've seen him in a tailored, long-sleeved shirt; it's grey. He's wearing black pants. His hair is cut short and greased back to reveal his shiny, domed forehead. His large ears stick out. I find myself measuring them in my mind and ask a colleague for his opinion. We agree that they are three inches long and stick out a full inch. His face is shiny and pink and expressionless; he looks at no one and he looks nowhere. He just picks up his writing pad and looks straight ahead or down at his pad, unfocused.

It is now 9:30 a.m. After a few remarks to the lawyers, Judge Williams asks the clerk to call in the jury, and fourteen people file in—twelve jurors and two alternates. "I see we have a full turnout," Judge Williams remarks, "but we only have room on the voyage for twelve." He excuses the two alternates, and they leave for good. That leaves five older men, between, say, fifty and seventy-plus; two younger men who seem to be in their thirties; two younger women who look as if they could still be in university or may be just starting their careers; and three middle-aged women. We do not know their names. As far as I can tell, they are all white. They look worried and uncomfortable, and they sit very still. They are not whispering to each other or even looking at each other. While we wait for the proceedings to start, we talk quietly about the most likely candidate for jury foreman. We think it will be the man at the far end of the first row, a man in his sixties, I'd say, with short, curly white hair and a short beard.

The judge asks the lawyers to introduce themselves. Ritchie and his team stand and bow to the jury; Petrie's team does the same. For the next half-hour or so, Judge Williams talks to the jury about their job: This is how you are to listen, take notes, observe the demeanour of witnesses. Don't read the papers or watch the news or talk about the case to anyone except each other. (But because the jury is not going to be sequestered, something that happens in many sensitive trials, no one can prevent them from reading anything they want or watching television.)

Come to me if you have a problem or a question, the judge continues. Then he goes through some of the arcane rules of a trial, which are probably new to most of them—the difference between direct evidence and circumstantial evidence, for example, or first-degree and second-degree murder—and he tells them that the questions being asked by the lawyers and the comments they might make don't constitute evidence; the evidence is what the witnesses say.

"Use your common sense and experience," he tells the jurors. "Consider the evidence with an open mind."

Williams is also careful to warn them that what they are about to hear will be difficult.

"Some of the evidence to which you will be exposed during the trial will be shocking and is likely to be upsetting. I must ask each of you to deal with that the best you can. It may arouse feelings of revulsion and hostility that can overwhelm the objective and impartial approach that jurors are expected to bring to their task.

"You should be aware of that possibility and ensure it does not happen to you."

In a housekeeping note, Judge Williams tells the seven men and five women that the court will sit from Monday to Thursday each week, and that they will have a couple of weeks off in the summer and another week some other time during the year the trial is expected to last.

Finally, he turns to the prosecutors and invites them to begin their opening statement. Derrill Prevett stands up, walks to the podium and stands silently for a second or two. We hold our breath, our pencils poised over our notepads, our tape recorders on so we can check the accuracy of our notes later. Whatever we expect, it is not this. Prevett doesn't speak for long—maybe an hour and he doesn't mention the other twenty women Pickton is accused or killing—but he hammers out the Crown's case in brutal, unflinching language. It tells the jury and the Canadian public exactly what this case is all about, the case that has been shrouded in secrecy and guarded by draconian publication bans for five years.

Prevett says that when they searched Pickton's pig farm, the police found the skulls of Sereena Abotsway and Andrea Joesbury stuffed inside two five-gallon plastic pails inside two freezers. The heads had been cut vertically in half with a saw, and the women's hands and feet had been placed inside them. He says that Joesbury and Abotsway are two of six women the police believe were killed by Pickton, and that DNA analysis has identified the remains of each of these six women. And he adds that Pickton admits the women are dead although not that he killed them. No mention is made of the other twenty women Pickton is charged with killing, nor of the trial on those counts that will follow this one.

Prevett tells the jury that the remains were found either inside Pickton's trailer or in the ground nearby. The search of Pickton's trailer uncovered a tote bag that contained syringes and an asthma inhaler belonging to Abotsway; a search through garbage below Pickton's window uncovered four more of Abotsway's inhalers. Swabs taken of blood-stained clothing in the trailer matched the DNA profile of Mona Wilson, another woman Pickton is accused of killing. Searchers also found running shoes and a cross that belonged to Wilson. In the laundry room of Pickton's trailer, the police found a revolver in a zippered gun case, its barrel covered in plastic wrap with an elastic band wrapped around it. The revolver had one spent casing and five other rounds. A dildo fitted over the barrel carried DNA from both Pickton and Wilson. Wilson's remains were found in a bag at the bottom of a garbage can.

Another search uncovered Brenda Wolfe's lower jawbone and teeth in the ground in a trough beside the farm's slaughterhouse; in July 2002, other bones, mixed with debris and manure, were found in the slaughterhouse, including a bone from Georgina Papin's hand, as well as thirteen other human hand bones, and three teeth matching the DNA of Marnie Frey. Other human bones found near the slaughterhouse could not be matched to anyone identified as missing by the Missing Women Task Force, Prevett says.

"These murders of these six women were the work of one man, the accused, Robert William Pickton," Prevett states. "He had the expertise and equipment for the task. He had the means of transportation available and the means for the disposal of their remains."

Although the trial is about the six victims he has named here, Prevett tells the jury that searchers uncovered a heel bone and a rib bone whose DNA matched that of a skull found in a slough in Mission in 1995. Saw marks on the skull, he says, match those of saw marks on other bisected skulls. This victim remains unknown and is called Jane Doe; hers is the count quashed during the voir dire by Judge Williams.

Prevett then tells the jury what happened after the police arrested Pickton on two counts of murder on February 22, 2002. He was placed in a cell with an undercover police officer, Prevett explains. "During the afternoon and evening of February the 22nd, Mr. Pickton and the undercover officer came to know each other. The officer related his cover story to the effect that he was in custody awaiting transport back East to face outstanding charges for violent offences. Mr. Pickton explained that he'd been arrested for two murder charges and that the police are looking at him for forty-seven others. In the course of telling [the officer] about his past, Mr. Pickton repeatedly tells his cellmate that he believes he is nailed to the cross. He also tells him he is being considered as a mass murderer—his words; you'll hear them."

Next, Prevett says, Pickton was taken to an interview room for questioning. "The interview begins with Sergeant [Bill] Fordy speaking with Mr. Pickton, and the accused explains to Sergeant Fordy that his trade is a butcher's—he butchers pigs; he has been doing it since he was thirteen years old—and he describes roughly how he does it. As an aside, there'll be evidence that when he butchered pigs he would sometimes have the assistance of his friend, a man called Pat Casanova, and the Crown anticipates that Mr. Casanova will testify at his trial. When you see and hear this portion of the interview, you'll see it's marked by the accused's denial. He claims he knows none of the women with whom he is being investigated. He states that he knows nothing and that he is just a pig farmer."

Another officer, Staff Sergeant Don Adam, questioned Pickton as well, Prevett says. "Staff Sergeant Adam asked him about the photos of women displayed on a large poster board which has been brought into the interview room and asks him, 'How many do you think you recognize? Like, if you were free to talk right now, how many could you reach out and touch? No, but I mean, that you killed.' Mr. Pickton responds, 'You make me more of a mass murderer than I am.'

"Some minutes later, Staff Sergeant Adam suggests to Mr. Pickton that the reason Mr. Pickton finds himself in this situation is that he didn't do a very good job in cleaning up a girl's blood. You'll hear Mr. Pickton respond, 'That's right, I was sloppy.' Mr. Pickton goes on to say that bad policing is the reason why it took so long to catch him. Staff Sergeant Adam questions him about his motives for killing and whether he ever thought of quitting, and Mr. Pickton states that he had one more planned but that was the end of it. 'I was going to shut it down. That's when I was just sloppy, just the last one.'

"In furthering his cover story, [the undercover officer] tells Mr. Pickton that the police have him [the officer] on an attempted murder charge and are investigating him for others as well. Mr. Pickton responds, 'But you're nothing like mine.' The officer tells him he is looking at some serious time if the police are able to put things together. Mr. Pickton then gestures with his hands, showing five with the fingers on one hand and a zero on the other. [The officer] asks, 'What's that—five, zero: fifty? Ha ha.' Moments later, Mr. Pickton verbalizes what he had earlier gestured. He says, 'I was going to do one more. Make it an even fifty.'"

When Prevett winds up his opening statement to the jury, the next step would ordinarily be for the Crown to outline the evidence in the case and then start calling witnesses. But the defence had won a battle ten days earlier when Peter Ritchie convinced Judge Williams to let him make an opening statement as well. Courts have the discretion to allow this, the judge had said in his ruling, and he was doing it in the interest of fairness.

"The case at bar can quite readily be characterized as special or unusual in that it is anticipated that the trial will run in the order of twelve months," Williams wrote. "The Crown intends to call more than two hundred witnesses, meaning that it would be many months before the defence would otherwise be able to give its opening statement. It is generally accepted that the benefit of an early defence opening [statement] is that it enhances the jury's ability to appreciate in a meaningful way the evidence which is led and to relate that evidence to a consideration of the issues."

Although the prosecutors had not objected to the defence making an opening statement, they appealed to the judge to impose three conditions on it: that the defence disclose the evidence they planned to lead with; that they give a copy of their opening statement to the Crown; and that they not be allowed a second opportunity to deliver an opening statement when the Crown finished presenting its case. Judge Williams rejected all three conditions, although he did ask Ritchie to give him a copy of the opening statement to approve before he made it.

Now, Peter Ritchie walks slowly over to the podium, hesitating a moment or two before he speaks. The people in the courtroom, still reeling from what they just heard from Derrill Prevett, are absolutely silent. Ritchie begins by promising the jury that he will be brief. Just a few minutes. Then he asks them not to be overwhelmed by the prosecutor's opening statement. "The defence position is that Mr. Pickton did not kill or participate in the killing of the six women he is accused of killing," Ritchie states. He asks the jury to pay particular attention to Pickton's level of intellectual competence and level of understanding while they watch the videotapes of his interview with the police. "Pay close attention to what Mr. Pickton says and the manner in which he expresses himself," he says.

"The picture that Mr. Prevett has painted to you is not a full picture. It is the Crown's contention they can prove those facts, but at this stage it is only a contention that the Crown can prove these facts. This case will unfold slowly," explains Ritchie. "The case is complicated. You will hear about other people in this case, and their roles can be significant. Some may have, you may find, their own motives. Do not move quickly to conclusions." He advises the jury to pay attention to the DNA evidence, especially when it concerns where Pickton's DNA appeared or where the DNA of other people appeared.

Ritchie's opening statements last about twenty-five minutes. As soon as he finishes, the judge turns the case back to the Crown prosecutors, and Mike Petrie calls his first witness, RCMP Staff Sergeant Don Adam, the head of the Missing Women Task Force.

—

We have all waited a very long time for this trial to start. As the day moves along, with its dreadful revelations, I find I need a few moments alone to sort out my emotions. I thought this would all be more complicated, but it's not. I feel mostly relief. Although details surrounding the remaining twenty first-degree murder charges won't come out until the second trial starts, the main elements of the story that we have all had to conceal for so many years are now known to the public.

Until this morning, I was worried about a number of things. As a journalist, and one who hates being scooped, it has been difficult for me all these years to see stories coming out on this case; I wanted to be there in front, writing them, breaking the news myself. I always knew this day would come when dozens of good reporters would fly out of the court and start filing their stories while I was getting into my car to return to my hotel and another long evening of work on the book. But the day I started work on the Pickton case almost five years ago, I decided my assignment *was* a book, not daily reporting. I told other reporters that this was what I was doing. I needed them to know we were not competing. Still, it has been hard for me. But now, as the first day unfolds exactly as I knew it would, I realize it is okay. I don't mind any more.

Five years of waiting for this day has also meant frustration about some legal decisions, especially what could and could not be reported even after the trial began. It was discouraging to deal with all the delays and rulings. I would sometimes turn up at court to learn that the day's sitting had been cancelled at the last minute. I began to feel like a fraud as I fell further and further behind on the deadlines set for my book, even though I knew it couldn't be helped and was not my fault. Sometimes, in dark moments I would never admit to anyone, I felt I wasn't even a journalist any longer. What I am, all I want to be, is a reporter. Waiting for so long, and knowing that the severance of the counts would mean a longer wait than I ever dreamed of, was terribly disheartening.

But now, in this place, with the jury seated and the lawyers laying it all out, I am, in every respect, exactly where I should be.

ACKNOWLEDGMENTS

When both Pickton trials finally end and the investigation wraps up, I will be able to thank all the people who have helped me with my work on it over the past five years. Until then, I would like to thank a smaller group whose help made this book possible.

As she has been since I started in 2002, Elaine Allan has been at my side with advice, contacts and friendship.

The journalists who have been working on the story for so many years were always generous and welcoming and they include Greg Joyce, Dan Girard, Kelly Ryan, Darlene Heidemann, Bob Matas, Lori Culbert, Neal Hall, Ethan Baron, Deborah Jones, Jeremy Hainsworth, Pierre Claveau, Natalie Clancy, Allan Dowd, Jane Armstrong, Steve Smart, Rob Bencze, Dave Lefebvre and Janet Dirks. Trude Huebner was an essential guide to the Pickton family and Port Coquitlam and I have always valued her sense of humour and support. Television producer Liz Fox, a good friend who retired from the CBC a few years ago, often came to court with me, took notes, kept clipping files and always offered good advice. Journalist Justin Beddall, who introduced me to Albert and Vera Harvey, has been another great pal.

But at the very beginning Lindsay Kines, whose stories finally forced the Vancouver police to take the missing women's case seriously, helped me find my way; his friendship and advice have been a godsend. I must say the same for my friend Jan Wong, a former colleague at the *Globe and Mail*. Even though she lives in Toronto and doesn't know the Pickton story well, her advice on how to tell this personal story has been invaluable.

I am grateful to Vancouver lawyer Raman Johal, who found the Pickton wills for me in the B.C. archives, and journalist Jonathan Woodward, a journalist involved in the documentary version of my next book, *The Pig Farm*, who unearthed the coroner's report described in Chapter 6, also buried in the archives.

Ron MacKay in Ottawa, Canada's first criminal profiler and my consultant on this book, has not only provided wise and expert advice on many occasions but has extended support that I can never repay. In very dark hours he was always there for me. So was Larry Campbell, Vancouver's former mayor and the provincial coroner who understood the grief and despair of the Downtown Eastside.

The families of Vancouver's missing women are an extraordinary group. I cannot find the words to say how good so many of them have been to me over the years. My hope is that before long I will have met or talked to members of every family.

I also need to thank the fine people who work in the court system in B.C. The sheriffs in the New Westminster and Port Coquitlam courthouses under the leadership of Mike McCafferty and Kerry McIntyre, the media team that includes Tom Collins, Mark Jan Vrem and Kathy Quon, the Victim Services workers including Freda Ens, Marilynne Johnny, Rita Buchwitz, Norma Parr and witness wrangler Fiona Flanagan, are all part of a civilized and humane service who make the unbearable bearable.

And in this group I must include the lawyers working on both sides of this case, the teams led by Crown prosecutor Mike Petrie and defence lawyer Peter Ritchie. The past five years have not been easy for any of them.

During the years I have been living part-time in Vancouver, so many people have done so much to make me feel at home. My brother Chris Dahl and his wife Jan Bell-Irving have included me in family dinners and watched over me like parents. My Friday nights in West Vancouver with a group of merry women at La Régalade or Carmelo's would make a book in itself. Vince Gogolek and his wife Karen Hoffman, Basil Stuart-Stubbs and his wife Brenda, Ruth Wright, Sisley, Larry and Sherry Killam, Allan and Angie McDougall, Rafe and Wendy Mair, Ken and Elaine Carty and my brother-in-law Ken Cameron and his wife Shirley are just a few of the people who made my life there so content.

The Pickton File was the brainchild of my editor, Diane Martin, the vice-president and publisher of Knopf Canada and one of the few people I know who really understands the story and cares about it as much as I do. She has sat in court with me, explored the streets of the Downtown Eastside, and met many of the players I mention in these pages. I don't know how I can ever thank her enough for giving me the privilege of working on this story. Louise Dennys, the chairwoman of Knopf Canada and Vintage Canada and the executive vice-president of Random House of Canada, has also been just as unstinting in her support and kindness over many years. Sue Sumeraj, the copyeditor on this book, saved me from many embarrassments, as did managing editor Adrienne Phillips.

And Simon Chester guided us all through the legal minefields of a story that is still unfolding in court and I am grateful to him for this—as well as for help and friendship through some very difficult times. Linda McKnight, my beloved friend and agent for so many years, has often made me crazy with her common sense but she is, unfortunately, never wrong.

As always, I thank my family here in Toronto, Tassie and Michael, Amy and John and my husband David, who make everything possible.

Toronto
April 2007

INDEX